D0585497

JOSHUA

John Dennen

JOSHUA

YELLOW JERSEY PRESS
LONDON

1 3 5 7 9 10 8 6 4 2

Yellow Jersey Press, an imprint of Vintage
20 Vauxhall Bridge Road
London SW1V 2SA

Yellow Jersey Press is part of the Penguin Random House group of companies
whose addresses can be found at global.penguinrandomhouse.com.

Penguin
Random House
UK

First published by Yellow Jersey Press in 2017

www.vintage-books.co.uk

A CIP catalogue record for this book is available from the British Library

ISBN 9781787290075

Typeset in 13/17 pt Minion Pro by Jouve (UK), Milton Keynes
Printed and bound by Clays Ltd, St Ives Plc

Penguin Random House is committed to a sustainable future
for our business, our readers and our planet. This book is made from
Forest Stewardship Council® certified paper.

Contents

PART ONE

The Picture of a Champion

The lights are hot. Twenty thousand people in the arena shift in their seats. They are hushed, quiet. Nothing is more deafening than a crowd that size waiting in silence. A bell rings out. It chimes once, twice and on, a last salute. Memories of Muhammad Ali stretch to every corner of the world, including England. Here, in London, under the dome of the O2 on the banks of the Thames is the first heavyweight world title fight since the death of the sport's greatest champion. The bell tolls a tenth and last time and the crowd erupts, the final honour.

All heavyweights toil in the shadow of their great predecessors. There can't be another Ali, there never *could* be another. But there are always more champions.

The crowd stamp their feet on the floor, they clap their hands, they shout their voices hoarse. This audience has certain demands of its heroes. They have to fight. They have to suffer. They have to bleed and they must hit to hurt.

Anthony Joshua will walk out before them. With his challenger, a polite American, Dominic Breazeale, already in the ring, Joshua will step out on to a raised platform, a stage. A vast screen behind him will flash with his name. He will stroll easily forward and back, raising a glove to knots of people spotted in the crowd. Too late to pause, too late to think of anything much: the show has begun. Lights flash, rolling round the arena, the snarl of a lion roaring plays out clearly, specifically requested by Joshua. This is the 'Lion's Den' after all. Just to underscore the extravagance, pyrotechnics, for little apparent purpose, ignite either side of him.

And so he makes his entrance, still recognisably himself, smiling here and there. He doesn't see the crowd now, it's too dark beyond him. He can't see the old faces that throng the ringside. Old team-mates, old friends, old enemies, too, are all sitting close, watching among thousands and thousands of new fans, new supporters, all shouting his name over and over. He doesn't see all that, doesn't hear the deep roar of the crowd.

Security guards, stony-faced, fall in alongside him, marching him through a passageway hemmed in by fans. Above him, lit brightly, is the ring. In it, waiting for him, is the fight. His first challenger. Joshua's face only hardens now. He steps up, his boots on the canvas. He slips through the ropes.

His robe, broad across his shoulders, catches the light, shining bright white. This is the picture of a fighter. Joshua stations himself in the home corner, his team fanning out behind him. He peaceably crosses his hands in front of his body, waiting, almost formally, for the inevitable. Breazeale, meanwhile, busies himself shadowboxing. The challenger, a converted American football player, is more comfortable than he has a right to be. But he doesn't look a natural fighter. He shifts his gloves through the air, snapping punches at nothing in particular.

The announcer takes up his familiar refrain. 'Let's get ready to rumble' reverberates across the arena.

Joshua's face is framed by the ropes. He looks out directly through the strands. Can he see the people out there? Or is it only darkness? Is it just him in there? Him and the fight.

* * *

A fight is a curious thing. It is a lonely business, no doubting that. There is nowhere to turn, nowhere to hide, no one else to ease the pressure. No one, aside from the man in the opposing corner, really understands what the boxer goes through in his fight. It's up to the fighter to force himself through the pain. Away from the ring, back in the gym, there is a team; sparring partners, coaches, support. But their help, by definition, is limited. It's Joshua who has to throw the punches, who has to take the hits, do the extra circuits on the track. When he does eventually enter the contest, it won't be so much his opponent he's fighting. It's a reflection, a mirror image of himself, of the work, of the suffering he's bled into this particular engagement. If he can shed his doubts and fears, if he can impose his style on his opponent and their contest, he wins.

This camp, though, is taking a toll on him. Joshua is a big man. When he enters a room he towers over its occupants. That's the thing about being big – everybody sees you. And Joshua is unmistakable. A hefty six foot six, it would take a lot to knock lumps out of him. But on this occasion, just a week before the first defence of his world title on 25 June 2016, he is weary. He is feeling the pace. No boxer wants to give away weakness but Joshua can't help mentioning time and again how tired he is. The training isn't over. He has more sparring to come, further training. He'll only catch a rest the following week, in the final two days before the fight itself.

A media lunch had been organised in Sheffield, eight days before the world title fight. Naturally I was in attendance for *Boxing News*, the magazine I've been working for over the last seven years. Anthony strode in, drawing everyone's attention. He's not just taller and far wider than anyone else in the restaurant, he is a big name now, a big star. He has the forbidding aura of someone who is recognised almost everywhere he goes, who is famous, someone who can generate £15 million, closing in on $20 million, with a single fight. Someone who doesn't just carry financial clout, but whose physical power has meant none of his professional opponents, at this point, have made it to the final bell.

Taking a vacant seat next to me, he leaned eagerly over a plate of food. I muttered my usual platitudes, about whether he'd have a break, a holiday, after the fight.

'I'm not being funny, John,' he said grimly, 'but the media lunch hasn't started yet.'

Blinking, silenced, I turned back to my lunch, chastened, only to notice Joshua laughing with a familiar deep chuckle. Mentally at least he felt laid-back. Smiling, his enthusiasm for the job, for the fight, was apparent. Discussing the arena, the atmosphere as he made his ringwalks, he gleefully shadowboxed in his seat. When you're in it, in that moment, evidently it's hard to take in. 'Is it good?' he asked.

'It's the best part,' I replied, somewhat uncharitably. What I should have said, what I do then say, is it's like nothing else. There's nothing like the roar of the crowd, willing their hero on, into a major heavyweight fight.

The talk meandered on before the media roundtable began in earnest. Still light-hearted, Joshua said quietly, 'I'm not the amateur you used to interview.' On that score he was absolutely right.

He is known. It takes a while for the Joshua team to roll out. There are always hands to shake, people to meet, fans to greet. In this instance they wound their way out of the hotel through a wedding reception. That appearance was enough to disrupt the celebration. The bride rushed up to ask him to pose for a picture, closely followed by the bridesmaids, then elderly relatives. He's a public figure; to him these are duties and he carried them out with a smile.

Such public outreach came from the top, it came from him and it was paying off. A week later hundreds pressed forward at Covent Garden Market in London to see him weigh in in the open air on a warm summer's afternoon. He didn't have a weight limit to make but this was one of the rituals of the sport, giving the people a chance to see, and to appraise, the fighters on the final day before their contest. He went face-to-face with his challenger, his last staredown with Breazeale before they were in the ring. Normally Joshua loomed over opponents, a silent, intimidatingly impassive presence. But on this occasion he spoke softly to the American, turned and gestured to the crowd.

'You talk about these different processes, learning through experience how to deal with that, and now once I get it right I'll be able to play these opponents at their own game,' Anthony said. He wanted to take control of his opponent. He was telling him to embrace the occasion. Breazeale declined to accept the invitation, just glaring at Joshua, breathing heavily. They were parted and Joshua snatched up his world title belt and held it aloft in his fist, showing it to his crowd, an offering.

'He's seen in my face that I'm ready to go,' the American insisted, speaking in the clipped tones of the college athlete he frankly was. 'He was doing a little blinking. I was doing a lot more staring.'

But Joshua saw the fight. 'Even when I'm looking at him, I'm calculating what shot I'm going to knock him out with,' he said. 'A hundred per cent. Slip, with a left hook. That's how I am. I'm actually picturing boxing him, when I'm doing the eye to eye, thinking what shot will he throw. He's a big guy. He's going to throw jabs and then you have to keep your head moving and counter-punching.'

Stepping down from the stage, Joshua endeavoured to exit down a side street, but the crowd simply mobbed him, rushing round waving phones, trying to get a picture, a fist bump, just getting close to the champ. As security clustered round him, they picked their way through the people step by step, rather like, I imagined, a presidential candidate being manoeuvred through a campaign rally. In a way he was running for office – to be the heavyweight champion of the world. He had one of the belts, but there were three other major titles. In the meantime he just had to fight for the crowd, try to impress them enough to prove he was a true champion. It was a court of popularity and, if this weigh-in was anything to go by, Joshua was winning their support.

The champion liked to spend time with fans, posing for

pictures, shaking hands, bumping fists. On this occasion if he'd done so, who knows what kind of a riot, or stampede, that might have caused. 'It's mental. I haven't seen that for a while for a sportsman,' his commercial manager, Freddie Cunningham, said. The adulation was reaching rock star levels. On occasion they had fans just running after his car. 'Some kids made it through four traffic lights, down the main road, like a mile and a half, and they kept making every light. I couldn't believe it,' Freddie continued.

But the support he'd accrued, that was palpable the following night. Boxing crowds tend to drift in late, perhaps only arriving for the particular fighter they support. For this event the queues were building early on, fans massing to take in the excitement five hours before the main event was due to start. By the time Joshua was in the ring they were delirious on that heady cocktail of anticipated violence.

His cornermen reached up to strip the white robe from his shoulders. Joshua stood there, broad across the chest, chiselled. 'Carved in mayhem' was another of his expressions. Breazeale, his opponent, may have been taller but at that moment Joshua seemed far the bigger man. He looked up now, to zero in on the opposite corner. Stripped to the waist he advanced on Breazeale to touch gloves, one more pre-fight ritual, only to throw fists in earnest in a few moments' time. Joshua backpedalled to his corner, waiting for the first bell. He squatted down on his heels, his long arms stretching up to the ropes. He bent deeply at the knee, carrying his 243-pound bulk lightly. The crowd roared again at the sound of the bell, propelling him up on to his feet, forward into the centre of the ring.

Breazeale stuck his jab out, trying to hold Joshua off. The American was hesitant; Anthony's lead jab hit out cleaner, faster. With a straight left-right combination, the one-two punch, Joshua drove him back, too far back. He threw a left to follow up, hooking it round from the side. It curved away from Breazeale, falling short, catching only the light.

Breazeale tried a one-two of his own, only to see it easily blocked. Joshua went looking for him, flinging two straight right hands. The American cupped his gloves over his face to protect himself. Joshua's heavy right cross, the back-hand power punch, shuddered into his guard. He cuffed a left hook at Breazeale, catching the edge of the American's right glove. The hook comes round from the side, harder to block than a straight left or right despite being a slower punch. An ideal shot for prying apart a stubborn guard.

Joshua opened up with a firm four-punch combination, bombarding Breazeale's defences. He even ducked a defiant jab, wheeling away underneath it, enough to whip up a round of applause from his supporters.

Joshua's jab shot through to start the second round. He doubled that, punching Breazeale's guard so he could hammer his right to the body. He lanced his cross in again to set up his left hook. The American felt it. The crowd sensed his hurt, a rumble of sound starting to reverberate round the arena. Joshua followed their prompting, stepping up his attack. A burst of punches rattled off Breazeale's gloves.

The Briton scored with another clear jab. It landed clean. The shot moved fast but there was real weight behind it. At once a red mark swelled up around Breazeale's right eye. The left, for an orthodox boxer, was normally the weaker hand.

Joshua wielded his like a piston. It thudded out and Breazeale, a lesser fighter, could never figure out how to escape it.

Joshua stepped forward quickly. He sent in a sudden uppercut, a blow that, as its name suggests, cuts upwards. It sliced through the gap between his opponent's elbows, a short shot that swept through a tight arc. It snagged Breazeale's chin. At first glance it didn't look like much. But its effect was delayed. A second later Breazeale lost control of his legs. They wouldn't obey him. Instead, for an instant, they loosened beneath him. His knees buckled. He wobbled backward, putting distance at least between himself and Joshua. Through an effort of sheer will Breazeale kept himself upright. But he listed, trying to reclaim his balance. He lurched away, stumbling into a neutral corner. He needed to lean his back on the corner post just to keep himself on his feet. Joshua advanced on Breazeale, a shadow looming over him.

The American, however, was spared. The referee stood between them, an error, although he was taking a close look at Breazeale to see if he ought to intervene and save him from Joshua. It served as a block, shielding Breazeale for a few crucial seconds. He reeled out to the clear space of the centre ring. Joshua sent a right after him, and piled forward to press his attack, a hint of recklessness that saw Anthony catch a wayward punch. Breazeale clinched, desperately holding on to Joshua's arms to survive the second round.

Joshua normally rushed his bouts. He was never willing to spare an opponent when he had him on the hook, lest he manage to regroup and come back at him later. There is always danger the longer a heavyweight fight continues. The big men have heavy hands. Give an underdog more time and the more chance he has of landing a knockout blow, however lucky. In this weight class an unknown like Hasim Rahman can take out as great a champion as Lennox Lewis with a single punch, as he did in 2001.

Joshua rarely gave his opposition much time to linger, typically snuffing out any potential threat as quickly as he could. But before this first world title defence he had promised something else. Instead of a ferocious assault, Anthony wanted to lay down a defensive foundation; he wanted to be in control of the fight before he disposed of his challenger. So he measured out Breazeale. He was methodical now, but no less impressive for that. His jab zeroed in on Breazeale's right eye, the swollen damage starting to close it. Joshua's right flew across. But even as he attacked, he still palmed a Breazeale jab down.

The American tried to unload shots of his own but Joshua screwed up a right to stop him in his tracks. Breazeale held that ground, looking to hit back. Joshua jabbed him down, scored with a cross. Stubborn still, the challenger responded with a jab. Joshua flung that sweeping uppercut through the air. He worked to usher Breazeale to the ropes. Normally trapping them on the strands left his victims vulnerable as Joshua stormed forward. But here, with his back resting on the ropes, Breazeale gamely traded blows with him. Joshua nevertheless had the edge, hammering his left and right home. He kept his eyes wide, focused on the job. He unleashed a fast combination in close and all the time kept Breazeale on his jab. Still the American couldn't step round it, couldn't slip that lead left.

Joshua built on his work, unhurried, patient enough to back off from a feint, letting Breazeale recover himself. He doubled his jab to let his right hook crash round the American's guard then stepped in with his jab again, this time to tee-off his uppercut. Joshua could still drag his right hand back fast enough to block an oncoming left hook. Breazeale unearthed defiance, hacking at Joshua with his backhand uppercut and firing off a left. He made it through the fourth round, something only one of Joshua's previous professional opponents had managed before. Perhaps exultant at the feat, Breazeale stood firm at the bell muttering darkly at Joshua, his face contorted with the pain and the effort.

Breazeale might have been standing up to the bombardment, but he wasn't winning. Joshua in truth was subjecting him to a systematic beatdown. It was a question of how long the Englishman could maintain his patience.

Joshua was commanding but his defence was not impregnable. As thickly muscled as his torso was, his body was the point to attack. Breazeale worked punches through to his midriff. For an instant Joshua felt those. But again Breazeale wandered on to a left hook. Anthony was moving, he slipped a right cross. All the while his jab tore through again and again. For a big man Anthony could shift sharply. He ducked beneath a lead hook and bobbed back to strike in his own left.

The American sat rooted to his stool at the start of the sixth round. He was slow to rise, slow to emerge from his corner, feeling the pain. Then he walked straight into Joshua's double jab. Anthony applied it cruelly, relishing the damage he did with it. Breazeale couldn't escape it and Joshua, licking his lips at times, sent his jab slicing heartily through the openings. It allowed him to blast his backhand straight to the body or set up a one-two. 'You've got to pop that jab, man,' he once said.

'It's a smokescreen for this bad boy,' he added, brandishing his clenched right fist. Breazeale tried to swing back, heaving a left hook over, to no avail. Joshua began to break him apart, hitting a left hook over to open his prey up for a straight right cross. Breazeale was left wearily trying to rekindle that stubborn resistance. The bell ended the round and the American again attempted to hold his ground and stare Joshua down. Bruising twisted Breazeale's face into a grimace. Joshua simply patted him on the back and ushered him back towards his own corner.

Such mercy was short-lived. In the seventh round Joshua suddenly increased the intensity. Upping the tempo, he threw the jab-cross. At once another straight left scorched through after it. The punch slammed in hard, snapping his head back. Breazeale, now woozy, found himself on the ropes. This time he couldn't fight his way off. Joshua was quick. He sprang on the American, letting loose fast punches, cuffing him heavily down to the canvas.

Breazeale had to beat the count. One . . . Two . . . Face-down still, Breazeale scarcely moved. Three . . . Four . . . Yet he had a stubbornness deep-rooted within him. He stirred. Five . . . Six . . . He hauled himself off the deck, on to his knees and up on to his feet before the referee counted eight.

Joshua stayed on him, maintaining that intensity. He launched a cannon-like right hand and with both fists battered the American to his knees once and for all; a fast blur of white leather and Breazeale was down. Joshua strode away casually, like a gunslinger marching across a saloon bar floor.

Sixty-one seconds into the seventh round and it was over. Joshua raised one arm in the air to celebrate before the referee had even finished his count. As suddenly as he had switched his attack, unleashing rapid flurries to end Breazeale's challenge, the atmosphere in the arena changed. For the crowd Joshua had delivered the knockout they expected. As they exulted, cheering, shouting, at this moment Breazeale was no longer the enemy. He was just a man, cutting a forlorn figure as he picked himself off the canvas. A man who had come up against the limits of his ambition. Through boxing the American had actually made a connection to the father he had never known. His father had been in and out prison, and out of his life, during Breazeale's youth. Only later, when the young man had already become a boxer, did he discover that his father had been a fighter, too. With this challenger now bludgeoned into submission, at a time like that you also remembered that his wife and child were in the crowd. You hoped Breazeale had been well paid for what he suffered. You hoped he'd be the same afterwards.

The mood in the ring had changed as well. Joshua could walk to the opposing corner smiling now. He touched fists with Breazeale's trainers and they could exchange grins, relieved that that was it, the worst was over, and their man might just have shared the ring with someone special. Joshua's world title belt was returned to him and he stretched up, raising it high above his head, presenting it to his crowd once again and smiling broadly still.

He shrugged off the necessary, concentrated cruelty of the fight. Warm satisfaction settled over him as he sat back, feet up, in his changing room after the battle was won. Usually after a knockout victory he got on the pads to complete the rounds which had been scheduled for the bout but remained unfinished in the ring. He spared himself that now. Joshua might have controlled this contest but the camp, the weeks of training he had endured to make sure there could be no doubt as to the outcome of this fight, had been hard, harder than ever. That work was now done. His title belt sat alongside him, lying ahead of him only rest.

It is summer and this is the picture of a champion.

Origins

London, 2008

Few great adventures start in Argos.

Anthony Joshua left Watford when he was eighteen. His mother, Yeta, moved to London and the six foot six teenager went with her. Joshua didn't plan on leaving his friends or his life behind, but when he went back he wanted them to see he'd grown in stature. Which was why he found himself in Argos, his big hand holding a little pen, filling out a slip of paper to buy a bench press, some weights and other training paraphernalia.

His mother would be a constant in his life and, if he was more distant from her when he was young, Anthony would find they grew closer as he matured. In Golders Green he may not have had new friends to hang out with but he had family. His cousin, Benga Ileyemi, had come round to his mum's house and the two exercised with these new weights. 'You know I'm doing real workouts at the minute,' Ben said. 'I'm going down the boxing gym.'

'Oh yeah, is it?' Anthony's deep voice replied.

In Watford he'd played football with his mates after school, like any normal teenager. New in this part of town, Joshua had little to do. So he went along to the Finchley Amateur Boxing Club to watch Ben and this real workout. Boxing had made a fleeting appearance in Joshua's life four years earlier. When he was fourteen the boys he'd grown up with all went down to Ricky English's gym in Watford. Young Anthony had tagged along, more for the fitness than anything else. Before football had entirely taken up his time after school, he managed three sessions in total before knocking boxing on the head, dissuaded not so much by the difficulty of the endeavour than by the far too hefty cost of six pounds a go. He never bothered going back.

Four years on, in 2008, he'd been in a boxing gym another three times but only watching. He could see it was serious. The coaches at Finchley had little interest in wasting their time with 'dead wood'. You came here to work or you went back home. And Anthony was still bored.

Ben lent Anthony twenty-five quid for his first pair of boxing boots. He dug out some vests from home, borrowed a pair of shorts from Ben, too, and stood on the wooden gym floor being shown how to wrap some bandages from the club round his fists.

The wrapping of the hands is one of boxing's rites. In the still moments before a contest, the boxer and his cornerman share a quiet moment in the changing room as the trainer tightens bandages round the fighter's tools of his trade, his fists. He makes his fighter feel strong. For Joshua the wrapping of the hands on this occasion was an initiation into another kind of family.

So new was Anthony to the sport that he didn't even watch it. If he had, he might have turned his TV on to the Beijing Olympics that year. He might have caught a glimpse of his future.

But in 2008 such high-minded aspirations were far from Anthony Joshua's thoughts. He wasn't thinking about international amateur boxing. He was getting to grips with the humble jab, the very basics of their sport. Finchley ABC had the grizzled coaches you'd expect of a boxing gym; John Oliver, a member of a family which had become a boxing dynasty synonymous with the club, ever ready to break into a smile beneath his thick, square-rimmed glasses, and Sean Murphy, whose face and flat nose bore the scars of a hard career as a professional fighter. When Joshua first entered the club, John Oliver had returned home with a smile on his face. He'd seen what he needed to see. He for one knew that a teenager had arrived in the gym who could become a special fighter.

But Anthony, of course, had to learn. Foot placement first for Joshua, standing on the wooden floor of the Finchley gym to get his legs about shoulder width apart, left foot to the front, body turned side on. Getting his fists up, sending the jab out, getting the twist on it, tucking his chin in. Making sure that when he brought the jab back, his gloves stayed high, keeping that chin safe.

Whether it was fate or luck or random chance that brought Joshua to the gym, it was his choice to stay there. He respected the seriousness of his coaches and the dedication of his new gym-mates. If he didn't feel like doing his roadwork, soon enough cousin Ben would have him on the phone, insisting Anthony come for a run. He'd found something here.

But the going was hard. His coaches got him in the club's ring for sparring. He was getting beaten up. 'You know what, I need to change,' he thought to himself. 'I need to sort this out.'

'It's easy not to do it the right way,' said Anthony, 'and make your time in the gym a lot harder. I remember one day, when I was eating chocolate and McDonald's and I wasn't living a clean lifestyle. But I was still training like I was Olympic champion. I remember saying, "This is getting tough."'

He realised he faced a decision. Do it properly. Or don't do it. Joshua continued, 'I said to myself, "Either I'm going to clean up my act, clean up my diet or I'm going to stay on the chocolates, stay on the McDonald's." That was the decision: do I want to make my life in the gym easier by living a healthy lifestyle and watching boxing videos?

'That was a turning point for me. I made a decision. I said I was going to focus on my training and get better and live the life properly.'

He had been in the gym six months before he was put forward for his first competitive bout. The club, considering his travails, was divided as to whether he was ready. Amateur boxing coaches are careful with their charges, matching them thoughtfully. They don't want their boxers harmed physically or their confidence damaged. And super-heavyweights can hurt one another. But Joshua's coaches were prepared to back him.

'You know the thing with boxing, your coaches can see the future. They can see what you don't see. So my coach saw that I was ready. I had something about me,' said Anthony.

Finchley was having a home show at the Boston Arms, a pub in Tufnell Park and no stranger to violence. The function room out back, the Boston Dome, could create quite a buzz, especially around a boxing ring. Joshua, as the super-heavyweight, would be on last, a routine he would have to get used to.

'A lion's always patient before he goes in for the kill,' Joshua laughed. 'I'm patient. I bide my time. I look forward to getting in there. The day's been set and I'm boxing on that day so, whatever time it is, it doesn't bother me.'

The two bouts before Joshua's had been thrilling ones, stirring up that heady excitement of the fight crowd. Finally it was Anthony's turn to go on. In your first contest, it's so easy to forget everything, all your training; all your practice deserts you when you first experience the unique stresses of entering the ring for a real boxing match. For Anthony this fight was a blur. He remembered his opponent coming out of the corner, coming towards him. He just threw a jab-right cross, a straight one-two combination. Watched his opponent fall. The room erupted. Anthony accepted their applause.

'This is all right,' he thought.

Harder Days

Chadwell, 2009

It wasn't all easy. Boxing soon becomes extremely tough. Anthony Joshua racked up a couple of knockout wins. But in the amateurs, sooner or later, everybody loses. The name Anthony Joshua meant nothing to Dillian Whyte – a rough and ready kickboxer making the transition to boxing – who competed for Chadwell St Mary, a small club east of London. Whyte had always been a fighter. 'I'm from Jamaica, I had a strong Jamaican accent so a lot of people thought it would be funny to take the mick until I started knocking people out. A lot of people thought it would be funny to laugh at the way I talk because I didn't speak proper English,' he said. 'As soon as I started knocking people out that changed.

'It's what I had to do to survive. I had to fight. Even in my house I had to fight because I've got big brothers and a big sister who used to whup my arse, so I had to fight my brothers and my sister growing up.'

A street brawler who'd grown up in Brixton, Whyte always

welcomed a scrap. 'I was working the doors when I was fourteen years old in south London,' he recalled. 'So I'm used to people being unpredictable and being crazy because you tell them they can't come in because they haven't got the right shoes on or something. I'm used to all of that crap so to me it's nothing.'

In 2009 he was twenty-one years old and trying to get his amateur boxing career rolling. 'We were looking for somebody to box, we couldn't find anybody and they said there's this kid from Finchley but he's dangerous. Obviously he's knocked everybody about, etc., etc. I said I don't really care. I'll fight him anyway. My coach said we'd find somebody else. We looked, we looked and there was nobody else. We said, all right we'll take the fight. We took the fight,' Whyte said simply.

The bout was set for a working men's club on Whyte's home show. The ring was small and a rowdy crowd, a couple of hundred strong, leaned forward, close to the ropes, growing increasingly lively as the evening progressed. 'People like to see two heavyweights going at it,' Whyte grinned.

Joshua was the taller man, but he was a callow boxer, tall, but yet to fill out round his shoulders and arms. There was a solidity to Whyte, shorter, squat, but as destructive as a wrecking ball. And he attacked with relish. He jabbed in quick, scoring first. Joshua threw a clumsy right cross, his chin popping up too high. His technique evidently raw: he was after all a novice. Joshua reeled off a jab of his own and pushed out another cross, aiming it at the body. Already in the first round Whyte was muttering venomously at Joshua. Less a boxing match, the contest was quickly turning into a brawl. Whyte looked for Anthony's head with big swings from either hand. He charged in and Joshua began to slug with him. It left him open to a right then a left hook. Whyte tagged him with that right again: the weight of the shot knocked him back off balance, falling into the ropes.

To start the second round Anthony tried to stave off the aggressor with a one-two combination, a straight left-right. But still Whyte came on, belting him with a furious left hook. He struck Joshua with a one-two. The shots clattered in, dropping him to the canvas. He was hurt momentarily. But then his pride kicked in. He bounced straight up to his feet. Whyte accepted the invitation. He swarmed over his opponent, bulling forward. Anthony's arms were tiring and Whyte released the faster punches. He was overeager, though. Too many missed the mark.

Joshua sucked in air to recover in the break between rounds. He dragged himself off his stool, digging deep to unearth new energy. His work was still loose and ragged. But his left hook hit Whyte on the way in. He landed a clear jab. A left hook from Whyte smacked in high but Joshua slung a cross right back at him. The success encouraged him. He came on more strongly. His right hit in again, he even ducked a jab. He landed a final left on the bell, but it was too late to affect the decision. Breathing heavily, his shoulders a touch stooped, Joshua's arms hung at his sides. The referee raised Whyte's hand, the unanimous victor.

Whyte forgot his animosity at once. As Anthony trudged back to his corner, he stepped across to meet him. He reached out to grab him round the waist, a movement so sudden for an instant it looked like an attack. But it was an embrace. He hugged him, lifted him up off his feet, a gesture of respect after a hard bout.

Ultimately, though, it would not prove to be a happy victory for Whyte. It prompted closer scrutiny of his past experience. His kickboxing background had come at a higher level than many had thought. He'd fought professionally. If the Finchley coaches had known this they would never have matched him with a novice like Anthony. The fallout would eventually see Whyte's amateur boxing card revoked, forcing him out of the sport and obliging him to turn professional, with no amateur titles on his résumé. 'How many boxers have gone into amateur boxing that's done kickboxing? Loads,' Whyte lamented bitterly. 'As long as I'm in boxing, I'm going to have a hard, tough career. I just need to be strong and keep pushing forward.'

Joshua for his part had proved something. His technique had had none of the precision Sean Murphy expected. John Oliver would only send a boxer to the ring expecting him to win. Yet Joshua had demonstrated an ineffable quality. He had what boxers call heart. Knocked down, hit hard, he clambered up and fought back. He even finished strong. It was a sign of a promise.

'I fought a guy that was more experienced than me,' Anthony noted. 'I realised boxing wasn't as easy as I thought, so I thought I had to up my level.'

His coaches would keep on testing him. As well as putting him into novice championships, which Joshua duly won, they put him through it in training. He was still just learning the ropes. But they made it punishing for him in the gym. His trainers got wind of a six foot nine heavyweight from Manchester who was in London for sparring. The fighter had only recently turned professional, and no one then knew that

Tyson Fury would one day become the heavyweight champion of the world. The big Traveller was just beginning to make a name for himself, boxing on undercards screened on ITV. Joshua was still a novice but his coaches decided to sling him in to a spar with Fury. There was another lure for Joshua, too. The Mancunian was offering his Rolex as a prize to anyone who could knock him down.

'If you want that Rolex,' his coach said, 'take it to him.'

Joshua did so. He went for him. 'We had a little war,' Anthony chuckled years later, 'it wasn't really a technical thing, it was holding on with one hand, trying to hit with the other, lowblowing me and all that.

'This was about 2009, I wasn't on GB. I was really inexperienced back then. I had my first fight November 2008. I was really inexperienced but we just went to war. I didn't know who he was. I was never a maniac boxing fan. I just thought there's this big guy, he's from Manchester,' he added. 'We had a good spar.'

Not that anyone suspected it at the time, but seven years later both men would win versions of the world title and Joshua would remain eager to renew hostilities. He wanted another shot at that watch. 'I've got the G-Shock on,' he laughed. 'I need that Rolley.'

The Taste of Victory

Liverpool, 2010

Anthony Joshua would ascend to the summit of the sport with astonishing speed. It says something about my talent-spotting abilities that I hadn't detected any such brilliance in him. Watching the 2010 ABA super-heavyweight final, the last bout of the annual senior national amateur championships at York Hall in Bethnal Green, my focus was on his forlorn looking opponent in the opposite corner. By reaching this stage of the national competition, Dominic Winrow had already done sterling work putting boxing on the map in the Isle of Man. The island has only two boxing clubs so it's hardly easy for Manx ABC, whose boxers travel to the mainland by boat, to get sparring, bouts, or, indeed, boost its reputation.

Winrow was a likeable bloke – a newly qualified PE teacher – and ready to settle down with his new wife. Ginger hair cropped short, he had a problem quite common to the super-heavyweight division. He was chubby. The only stricture of that weight class is to be over ninety-one kilos. Unlike members of any other division, their weight is unlimited. It means a lax diet won't stop a super-heavyweight from boxing. Modern angst about heavyweights revolves around their decline and that is bound up in the appearance of many, particularly professional, contenders. They don't look like athletes. They're fat.

Anthony Joshua is not fat. Seeing him in the ring for that final in May 2010, it wasn't his height that caught the attention, though he is tall. It was his breadth. Massive, heavy shoulders, thick arms hanging down to his waist. I found out later he was a mean sprinter. It marked him out as an athlete. Born in another country he could have made a fortune charging across the turf with an American football in his hands. Born in another time you could imagine him swinging an axe on an ancient battlefield.

His unblinking stare completed the fearsome aspect. His eyes were wide, the whites clear. They blazed at poor Winrow and that concentration was not to be broken. 'I watched a lot of Tyson. You never take your eye off your opponent in the corner. It's the staredown,' Anthony would say.

Winrow's knot of supporters had moved to the ringside seats right alongside me. They were loud, cheerful, enthusiastic. A woman took off her shoes to clamber happily up on to a chair to cry out Dominic's name. But just looking at Joshua I feared the worst for Winrow.

The intimidation – Anthony just standing, staring – worked. Winrow stayed within himself. At the bell, Joshua charged out of his corner, slamming great fists down on his prey. Winrow tried to box properly, kept his mitts up to form a shell-defence, hoping to ride out the early storm. It was a vain hope. A blow, glancing along the top of Winrow's head, had his legs jittering.

Joshua was simply too strong. Wide shots that might have left him open to counters cannoned off either side of Winrow's head, those huge shoulders heaving behind them, generating force. It was over fast. Joshua stopped Winrow in the first round.

Even then I didn't realise Britain had its next super-heavyweight hope on its hands. Yes, he was a level above Winrow, on physicality alone. But that isn't enough. Power has to be controlled. That is especially true in boxing. Raw strength needs skill to be translated into any kind of outcome in the ring. On the night it was teenage featherweight Martin Ward and other finals in the lighter divisions generating the buzz. Joshua only made the final sentence of an online BBC report.

Anthony was senior ABA champion only a couple of years after taking up the sport. His potential was clear. But the domestic super-heavyweights were nothing like the beasts that lurked in international competitions. I had to assume Joshua was far off that level. Not that I wanted to. In the pros there is nothing like the heavyweights, the equivalent of amateur super-heavies. Competitors at that size always carry the threat of a knockout, regardless of how dire their predicament in a contest may be. Big men bring big money, too. A promising American heavyweight prospect would cause such a stir that Floyd Mayweather actually fighting Manny Pacquiao might no longer seem the only thing that could save boxing. A bright, charming, English-speaking heavyweight prospect, from the battling island on the far side of the Atlantic, would be the next best thing.

But I had to be careful to take note of what was really in front of my eyes, rather than what I wanted to see. Anthony Joshua was still raw.

And Joshua had yet to experience international action. In days of yore winning the ABAs granted instant elevation to the national side. In the modern age, of course, the Great Britain team is far more advanced, categorised into its Development and Podium squads, constantly monitored. Domestic success is now just one more criterion for the GB assessors.

Joshua's exploits earned him that call from Sheffield. He went up to the Steel City, invited to train with the GB Development squad. It was a shock to him. The boxing facility at the English Institute of Sport was a world away from his home club. The gym in Finchley looked like a chapel. It had a vaulted roof, wide wooden floor, punch bags bolted into the wooden beams. A side room, with mats on the floor and a few assorted weights, led to a changing room that barely had space enough for your kitbag. That's boxing. You need your coach's brain, your body and a pair of gloves. Luxury can't make you a fighter.

But it can sometimes help. The GB gym in Sheffield is a modern cathedral. Three full-size rings occupied the floor, the shining new bags hung all the way from the high ceilings, so boxers could circle them fully as they worked. The hall extended into an area for strength and conditioning, containing gleaming devices for exercise that Anthony had never seen before. A back office looked out on to the training floor. A treatment room housed their physiotherapist. As well as a crack team of coaches, they had a performance psychologist on call, a doctor, a nutritionist, everything a boxer didn't even know he wanted.

Luxury in a boxing sense, but a new, difficult world for

Joshua. 'I trained hard in Finchley,' he said. 'I did loads of extra stuff when outside the gym and so on. But when I got to Sheffield and I had my first week there, I had to make a serious decision again.'

He was on the Development squad, training Thursday to Monday every fortnight but four times a day. He simply wasn't used to that sort of work. He had Paul Walmsley, a coach militaristic in his attitude, on his case. His first meeting with the tough Liverpudlian trainer was memorable. 'This guy, he's training and hitting the bag and I thought, "Fuck me. This is completely different to what I'm used to." We had to train four times in a day. I didn't even train as much as that in a week when I was at my local club. I thought, this guy's nuts,' Anthony said.

He had to ask himself whether this was for him. 'I might just stick to being ABA champion,' he thought. 'It was a touch of reality for me that this is what it's about. If I want to go to another level.'

Joshua could have walked away. He was already getting offers to turn professional. 'Only from chancers, not so much solid promoters. Like managers acting as promoters and that was it,' he said. 'Which was interesting because Jonny Oliver would always tell me to be careful of these people, so when it started happening I was already aware of it. That's why I kind of kept away and I stayed with the amateur circuit.'

His clubmate Dereck Chisora, the super-heavyweight before him at Finchley, had gone pro after winning the ABAs. With GB Joshua was only on a small grant, about £500 a month. There were other ways he could make more money, in and outside of boxing. 'When you're a young kid everything runs through your head. Because Chisora was pro at the time and he was making headlines. He's from my local club, he only won the ABAs and went pro so there was a formula that worked without doing all this extra graft.'

The training camp in Sheffield gave him no quarter. 'I would get dropped out there. I was getting battered,' he said. 'It came to a stage where I was thinking this ain't for me. It was tough. It was brutal.'

But then he added, 'The tough times, either you get disheartened or you come back and get better. I needed to get beat up.

'You start to adapt.'

What he had achieved in the past was simply his pass to the GB gym. It meant nothing here. 'Someone said to me, "You can't take your ABA Championship to a Russian or a European champion because they won't respect you,"' Joshua recalled. 'You need to aim higher.'

Mounted on the walls of the gym were images of Britain's past Olympic heroes. The display charted them chronologically, finishing with a blank silhouette of an unnamed boxer. Above read the words: 'London 2012'. Below: 'This could be you'. It took Joshua a while to embrace that concept and seize the top spot. Back in May 2010 he wasn't even the number one super-heavyweight in Britain. A man called Amin Isa occupied the super-heavyweight berth. You sensed that he was just a place-holder, there until someone better came along.

Isa wasn't considered worth sending to the European Championships of that year in Moscow. I had seen him box, in the less exalted environs of Fairfield Halls in Croydon. Isa is tall but spindly for a big man. He didn't impose himself in the ring, so much so that speaking to him up close I was surprised at the real size of him. He didn't carry the menace of a heavyweight boxer. In Croydon I watched Isa boxing Dominic Akinlade, a solid lump of a super-heavyweight. Akinlade, a bus driver from the London institution that is the Fitzroy Lodge Amateur Boxing Club, brought a diffident attitude to his boxing. He occupied the centre of the ring but moved little from there.

Isa decided to showboat, staying on the outside, switching to either stance, trying to inject some flair into the bout. He made his work ungainly, his aspirations at nimbleness let down by the lack of grace, and speed, in his feet, legs and hands.

And yet his tools were such to put him near and, for a time, at the top of the domestic super-heavyweight talent pool. He didn't possess the aura of a world-beater, though he was sent to the Commonwealth Games later in 2010. For Great Britain the Commonwealths are significant, though they do not rank high in the amateur boxing firmament. Its entrants do not include the fearsome Russians and Ukrainians who populate the European Championships, let alone the Kazakhs, Cubans and more who illuminate the Worlds. In that sense the attention victory at the Commonwealths brings a British boxer is disproportionate to the challenge.

The reason for the fame it brings? The magic ingredient of television. Amateur boxing has grown ever more obscure. Days when the ABAs were broadcast on TV, not to mention held at august venues like the Royal Albert Hall, are from another era. More than most sports, boxing needs airtime to breathe life into it. The Commonwealth Games, involving as they do multiple events as well as amateur boxing, are a mini-Olympics and the BBC brings the full spectrum of coverage to them with relish. And the boxing event is fertile territory for the home nations to harvest some shiny medals and reap some long-overdue press coverage.

Some seized the moment to assert themselves. Isa fizzled out at an early stage. As the reigning English amateur champion, Anthony Joshua had an argument for being the one who was sent. 'He didn't have any experience,' recalled GB performance director Rob McCracken. 'I tend to err on the side of caution when you're putting boxers into international competition. But great kid, real nice personality, nice way about him, very humble and he's very popular, not just because he's a very good boxer, he's a very nice human being. People warm to him. He's charismatic.'

He continued, 'You just see what they've got and then you start working with them.'

The GB Championships followed in November 2010 soon after Joshua's arrival on the GB Development squad. It was a new tournament, held at the Echo Arena in Liverpool, which ranged the country's number ones against the best of the rest from England, Wales and Scotland.

Holding a GB Championship-type competition was unusual. While the British team members were often held back from the ABAs, here was a tournament that pitted the national side against those judged to be the best available challengers, in a competition for all to see and with international-style computer scoring. A rich prize for those not on the GB squad was on offer, the chance to win an assessment with the team in Sheffield.

For those already on the elite Podium or the Development squad, it was their opportunity to solidify their standing.

Professional fighters collect their purse no matter how they perform in the contest. For these amateurs their form does dictate what they earn. Elevation to Britain's Podium squad meant they could train full time at the high-tech gym in Sheffield's English Institute of Sport. Win medals at major tournaments and they could be moved up a payment grade. The Development squad are there every other week, and their funding reflects this part-time status. The GB Championships offered Anthony Joshua a launchpad to propel him up the rankings.

Joshua would box Isa for his place on the team. In a nervy bout, he could not pin his opponent down. That power of his did not tell. Anthony Joshua may clearly have been the future but watching them box you had to worry about him losing here and see his emergence postponed to an even later stage of the Olympic cycle. Their jabs battling for supremacy decided the contest, with a margin of only a few points. Anthony took his chance but he did not dazzle.

Nothing flashy: simple straight punches carried the day for Anthony. At the time that was less impressive than I'd hoped or expected. But those basics would be exactly what Joshua counted on for his defining contests the following year. A reminder that in this version of the sport, when computer scoring totted up punches landed, you don't get rewarded for style. In amateur boxing it doesn't matter if it's by a point, a landslide or a knockout: winning is everything. The hints were there of what was possible for Anthony Joshua. I just didn't pick up on them.

Alternate Histories

Ankara, 2011

Does an athlete choose to be great? Is there a moment when he suddenly decides that doing anything, being anything less than excellent, is unacceptable? In the space of a couple of years Anthony Joshua had moved far. His club convinced him he could become a champion in Britain. Even he had doubted them at the start. Slowly he became a believer. He joined the international squad and speaking to him at the GB gym in Sheffield in the weeks leading up to 2011's World Championships, there was a clue to his thinking.

'History is calling for a great heavyweight right now,' he said.

I thought he was merely acknowledging the desperation the sporting public had to see a genuine heavyweight prospect, one who was in shape, strong and had power. There's always a fuss whenever a big man looks like he can swing a punch, mainly due to the oft-lamented lack of decent heavies and the glamour that boxing's premier division, even in this tarnished day and age, still retains. I assumed Anthony was referring to the weight of expectation that would be thrown on his shoulders as soon as he was accepted as GB's number one super-heavy. I never suspected that, in distant Azerbaijan at the World Championships a few weeks away, he was going to force his way to the very top of the sport. He'd decided to heed the call.

But nothing in boxing is ever guaranteed.

It is the victor's story that gets told. Defeated in the GB Championships in November 2010 Amin Isa became a mere footnote in Anthony Joshua's history. I never saw Isa again. He drifted away from the sport. Later I heard that when at home in Brixton he would only run at four o'clock in the morning when no one was around. His estate was so dangerous he didn't want anyone to know he boxed. His fear was that, if they didn't care to differentiate between an amateur and a professional, people would think he had something worth taking. I imagined that Isa had soon abandoned boxing. The respite the sport offers some is, occasionally, only fleeting.

There are many frightening things about boxing, not least two highly trained young men flying at each other with dangerous intent. Lives can change in the blink of an eye and some people who leave the game will never know what they could have gained.

Anthony Joshua will become a heavyweight star and an exceedingly rich man. Rewind to early 2011 and all that so nearly passed him by. He was caught driving a car in possession of cannabis, drugs of the recreational variety. How could he have been so foolish? A valuable lesson in how having the wrong people around you can ruin you.

Before boxing, street fights, for someone as big as Joshua,

had not been hard to find. Trouble had never been too far off. But now the past threatened his future. Association with the d-word is an electric shock to sports administrators, even if Joshua had only been found with cannabis. He was suspended from the Development squad. If that ban held, you could only imagine what path in life lay ahead of a six foot six behemoth, with his sport taken from him and the temptations of petty crime already beginning to bite. It was an alternate life, a darker one, that beckoned him.

The decision to suspend Joshua almost drove him out of boxing. 'It was quite disheartening due to the fact that everyone makes mistakes. It was a silly mistake, it was only possession, it wasn't with intent to supply. It was possession and I got a caution. I did my community service but they banned me from boxing altogether, amateur boxing. I was like, "Wow, do you know what, forget this then." If I can't even win an ABA title and turn pro or whatever, I thought I can't be bothered with this because I'm already being labelled. So I was going to quit,' he said simply. 'It was all part and parcel of what I was going through at the time. It builds character.'

Somehow Joshua managed to keep himself preternaturally calm about his predicament. He might have hoped (but he didn't know) that the GB back office would do what they could to take the sting out of the situation. That there was a place waiting for him on the elite Podium squad, if he could just win his second national title. Officials at the very top of GB Boxing had already shown a disposition to stick their necks out for young boxers with great potential.

At any rate, Joshua would indeed go on to demonstrate scarcely believable coolness of thought under pressure.

But in March 2011 he was standing in a small changing room in a school's sports centre in Dagenham looking through a window on to the finals of the London stage of the ABA national championships. He was still suspended from the GB Development squad as part of their disciplinary process. Boxers, however, enter the ABAs through their clubs. Joshua therefore persisted with a second national championship campaign. Flanked by his Finchley coaches Murphy and Oliver, he could only darkly contemplate his uncertain future. The controversy was still fresh so Joshua kept himself away from the meagre audience strung out round the ring. Appeals would go back and forth about whether he should be competing in this championship at all, because of the charges he faced. He was nearly ejected, but that was before his team swung into action.

Joshua's arrest and suspension could have changed everything for him. He'd made a mistake. but he also knew to learn from it. 'It was a shock to me and it hurt me and I think it made me stronger. I was able to move on from it all. That was another decision and turning point in my career when I thought I've really got to focus on my training and get my head down,' he said.

'That's what I'm saying about where I come from. I needed that change, I made that change, I focused. Saturday nights, I was running past clubs and people were looking at me like I was crazy. That's what I was doing with my Fridays and Saturdays. That's what it takes.'

He made the switch. You've got to think like a champion. You've got to train like a champion. You've also got to live like a champion.

It was a stark reminder that there are no shortcuts. When he was on the Development squad, Joshua struggled financially.

He was catching the train up to Sheffield, lugging three bags on his shoulders, a suitcase in his hand. The Podium boxers were put up in a better hotel, the Premier Inn. Joshua was stuck in the grim Etap. He remembered sitting at his window, looking out. Thomas Stalker, the team captain, and other Podium boxers were laughing in the street, climbing into Stalker's smart Range Rover before shooting off down the road. 'We were stuck in the Etap and they were in the Premier Inn living the high life,' he remembered.

'Man, I need to make a change or something,' he thought. 'I need to get where them boys are.' Later he met them and asked, 'Tom, what do you do? How do you make so much money?'

There were other ways, of course, beyond being a part-time member of the Great Britain squad, for Anthony Joshua to make some cash.

'You've got to work hard,' Stalker happily explained. 'If you want to be number one in the world.'

A boxing team doesn't necessarily need a captain, but Stalker, a fast-talking, indefatigable Liverpudlian, had inhabited the role. In his first bout at the 2010 European Championships the light welterweight had toppled the reigning World champion. That inspirational effort gave the whole team a momentum which ultimately saw them scoop five medals, a breakthrough performance for GB Boxing at a major. Stalker would remain the heart of the team. He made time for his squad-mates, sharing his experience with them, always ready to talk.

Joshua needed to get on the Podium squad, the elite, full-time team. 'Tom's a good captain,' the super-heavyweight later reflected. 'All the boys on the Podium, they're all there for a reason. It just rubbed off on me.'

Stalker and Joshua had an understanding. Like Anthony, Stalker had taken up the sport late. Most of boxing's top talents begin young, having their first bout at around eleven or twelve years old. But Stalker spent his teenage years on the streets of Liverpool engaged in a very different kind of activity. He stole cars, mixing with a crowd who were only going in the wrong direction.

'A few of my mates used to pull up beside the police in Liverpool in a robbed car and put two fingers up to them and get chased around Liverpool. I've been in a few of them thinking, "Bloody hell, I'm going to die here," ' Stalker said. 'It's not big and it's not clever doing it. But at the time, if you're in with the wrong crowd, that's just what you do.

'I never used to think of the consequences. I used to think it was fun, it was exciting. It's not exciting. It's daft, it's dangerous. I'm just glad that I didn't ever hurt anyone.'

They would sell a stolen car for a few hundred pounds and go out with the money. 'You're not having much money and then you're getting like five hundred pounds,' Stalker continued. 'We'd party. You're living in the fast lane but it doesn't last because you can't get away with that for that long. You can only rob so many cars before you get caught. And that's what happened.'

Reality was fast catching up with Stalker as he fled from a farm in Southport, to the north of Liverpool, in a stolen jeep, with not only the police but the man they'd just robbed in pursuit. 'We got chased all over Southport by the fella in his mate's jeep and the police. We ended up getting caught. That was it because I knew it was bad. I thought if I do one more car and I get caught, one more car and that'll be me going to jail for six months or a year. I chose not to go that way,' Stalker said.

'We could have killed someone in that car. We could have crashed. I never used to think of that.'

Stalker's girlfriend was pregnant and he refused to let his life carry on as it had. He had no qualifications from school. He hadn't even taken his exams. The best job he could manage was as a kitchen porter at the Marriot hotel. To keep himself away from the streets he walked into a gym, his local boxing club, St Aloysius in Huyton, an area better known for producing footballers like Steven Gerrard and Joey Barton.

He had only taken up boxing at the age of eighteen. He didn't have his first bout until he was nineteen, meaning he had no junior experience. And, by his own admission, he was terrible. After his first year his coach didn't even want him to have that initial contest, saying he wasn't ready.

'I weren't good in the gym but when I got in the ring I knew how to win and I won and that was it really. Any bout, an Olympic bout, it doesn't matter, it's still a great feeling winning. That feeling,' he said. 'The best sort of buzz you can ever have is fighting and training. The best thing in life is training for a fight and winning the fight.'

He stayed at the gym. He began living right. It's not too much to say the sport saved his life. 'I was basically in with the wrong group of people,' said Stalker. 'When you're with the wrong crowd, even though I'm not a bad person, you can become a bad person. Because you're with a gang of people that are going nowhere. All my mates, my old mates, they're all in jail, doing like ten years.'

Instead of walking a path that would have led him inexorably to the same end, Stalker became an athlete. 'Boxing has made me disciplined and become a better person,' he insisted.

For Joshua winning a second ABA title proved crucial. Not only by the end of the tournament did he see his suspension from GB Boxing lifted, a ban which would stretch from February to June, but he and a friend at the opposite end of the size spectrum, another Londoner, light flyweight Charlie Edwards, would be elevated to Britain's Podium squad and entered into the major internationals.

Joshua's victory at the national championship assumed an air of inevitability. But nothing in his career has been inevitable. He had to get through the London stage of the tournament. He strode out on to the gym floor of that sports centre in Dagenham. A tall but, at that time, comparatively slight Joe Joyce, who carried a dramatic scar round his eye, had jabbed and moved his way round Dominic Akinlade to reach Anthony Joshua in the London final at the Dagenham school sports centre. Akinlade, uncomfortable, elected to switch stance and box southpaw, that is leading unusually with the right hand instead of the left. That might have thrown Joyce off. Against a southpaw you step to the left, away from the unorthodox cross. Stepping into Joshua's backhand right was a big mistake. He received a terrible shelling from Anthony's fists. Joyce had many talents (he had completed a fine art degree, been a cheerleader in the US, a diver, learned kung fu in China) but they came to naught. Joshua bombed heavy, straight punches down the middle until the referee wisely stopped Joyce on his feet in the first round. 'I got caught with a few shots,' Joyce sighed. 'I got stopped three times' – for standing counts – 'obviously three times it's over.'

Joyce would fill out. In 2016 he lost a controversial decision in the final of the Olympic Games. But all the way back then, five years before his final in Rio, going into that bout with Joshua he had ambition. 'I was quite confident, I thought I'd beat him,' he smiled ruefully. 'It all went really quick.'

In the quarter-final of the championship, where the London champions boxed the winners of the armed forces championships, Joshua's opponent declined the bout. Eminently sensible as well – it doesn't mean the soldier wasn't game, just that good coaches will not overmatch their charges at too early a stage in their careers.

By the final Joshua was in Colchester. Gratifyingly, his cousin Ben won the ninety-one-kilo national title immediately before he stepped out under the lights in front of a lively crowd at the Charter Hall. Joshua lined up opposite Fayz Abbas, an Iraqi boxing for Manchester club Northside, and desperate to make a name for himself to turn pro. 'He was trying to intimidate me,' Anthony noted of their behind-the-scenes encounters before the contest. Whether that was staring Joshua out, or trying to start a fist fight, quite how Abbas would manage to intimidate him remained a mystery to me. Joshua just had to maintain his wide-eyed glare to look fearsome and Abbas, sturdy but a touch fleshy, was not the same sort of physical specimen.

But again Joshua simply outpointed him. He kept his punches straight. Kept it long, that is to say kept Abbas at the end of his long reach. He could have let some blazing shots go but elected not to. He may not have been the consummate technician in there, but that was the template he was boxing to.

'Imagine Abbas had come and beaten me now,' Joshua said. 'Because Amin didn't do too well they're looking for a dominant super-heavyweight. It was open for anyone to claim. That's why those wins, ABA Championships, Amin, Joe Joyce, they were pretty crucial wins in order to get me silently respected with the right people. They didn't say it but they put me forward. Then it was just me trying to prove myself again and again.'

I didn't feel uneasy at Joshua's performance against Abbas though I did have a vague sense of disappointment. The crowd wanted to see Joshua's power unleashed. The super-heavyweight, though, let his wiser head prevail. It was hard for him to get matches domestically; he'd already had too few bouts for his liking in this championship. If he'd decided to get a full-distance, three-round contest under his belt, that was a sensible call.

It doesn't sound much, three three-minute rounds. But even a normal person trying it, to the best of their ability, will find themselves drained frighteningly fast. How hard is it to hold your hands up by your eyes, up past your chin? It's nothing. At least it should be nothing. But in the confines of a boxing ring, in the heat of competition, with the extra weight of the gloves, those hands can suddenly become impossible to raise, even when you desperately need to shield your face from another man's punches. Fear, from being in the fight itself, can power neither your lungs nor legs the way one would like to believe. You need to do the work ahead of time, you need the stamina, the body conditioning in the bank. Without it you're doomed.

A hard round working pads held by a coach or pummelling a hanging bag can sap your arms of strength. And that weariness comes without the tension of combat, the nervous energy that drains the muscles when a contest is barely underway. No amount of experience will rid a boxer of those nerves, though they can learn to manage them better. Boxing is a sport that exhausts you to the bone.

How the pros can go twelve rounds is remarkable. They must modulate the intensity of their output at their discretion. It is a marathon, which doesn't necessarily mean the amateurs have it easy. They are in a sprint. Or, more accurately, a sequence of three sprints, at middle-distance intensity, with a minute's pause to recover and regroup in between.

Anthony's suspension, reinstatement and elevation to the elite squad, as gratifying as the turnaround was, left him with only ten days on the Podium squad to get ready for his first major tournament, the European Championships in Turkey. 'At the time I was suspended completely, so my head was everywhere,' said Joshua. 'I didn't really know all the boys then so that was an experience.' Stepping him up to the elite level may have been reassuring but it left his body playing catch-up, needing to make the adjustment.

Never before in his life had Anthony needed to box three times back-to-back. In Ankara he'd have to do just that against the most challenging opponents he'd ever faced. 'The lads that have been to championships before, I asked them obviously and I got a little bit of an idea of what it would be like. But it was different, the travelling, the adrenalin. It's hard to sleep at night. Those little things. In an ABA Championship you're boxing once every two weeks,' said Anthony. Out here GB even had him training before bouts to sharpen up.

The team had suffered a hit before they even reached Ankara for the 2011 European Championships. They had lost Robert McCracken, Britain's head coach, lost him, that is, from the corner. McCracken, as well as being the performance director of GB Boxing, was the trainer of a professional. No ordinary pro, by any means, Carl Froch was the WBC's super-middleweight champion at the time. McCracken was renowned for his calm words in the corner and his guidance had helped steer Froch through some blood and thunder twelve-round fights.

While McCracken may have cared little for journalists or what they thought of him, his concern for boxers was quite incredible. The day Froch contested that WBC belt, McCracken's mother died. He didn't tell Froch, refused to disrupt his charge on the most important night of his life. He left his own grieving till after the fight. He did his job.

McCracken, once a fighter himself, was a hard man, a cool customer, but clearly someone capable of extraordinary class. Froch would be the best man at McCracken's wedding some years later in 2012.

There was customary outrage from the amateur boxing old guard when McCracken was appointed to GB. The hostility between the amateur and professional codes is long-standing: it was only recently in England that a trainer was allowed to coach boxers in both sports.

AIBA, the world governing body for amateur boxing, still maintained a firm separation from the professional sport and for that reason stripped McCracken of his licence, even though he had been the GB performance director since 2009. While he could work in the gym with the team, the move effectively banned him from the field of play in competition, removing him from the corner during his amateur boxers' bouts. The timing was curious. McCracken had been Froch's trainer for as long as he'd been on GB. Why, two years on, AIBA all of a sudden decided to ban him, just ahead of a major tournament, was anybody's guess.

Boxing is unique in that the coach doesn't just step back

and observe how his best-laid plans pan out. He's intimately involved. The cornerman has the final word with his boxer before he goes out and, in the amateurs, has two opportunities within the contest to explain, cajole, advise, direct or urge his man on. In part, it accounts for the peculiarly intense bond between a boxer and his trainer.

McCracken was an acknowledged master of the art and his absence was a direct blow to Britain's medal hopes, not only at these Europeans but for future championships.

In Ankara, Anthony Joshua was having to get to grips with his first major tournament and the new customs and habits of being an elite GB boxer. In Turkey he shared a room with light flyweight Charlie Edwards. At such an early stage in their international careers little was expected of them. They were at the Europeans for experience, a confidence building exercise, with the European Olympic qualifying event in distant 2012 a more realistic target than the World Championships, which would also be the first Olympic qualifier, a few short months later. In Ankara the two friends went out to fight, one after the other, coming back to the room to report back on how they'd got on.

And they were doing well. They were winning. Charlie, incredibly for an eighteen-year-old in his first major, made it all the way to the semi-final, picking up a bronze medal. Joshua was not so impressive. Outscoring the German and Irish representatives handily enough, he ran up against Romania's super-heavyweight, Mihai Nistor, in the quarter-final.

That was when Joshua's body betrayed him. Exhaustion caught up with him. His muscles seized up, his limbs would not respond. He'd got himself ahead on points, but he couldn't hold his gloves by his eyes, above his chin. The hands came down. He could see Nistor's punches coming but he couldn't stop them. They weren't hurting him but he was conscious of the impacts. He could feel his head jarring on his shoulders, his chin being forcibly turned to the side.

He had worked well in the first two rounds, flicking out straight punches, landing the type of long cross that scores well in amateur boxing. But he never forced Nistor back. Indeed, it was Anthony boxing off the back foot. He leaned away to get clear of those hooks. But he was letting too many through. The Romanian was a southpaw; his stance unorthodox, he led with his right hand. Short and squat, Nistor's hands were heavy. His hardest punches connected in the third round. That backhand left hooked across, jolting Joshua. The referee issued a standing count. Joshua got his gloves up, to show he was ready to continue. Nistor kept on him. He bowled in his left again but it flew wide. Nistor, however, drove the Englishman into a corner. Another left hook, with all the Romanian's weight behind it, smacked into Anthony's jaw, shaking him into the rigging. He had to grab the ropes with both gloves to steady himself. He wanted to go on, he never went down. But the referee called it off.

Straightaway Joshua moved to congratulate the opposing corner, even though disappointment was etched all over his face. It had been an emotional encounter for both boxers; Nistor was almost overcome at managing to dig out the victory. Once the referee had lifted his arm in victory, the Romanian shook hands with Joshua and they embraced.

Anthony could think over the whole tournament, his first European Championships and his first major international competition. 'The first bout I felt a bit tired, maybe because it was the first. Second bout I felt amazing and in the third bout . . . This is all taking place in four days. I was just tired. In that last round, I was just tired,' he recalled.

'I was six points up and that was for a medal. Imagine if I had trained hard for these Europeans and I was focused. I just felt like everybody who had doubted me with my troubles . . . all that had gone on and me being stopped – you know what, watch what happens next.'

It was a good, not a great, tournament performance. And that, Joshua decided, was unacceptable.

Shock and Awe

Baku, 2011

Boxers suffer. No other sport compares. It is risky. Those who box know they have only their will and their skill to prevent themselves from being hit, being hurt, knocked down or knocked out.

The boxing ring is a lonely place to fight. In few other arenas are limitations of skill and character so painfully and so publicly exposed. The game is contact and pain. In no other sporting endeavour is a small lapse so brutally punished. Miss your attack, drop your guard and prepare to eat a fist thrown by a man whose business is knowing how to hurt.

There's a reason why boxers are so supremely conditioned. Their fitness training is an arms race. If one man tires, while the other stays strong, the exhausted man is in danger. That's when he lowers his fists a fraction, that's when he makes mistakes, cuts corners. That's when his opponent's punches land, when his opponent's punches hurt. Exhaustion stops you defending yourself. Exhaustion leaves you no strength to repel your attacker. If you tire you lose.

International boxers accept pain. They have to. But this British team, at its heart, would not tolerate failure.

In many ways boxing is a simple morality tale. Nothing comes for free. If you want something by all means take it. But you can't take it without the work. You can't cut corners. You do get out what you put in. Your work translates into your ability. Britain, in this generation, had boxers with the right mindset and the right skill set. They also had a system that put them in a position to be successful.

Bringing in Robert McCracken as performance director was one step in the moves they were making to professionalise their international set-up. They had seen the state-backed programmes that had made the Russian team such a force. (In later years allegations of systematic doping would be levelled at multiple Russian Olympic sports, tarnishing the country's reputation.) But there were many overseas programmes to admire. The marvellous Cuban school produced imperious boxers. You only had to look over to Ireland to see a high-performance unit that had brought major medals to a team with a limited pool of athletes to draw on.

British policymakers do share a characteristic with their opposite numbers in the former Soviet Union: they value the prestige that comes with international medals. Public money, via UK Sport and the National Lottery, would be funnelled into the boxing programme. But the coaches understood it wasn't only the boxers, who for the sake of their funding and their selection for the team, were in a results-orientated business. The coaches' own positions depended on medal hauls and a healthy outlook for the Olympic Games. Pressure stayed on them because they had been given all the tools they could wish for. The million-pound, fully staffed gym in the English Institute of Sport, for instance.

For boxers from gritty small-town gyms, where they have to rise at the crack of dawn to run, do their roadwork, go to work to earn, before getting down the gym to box for two, three hours, this facility in Sheffield is the promised land. But that doesn't make the training hurt any less. Boxing is not like other sports. Being hit in the face gets to you, in a way that even a full-bodied tackle into the turf does not. The training is near-fanatical. You can't live a normal life and box. You have to watch what you eat; making weight is a constant stress. Boxers don't drink alcohol. There are the obvious reasons – the calories, the dehydration, it dulls your reactions. But there is a near-religious fervour about the life. Drinking alcohol is a sin. Early mornings, to get in that dawn run, are a virtue.

Standard roadwork for a boxer is running far and for long. It makes some sense for a pro, who may have to contest the marathon length of twelve rounds. But pain is seen as good for the boxer. The run strengthens the legs, gives the lungs wind, but the goal is the suffering.

The GB training programme applies more targeted suffering. They're up by 7 a.m. for their running. But they'll usually be on their indoor track doing sprints, sets of hard three-minute dashes as well as steady-state runs. The team will do it all together.

Then they split into groups. Mid-morning they'll have a strength and conditioning session, which may include strongman circuits, that is to say flinging around tyres and sledgehammers. For some boxers moving up in weight they may have an extra period of S&C thrown into their day.

Their boxing session will come in the afternoon. This will be shorter and sharper than is traditional. The boxers will be divided into small groups of three or four, going into the gym at staggered times. Here they do their bags, padwork, sparring, whatever McCracken and his coaching team have decided for the day. Having a small group means there's virtually a coach per boxer. Even on the bags they can't take it easy. There'll be a pair of eyes on them. There is nowhere to hide.

There are also cameras. They have the gym rigged up so that GB's sport scientists can record and analyse the sessions, logging punches thrown per round, their accuracy and many more variables. This is more useful for sparring, especially when they have foreign teams over for training camps and the analysts can gather data on potential opponents. Their sparring is more complex than simply going to war, though sometimes they do just that. The coaches will give the athletes technical spars, where they have to fulfil different roles, practise different skills. They spar their rivals at their weight as well as those in neighbouring divisions. Occasionally they spar pros: super-middleweight champion Carl Froch, for instance, is a regular fixture in the gym.

Those technical spars are harder to maintain when foreign teams come over. A Kazakh will take the chance to knock your head off, in your own gym, if he can. He wants to have one over the Brit should they meet in a competition ring.

Typically the GB team are in their Sheffield gym Monday to Thursday before the boxers are allowed home for the weekend. Inevitably they'll be running or popping into their original boxing club once they've returned to their own part of the country.

Sometimes they'll be taken overseas to share training camps with other international teams in their homeland. These can be brutal. They want to learn from other nations, familiarise themselves with key future opposition in sparring. The GB management valued the links they'd built with Russia. The Russian team was perennially strong – their coaching methods influenced post-Soviet countries, the rising boxing powerhouses of Kazakhstan, Ukraine and Azerbaijan – and Britain needed to find a way to beat them.

That involved flying into the depths of Russia and entering their mountain base, running through snow in the mornings, staring at strange food, blood pudding and caviar. The Russian boxers are cold like their landscape. The Britons could strike up a conversation or enjoy a joke with the French, with whom they often joined camp. Not so the Russians. They're there to hurt.

The Russians aren't released, they don't have down time like the GB lads, they're all about boxing. The Brits say you need a break, mentally you need to switch off. Coming through those experiences, weathering the foreign training camps, is part of what brought the GB boys together. They were on enemy territory, in a hostile environment. They had to rely on each other. They had to look after each other.

That prepared them. At the Olympics they would be able to box at home, with all the world watching. But to get there, all the major tournaments, the qualifying events, would be in far-off foreign lands.

These camps also demystified the Russians. They may have needed to travel halfway across the world to do it but it meant the GB boxers didn't have to wait for a crucial competition bout to meet the planet's cruellest operators. The Brits could see inside their training camp, spar with them and remind themselves, really convince themselves, that the Russians were men like any other, with two arms and two legs. They could be beaten. If you had the ability. If you had the will.

The GB 2012 Olympic programme produced consummate tournament boxers, superbly fit. Their doctor, Mike Loosemore, who'd been on the team for years, had never overseen such superbly conditioned athletes before. There was only one weakness he'd identified. Their hands.

'Piano players' hands,' he said, to be more precise. When these young men, barely into their twenties for the most part, travelled to Baku in Azerbaijan for the World Championships, they would be boxing men not only from Russia but Kazakhstan, Cuba, the host nation Azerbaijan, old fighters with heavy hands who had their own strength, 'man strength' as boxers often termed it.

The GB boxers were young. They'd developed crisp power. They needed to channel it through their fists without harming those transmitters. Dr Mike had seen a spate of hand problems, but, rather than dismissing it as simply part and parcel of the trade, he instituted a policy. For a start he forced the boxers to sit through a seminar on how to wrap their hands properly, how to fasten the bandages round their knuckles, thumbs and wrists to support the fists beneath their gloves, a hard lesson to instil when the boxers had already come this far with their old habits. He made sure exercises were added to their regime specifically to strengthen their wrists and hands, from twisting weights up on a coiling rope to gripping together the levers of curious metal contraptions. At the end of every session of punching they had to plunge their hands into ice and hold them there. To keep those tools in prime condition.

Such was the depth of support, the backroom staff pulling together with the coaches and the athletes, all focusing on the goal, the looming World Championships which doubled as the first Olympic qualification tournament. It was no accident therefore that the team managed to keep themselves fit and healthy.

They needed to be. The Worlds would knock lumps out of them. Almost six hundred of the world's finest boxers would congregate in Baku, all desperate to reach the quarter-finals and thus guarantee themselves a place at the London Games. A series of battles is what would make this championship a war.

Azerbaijan is a strange place to hold a World Championship, even for amateur boxing. In 2009 the Worlds had been in Milan, in 2007 Chicago. Baku, on the shore of the Caspian Sea, was a far-out destination for the competition.

In Baku's old town ancient city walls, like something out of *The Arabian Nights*, rise up among boutique shops, a stone's throw from a Mediterranean-style promenade along the sea. Azerbaijan has oil, hence its wealth, but the inequality is blatant. Young Azeris speed down the dusty roads in bright, pricey new cars, while hunched old ladies scuttle out with brooms to sweep the sands from the asphalt. Shacks and rubble, plains and braying donkeys sit next to the shining, expensive new hotels.

Azerbaijan is corrupt. On a corruption index at the time it ranked below Mexico, Gabon and Niger, 143rd out of 180 countries, level with Russia, Belarus and Nigeria. Being told to arrive at the border with 'about' a hundred dollars was disconcerting for me. It was no less true. The border guard on the day of my arrival decided the cost of a visa was $101. Since I hadn't brought my cash in small bills, and he couldn't provide change, he made a small profit for no added effort. I'd arrived on a budget Aerosvit flight, via a lengthy detour in Kiev, one of just a handful of Western journalists covering the event. These Worlds were, though, significant. The tournament would not only decide the best amateur boxers on the planet but it was also the first of just two chances to qualify for the Olympic Games. I thought GB's seasoned boxers like Thomas Stalker and Luke Campbell, who in 2008 had become England's first European champion in forty-seven years, ought to reach the quarter-finals at least. Finishing in the last eight was the standard required to win a place at London 2012. But for someone as inexperienced as Anthony Joshua I saw this more as a reconnaissance mission, to learn what it took to succeed in high-level international competition.

Azerbaijan had been part of the Soviet Union until its collapse in 1991. The Communist legacy persists. Freedom of speech, freedom of assembly, freedom of the press are all harshly restricted. Heydar Aliyev, after whom the airport today is fondly named, rose through the KGB to become the first Turkic member of the Politburo, the body that ruled the USSR. He then took over Azerbaijan. He handed the presidency of the country, through an 'election', such as it was, to his son Ilham, who happened to run the national Olympic committee before he assumed his father's seat.

Bread and circuses is a rule that still obtains in the modern age. Repressive regimes like to burnish their image with sporting success. Medals matter, especially in Baku, which was bidding for the 2020 Olympic Games. Boxing was a sport where Azerbaijan could find success. It had some athletes. And as we know, with scoring notoriously subjective, home advantage goes a long way.

It was significant, then, that the 2011 World Championships, the first men's qualification tournament for the following year's Olympic Games, was moved from original destination South Korea to Azerbaijan and a new ruling was instituted that gave high seedings to the host nation of that tournament, which smoothed the path of the local boxers to the crucial qualifying contests.

In some quarters far more sinister forces were seen to be at work. That quarter, to be precise, was the British Broadcasting Corporation – the world renowned BBC. One of their flagship programmes, BBC2's serious and, at the time, highly respected *Newsnight* current affairs programme sensationally accused Azerbaijan of paying AIBA the princely sum of $10 million in return for two gold Olympic medals.

The BBC claimed that an Azeri investor, through a meeting facilitated by a minister in the Azerbaijan government, channelled $9 million into the North American branch of AIBA's World Series of Boxing offshoot. This, according to *Newsnight*, was for two gold medals to be delivered at London 2012.

Azerbaijan, however, did not subsequently win two gold medals at the Olympic Games. Such an audacious plot would, given the scoring system and restrictions on referees and judges, require an awful lot of officials to be corrupted in the course of a tournament. The practicalities of getting it done were vast, given that the specific judges were assigned their bouts randomly and ten minutes before their contests were due to begin. To make the conspiracy theory a reality, between forty and sixty officials would have to be bribed, pressured or turned. The problem for AIBA was that this story, from a reputable outfit, conformed to the worst suspicions about the nature of amateur boxing. That it wasn't a fair sporting contest. That it was bent.

The programme was aired in Britain the night before the World Championships began in Baku. It left the British boxing team in a deeply uncomfortable position. Would this episode prompt any retaliation? Would it ratchet up the tension between AIBA and Britain and could that fallout affect the GB boxers in the tournament? Would it prejudice the judges against Britain?

The boxers couldn't let themselves get caught up in fevered speculation. They simply had to focus on the task ahead of them. They could only control their boxing.

Anthony Joshua had found the 2011 Europeans exhausting, draining, infuriating, too, but alive with possibility. By the World Championships in October of that year he had changed his training, pushing himself further and harder. I remember seeing him stay on after sessions in Sheffield, doing extra drills, among other exercises strapping a harness over his head to lift weights with just his neck, learning the lessons of his encounter with Mihai Nistor in Europe. Mentally, physically, Joshua was different this time. He came to Azerbaijan ready to fight.

GB Boxing had carefully choreographed the athlete's routine for the day of a contest during a tournament. Their analysts, two of whom, Rob Gibson and Kathryn Stuart, were on the ground in Baku, amassed footage of their possible opponents. Normally they'd film during the course of a tournament but issues with television rights prevented them from doing so at the 2011 World Championships. Once they know the GB boxer's opponent they'll compile a dossier. The information they retrieve allows the coaches to analyse the opposition and then brief their charge.

The boxer has to go to the venue first thing on the morning of his contest to weigh in once again. He returns to the hotel for breakfast, an hour's rest before a team meeting at 10 a.m. Then Rob McCracken and the coaches sit down with the competitor to go through the video analysis and the battle plan.

The support team has to switch to more mundane concerns, getting to and from the stadium, not easy through the wild traffic of Baku. With shuttle buses organised for them, they were giving their boxers two hours to get to their stadium and their hotel was only eight kilometres from the venue. The Cuban team, for instance, was installed twenty kilometres away, a severe hassle especially when you've got to get there and back just to weigh in on the day you box.

The hotels were assigned randomly, though Matt Holt, the team manager, and Rob Gibson, the lead analyst, had travelled out for an advanced recce. This gave them a chance to see where they'd be likely to stay, calculate the logistics and make crucial contacts with the local organising committee.

A full staff had come out with the team for the tournament; nutritionist Mark Ellison was there, a significant presence as the boxers had to be at their fighting weight throughout the days of their participation and navigate the sometimes unappetising Azeri food. Dr Mike Loosemore was also there to keep the team fit and healthy. GB had had no problems for the Worlds, aside from Rob McCracken picking up a mild case of food poisoning when they first arrived. Even the psychologist, Pete Lindsay, was with them in Azerbaijan; his role was not only to work individually with the boxers but to make sure the different parts of the team functioned smoothly in unison with each another. They were lucky to have a group of characters who were not troublesome, not too often the case with a group of young boxers travelling overseas.

Their hotel had a conference room, which served as a space for them to train – to keep ticking over during the weeks of the tournament. In the bowels of the Heydar Aliyev Stadium there was a curtained-off room to warm up in. By the time the boxer gets there he is solely in the hands of the coaches. McCracken would be heading to his seat in the stands leaving the coaches who would man the corner to take the boxer through his final steps.

These four coaches were Paul Walmsley, Dave Alloway, Lee Pullen and Nigel Davies. Two of them would go out with each boxer into the arena. For their final warm-up, the coach takes the boxer through one last short, sharp drill on the pads, imitating what they expect of the opponent, simulating what they had discussed in the morning briefing.

At this point the trainer has become analyst, psychologist and mentor all in one. 'It's knowing what buttons to press with different boxers,' said Walmsley. 'There are so many different personalities and different ways of switching them on, tuning them in to what they need to do. As you get to know them on the squads and going away with them, you know what works and doesn't work. It's about building camaraderie with them.

'They've all got their own little idiosyncrasies.'

The team had an unwritten rule as well. After the first round never let yourself fall behind. After the first round never be down.

Anthony Joshua violated that rule.

Considering his opponent in the super-heavyweight quarter-final, that moment of fallibility was forgivable. He had spent three minutes boxing Roberto Cammarelle. The Italian southpaw was the reigning Olympic super-heavyweight champion, the reigning World champion after striking gold two years previously in Milan. At the Beijing Olympics he had decisively beaten the crowd favourite, China's Zhang Zhilei in the final and in the semi-final he had brutally dispatched Britain's last super-heavyweight hope, David Price.

Back in 2008 Price had been the main man. Now, three years on, he was a strong professional and had recently dropped Joshua in sparring. The Liverpudlian was six foot eight inches tall, he stopped the Russian Islam Timurziev at the Beijing Games to get into the medals and back then was on the verge of becoming the next big thing.

Cammarelle ended that abruptly. His cross crashed into Price's chin, depositing him on the canvas backside first, leaning back into the ropes, and left the Liverpudlian with questions hovering about his chin and punch resistance which would hound him for years to come.

After Joshua's stoppage loss to Mihai Nistor in Europe, he had been working on strengthening his neck, to prevent punches moving his head so visibly. My fear, as I sat nervously at a ringside desk, was that this particular aspect of his training would be put to its most severe test. I thought he'd do well to last the three rounds.

It was a reasonable fear to have. If Joshua had beaten Nistor in June he would have met Cammarelle in the European semi-final. His coaches wouldn't have risked him in that bout. They would have pulled him from the tournament. That they put him in now with the Italian showed they had significant faith in him.

The Londoner was a newcomer, with all the boldness that came with his youth. He hadn't even watched the last Olympics. It meant he didn't know who Cammarelle was. It also meant he had no respect for him. 'I always want to fight to the end. So I was, "Who the hell is this Cammarelle?" I researched and saw him socking guys for six and thought, "Okay I understand,"' said Joshua.

'I remember at the Worlds when I drew Cammarelle and they didn't pull me out. They let me fight him. I saw that my coaches had now gained confidence in me from training camps, from fights and so on, from my other fights before Cammarelle in the Worlds. I felt that extra boost.'

The Heydar Aliyev Stadium that hosted the tournament looks forebidding, a relic of Azerbaijan's Communist past. A huge block structure of dark stone and concrete. Within the stadium the seating round the field of play rose up in sheer cliffs. Vast images of the current president, Ilham Aliyev, and his father and predecessor, Heydar, from whom the complex, like the airport, took its name, hung down the walls.

Losing here to Cammarelle in this World quarter-final wouldn't be disastrous. Olympic qualification was harder for the heavies and super-heavyweights in this tournament; they had to reach the semi-final to be sure of a place at London 2012. All the other weights needed to reach the last eight, hard enough in itself. But if Joshua lost to an eventual finalist in the quarter-final, that would qualify him, and if you were going to bet on anyone to be in it at the finish, it would be World and Olympic champ Cammarelle.

Joshua, though, was not a man content to lose. He came back to his corner after their first round, his eyes wide, breathing heavy, feeling the sense of crisis. He had broken the team's first round rule. He was down by a point.

Coach Paul Walmsley stepped through the ropes. He had fifty seconds to speak to Joshua, fifty seconds to turn him round. Walmsley could see Anthony looked nervous, a touch overawed, giving Cammarelle too much respect. Waiting for the Italian, worrying about what Cammarelle was going to do, letting the champion come on. Joshua had to get back to his boxing. Walmsley couldn't talk at length, there was too little time and, besides, in the heat of battle Joshua would not be able to take it in. He had to keep the message simple. Keep it simple and repeat.

Sitting ringside, yards away, I could see Walmsley speaking urgently to him. 'Relax, relax. It's one point, only one point,' Paul said. 'Relax. Long, fast shots. Move. Block anything coming at you. Set your own pace.'

Joshua had to think back over the first round. The Italian may have been much-heralded but he hadn't felt a level above. Cammarelle swayed back from Joshua's long jab but when the Londoner had jerked down his heavy right, he had unsettled him.

Who could say what was going on in the Italian's head? Joshua may have already done enough to sow doubt in Cammarelle's mind. In his previous contest a little-known Venezuelan, José Payares, on his way to a wide points defeat, had managed to knock him down in the third round. In boxing a crack in your self-belief can splinter wide in an instant.

Joshua may have been breathing hard but the older man looked the less conditioned of the two. The period when exhaustion had caught up with Anthony, after he'd boxed on three consecutive days in the Europeans, had been banished. He was now a different animal. Already he'd boxed three men at these Worlds, stopping two of them inside the distance. He had every reason to feel primed, to feel strong.

The Italian pawed with his right-hand jab, as he often did to draw his prey on to a stern left. A clear right cross from Joshua to start the second round was a statement of intent. Cammarelle chased after him, trying to work straight, hard shots. Anthony's long jab kept him out. Again Cammarelle closed on him but the Briton landed a tight left hook. A couple of heavy shots clipped him but Joshua scraped the same hook across Cammarelle's face.

Joshua was boxing with him, he was living with him. The scoreboard swung three points. Going into the last round, Joshua was ahead 11–9. Cammarelle endeavoured to trade fire with him but he was catching arms. Finally the Italian backed off but left himself open to a long Joshua right. Anthony wrapped his arms round him when Cammarelle engaged, holding him still, the action of a tired boxer. But Cammarelle weakened faster.

The Italian flung a left, followed it with repeated right hooks.

Joshua's cross thumped back. Cammarelle rushed forward, his work ragged but still dangerous. He was desperate to rough up Joshua, who, swallowing a right hook, held once more. The twenty seconds until the final bell stretched long. Joshua lunged forward, only to step into a clinch. Neither was connecting, but Joshua had it: 15–13.

Just a few months earlier Anthony had been hammering Joe Joyce in a school sports hall in Dagenham. Now, in a stadium in Baku, he had delivered the most incredible upset of the championship.

I had been ringside for both and was left awkwardly jerking my thumb up in the air, a weird wave crossed with a salute. I was not in my finest form. This was Joshua's defining moment. In what would have been a journalistic disaster, I had nearly missed it.

The previous night at my hotel my love of free food collided with my customary wariness of foreign fare. The former impulse overwhelmed the latter. As enjoyable as gorging on the hotel's buffet was, it did not outweigh the misery of spending the night folded over my room's toilet bowl. The following morning I could scarcely move, let alone stomach the jolting shuttle bus ride to the stadium. Joshua–Cammarelle was on the slate for that day. I gamely hauled myself along that afternoon, just in case. I was more worried for Anthony's wellbeing in this one, considering a bout against Cammarelle more a case of whether Joshua would go the distance or be stopped and not for a second thinking he would actually win. Shows how much I know. But, rather than suffering a hallucination induced by the sickly fever of my food poisoning, Joshua really *had* beaten Cammerelle.

'I believed in myself. I stayed calm. The same thing we've done at the start of the competition is the same thing we've done all the way through. We just followed the game plan, listened to my coaches in the corner and we were successful again. When something is working you don't really want to change it. We didn't change anything,' Anthony said with his broad smile. 'Even though it was Cammarelle.'

The words on everyone's lips in Baku, the name rippling round the stadium and the name that would soon be heard across the boxing world was Anthony Joshua. A young, new, hard-hitting super-heavyweight had burst on to the scene. After nine minutes of action Joshua had that instant become the most sought-after property in the sport.

Time to Believe

Baku, 2011

The tension among the Britons boxing for their Olympic lives was unmistakable. The public never saw them at work. Here they were in Azerbaijan, on the far side of the world, in as high-level a tournament as there is on earth, untelevised, with no one at home watching. Outside of their grant money it was awfully hard for them to get sponsorship or funding. Such is life for an international amateur boxer. Make it to the Olympics and everything changes. There is no larger sporting event on the planet. Box in the Games, box for a medal there, and everyone will be watching. That degree of public exposure will change their lives.

It's everything they toiled for, everything they worked so brutally hard to achieve.

This squad had come to win. Rob McCracken had no intention of letting his side slump back into the tradition of mediocrity that had dogged British boxing teams in the past. Four of their boxers made it all the way to the finals of the

Worlds in Baku. But they were losing those gold medal matches. Even Hull's Luke Campbell, one of the most gifted boxers on the squad, had been limited to a silver medal in Azerbaijan. Britain's last golden hope at the 2011 Worlds came in the unlikely, but daunting, form of super-heavyweight Anthony Joshua. I had thought his heroics against Cammarelle had been enough; a splendid bronze medal was already more than I'd expected of him.

Joshua had different ideas. In the semi-final his right cross dashed across Erik Pheifer's nose. Broke it. Blood poured. The German was gone inside the first round. It was time to believe in Anthony Joshua. In his five bouts so far in Baku he had taken three out early. He'd need to carry his power into the final. In the last bout on the final day he was going in with the local boxer, Magomedrasul Medzhidov from Azerbaijan. The host nation had yet to score a gold medal in this tournament.

Other omens were not favourable. Midway through a contest earlier that day the Azeris ringing the arena stood to applaud as one. I was momentarily perplexed, for little action of note was taking place in the boxing ring. Staring more closely I saw their clapping hands raised, their eyes gazing up to the far side of the stadium.

There, high aloft in a viewing gallery of bright white stone, stood the President of Azerbaijan, Ilham Aliyev, the palm of one hand lifted to acknowledge his people. Two vast banners adorned the walls on either side of his platform, one of his father, the other his own image. He took his seat, alongside other assorted dignitaries, including the president of AIBA, Dr Wu, to watch the action far below.

By the time Joshua was set to enter, the atmosphere was gladiatorial. The Briton was not without support. The African nation boxers had been eliminated earlier in the tournament. They'd adopted Joshua as one of their own – he has Nigerian heritage, not to mention the outline of the African continent tattooed on his right shoulder. The Africans, the Brits and Europeans looking on loudly cheered his name. A knot of British oil workers, who'd met Anthony at the team hotel and had come to add their support, hollered, 'Josh'.

But nothing compared to the roar of the Azeris. 'Az-er-bai-jan.' Soldiers in uniform had filed in to fill row upon row of seats. They were out in force. Clapping together. Chanting together. Intoning the syllables of their country's name. 'Az-er-bai-jan.' It spread through the rest of the crowd. 'Az-er-bai-jan.' The people and their president had witnessed a Ukrainian soundly beat their ninety-one-kilo boxer in the previous bout. They couldn't bear to see their super-heavyweight fall. Into this maelstrom walked Anthony Joshua.

Already he had shown unnatural coolness of thought. Beating Cammarelle would have been enough to cue wild celebrations from anyone. Joshua kept himself calm then. He took long walks, spent time with his GB team-mates and stayed relaxed. 'If you get too carried away after that win, it's not the final. You've got to put today behind you and we've got tomorrow to focus on. I've got to put each day behind me and keep moving forward,' he said.

When he broke Pheifer's nose in the semi-final, he heard Walmsley in his corner urge him, 'Relax.' He restrained himself, didn't rush in. Charging in wildly, especially at super-heavyweight, is a risk. He boxed out the early end of that bout.

It brought him swiftly to the final, his sixth consecutive contest in this competition.

Joshua walked out into the arena. He shut out the crowd. 'I've learned about myself mentally throughout this tournament,' he said. 'I've learned how to try to stay relaxed, just put my heart into it and give my best.'

The roars grew louder, wound the tension tighter. 'Med-zhi-dov . . . Med-zhi-dov.' The president sitting above them, the crowd pressing closer, stacked the odds against Joshua. Azerbaijan's super-heavyweight could operate. Cuba's super-heavy Erislandy Savón had knocked French talent Tony Yoka cold. Magomedrasul Medzhidov had in turn beaten down the Cuban. 'I saw that he was very technical so I just directly attacked him to make him nervous' was how the Azeri explained that win to me. Medzhidov flung himself through incoming fire, left himself open but threw furious shots himself. A hard man, that toughness allowed him to rush in head on. But Joshua, we had seen already in this tournament, could hit.

The bout began. A left hook struck Anthony heavily, but his long, straight punches carved him space. Medzhidov missed. Another potent one-two and Joshua let his lead hook thump into the Azeri's guard. Medzhidov didn't charge him, dabbed a jab back instead.

For an instant Joshua opened up as he struck out. But his jab stopped Medzhidov coming forward. Anthony had followed the team's golden rule. He won the first round, won it 8–5. That was crucial. Or it should have been.

'After the first round I felt that I was losing the match and I just made every attempt from then,' Medzidov said. 'I felt that my country's president is here and it gave me more power.'

The Azeri rallied. Anthony's long right hand pegged him back for a moment, but Medzhidov drove Joshua into a corner. He caught the Briton there, jolting his head. Anthony simply fought back. He wasn't thinking about his boxing. He hit Medzhidov back down. A right hand from the Azeri hurt Joshua, the impact shook through to his boots. His footwork shuddered. Joshua nodded. Yes, he revealed he was hurt. But he showed he was here for a war. He came back at the Azeri, his punches looser, though, his guard lower.

'Of all the times for his hands to come down,' his cornerman Walmsley groaned afterwards.

Medzhidov wobbled him, prompting the referee to give Joshua a standing eight count. Anthony replied again, heaving a left hook across. He hurt the Azeri with a right slanting down. But Medzhidov would keep on coming. His own right hand found its way through Joshua's guard before the end of the second round. The local had levelled the score: 14–14.

Some boxers are assassins. Luke Campbell will ruthlessly close out a bout. He needs one strike to take the lead and will finish the contest, finish his opponent. If he suffers a score, it's hard for him to change his game. Pure skill, beautiful boxing, but it can be hard for him to break his style, break his patience and go to war when he needs to. He can do it, he *did* do it in his glorious Olympic quarter-final, but it means he has to work against himself. He's a finisher. He's an assassin.

Other boxers are warriors. They rise to the occasion. They relish the battle, take the licks and find something new. A boxer won't know this about himself, won't know if he's a warrior or an assassin until he's in the midst of his acid test. Until he's in the battle's heat. Then he finds out how he responds. He finds out who he is.

Joshua, it turned out, is a warrior. Medzhidov stuck his left over Joshua's attack but the Briton's cross, still sharp, shot straight to his chin. Medzhidov jabbed, brought in a right. Joshua had to hold. Again Medzhidov, punching his way in, shook Joshua's head, but a crisp uppercut from the rear hand relieved some of the pressure on him. Joshua's left hook turned Medzhidov away for a moment. Two heavy rights zeroed in. Joshua's hands came down, leaving him open but he held out his lead arm and boomed the right across. The bout had seesawed between them but Joshua had never let it escape. Before the close Medzhidov had slowed and Joshua, still in there, started striking him back, smashing his way back into the contest.

But he had needed one more shot. At the ring of the final bell it was 22–21. It was that close, that hard fought. But it was 22–21 to Medzhidov.

A one-point loss to the home boxer in Azerbaijan; many could consider that a win. Joshua had the World silver medal, extraordinary for a young man with little more than thirty bouts to his credit.

But he found no joy in that accomplishment. Like his team-mates, he had come to win. The sadness of his loss overcame him; immediately after the bout he couldn't bring himself to speak to the television cameras, had to walk away to gain command of himself. It was painful to see, painful after all he had given. Anthony deserved to feel proud of himself. But his grief was encouraging. It proved he had the desire. The desire to become a champion. You need that. You can't hide that.

He was of the same mind as his team-mates. With four medals this was Britain's most successful World Championship team ever. Yet none of the medallists were happy. None of them had taken gold.

'It was emotional. Boxing, I love it. This is what we do it for. The emotion's caught up with me now. It still hurts now. But I'm looking forward to getting back in the gym. I'm going to get stronger, faster, fitter, and I'm going to train my mind as well. I'm going to do my best once again. It just shows that Great Britain are on the map. Great Britain are on the map. We can do it,' he said, still in his red vest and shorts, taking in the stadium around him, the spectators milling about, thinking over the fortnight he and his team-mates had been through.

'The crowd are great. They're good. I like it here. It was a pleasure to be here.' He looked out and held up his hand, got a round of applause from lingering onlookers in response.

His chin, his heart, his character had survived the most exacting crucible. 'It's adrenalin. You take some, you give some. It doesn't affect you. Your heart's in it. When you're in there your heart doesn't understand give up. So I just kept on going. A steam train, that's the only thing that would have stopped me. I wasn't going to give up.

'It was a tough fight, he was a good fighter. A lot of people could have crumbled underneath that type of pressure but he kept on coming. It shows what home support can do. It can drive you and he took that energy with him into the ring.'

Joshua lingered in the arena. He stayed to pose for photos. People who, moments before, had been screaming their support for his opponent now wanted their picture taken with

Anthony. He was happy to oblige. He'd let the tears in his eyes dry and now could grin his broad grin. That kind of connection with a crowd is uncommon. That was a star being born.

And you had to think that while Baku is hostile territory, London 2012, for the Finchley boxer, would be home.

Heavyweight Tradition

Sheffield, 2012

The GB team could go home and let what they'd accomplished sink in. With their World Championship results – four medals in a single major tournament that is – as well as two successful European Championships, they could rightly aspire to become the greatest team in modern British boxing history. For Anthony Joshua and the four others who had locked in their qualification, there was another cause for celebration – they would be going to the Olympic Games. GB's first wave of boxers was through. When they touched down in England, each would be greeted by delighted friends and family, welcome-home parties, attentive media interviews and the warm knowledge that they had achieved what they'd left the country to do.

These men are fantastic athletes, supremely skilled in a sport so hard it's not just a 'game'. You never play boxing. You fight. In international amateur boxing that fight goes almost entirely unseen. It's a sport far removed from the mainstream.

Except for once every four years, when the Olympic Games come round. The difference for a boxer between being in the Olympics and being out is vast. It's a stark reality. Recognition or none. The Olympics is an end in itself. It is the biggest show on earth.

Winning a medal at the Games makes a life-changing difference to their earning potential as a professional boxer. It will save a boxer from the hard life of a jobbing pro and make him a prospect to be nurtured and groomed for stardom.

Professional boxing is a threatening world. Boxers become lost in it, drifting, cheated, mistreated. There were many pitfalls a young fighter ought to be aware of. Ought to be and yet, more often than not, he wasn't. A boxer can grow old fast. His youthful promise along with his options, like the payment he can command or the fights available to him, can dissipate far too quickly. The GB gym in Sheffield was a safe haven from that world.

The relationship that sustains any boxer is the one with his trainer, the man who coaches him in the gym and corners him for contests. For a pro, the trainer is on his payroll. Although the professional fighter too often forgets it, the boxer is the boss. Not so in the amateurs but on either side of the sport it's hard to stress too highly the bond between a trainer and his athlete. The boxer in his most desperate moments turns to his corner for guidance. His trainer is the only man who can help him when things go wrong. Day in day out, in the gym he seeks his trainer's approval. The trainer reprimands him, punishes him, praises him.

The feeling goes the other way, too. Outside of the boxers themselves, no one knows better how they've suffered, how hard they've trained, what they've been through, than their trainers. 'You want them to win so much,' said Podium squad coach Paul Walmsley.

A club coach and a professional trainer stand by their man for their entire careers, unless the boxer decides to move on. The GB coaches were in the unique and uncomfortable position of having to drop their boxers. They had to be ruthless: that's the nature of international amateur boxing. They had a country's worth of talent to shift through and they were paid to make sure the best coalesced in their Sheffield gym. If an athlete couldn't make the grade, he had to go. It was a brutal choice that would see the boxer lose his own funding. A dropped boxer would have to work to live and be forced to find the time to train on top of that. His hopes of winning a major medal were gone and with them any aspirations he had of landing a lucrative contract with a professional promoter vanished, too. Rob McCracken, the performance director, understood his duty of care.

Martin Ward, for instance, the young man who'd starred on the night Joshua won his first amateur title, turned professional after he failed to be selected for the final Olympic qualifier in early 2012. He might have been a teenage phenomenon in the amateurs but he would still face a long, punishing road, grinding his way to win the British featherweight title in 2016.

Boxing is a working-class sport. Boxers tend to come from nothing; they make themselves what they are out of hard work and belief. But so often they don't have other options. 'The great thing about the programme is it opens doors for them,' said McCracken. 'Even if they haven't quite achieved the success that they wanted to achieve, I think it prepares you for what's out there. There's education opportunities for them, there's course opportunities. There's job opportunities. A lot of this goes unnoticed because of the way the sport's developed and moved on, because of targets and winning medals.

'It also gives you a clue [as to] what you want to do or what you can become. A lot of boxers don't have lots of confidence, believe it or not, as people.'

The British team was full of youngsters, full of hope and promise. But boxing is scored with sad stories. Brave fighters, great men left with nothing. Old men left damaged, with nowhere to go and nothing to do. It may be right that at the start of their adventure this group did not think about the worst that might befall them. Their eyes ought to be set on their outer limits. But there are risks and someone had to be aware of them. Someone had to try to give them more options.

'They're ambitious. These kids are ambitious here. They want to achieve things in their lives,' said Rob.

'They're a great bunch and you just want the best for them. It's important that we equip the boxers as best we can while we're here. This is their life, they're going to go out in the world and make their way. Most of them are fine and more than ready for it. It is the one or two that need to be helped a little bit more while they're here. Hopefully they'll all go on and have successful lives. That's what's important.'

Boxers face the very real risk of being left with nothing. Few make good money and, besides, their competition years are short. To prosper in boxing they've shown they can apply themselves, shown what they can achieve when they work hard. They deserve help. After all their travails, they don't deserve to be left with nothing.

It is right for the team to have this life guidance but in the grand scheme of boxing nationwide it's not necessarily fair. This group has already been identified as the best in the country. They already have the best chance of making it through. It's those striving in their clubs in their hometowns, who don't get to taste the high life of international boxing, who could arguably benefit the most from this support. It's understandable for the coaches in small, shabby gyms to look at the set-up in Sheffield with an envious eye and resent its life coaches, nutritionists, physios, psychologists and the rest.

The GB gym has an abundance of resources and it is unsurprising that the grassroots gaze at all that money and are frustrated to see none of it trickling down to them. (Nor can it: UK Sport only funds elite Olympic programmes.) But from a certain point of view, Rob has it easy. He can pick the finest talent in the land. A club has to work with whoever comes through the doors. They give the boxers their core coaching in their formative years and yet it's McCracken's coaches who get to be in the corner in their finest hours, at the international tourneys, and enjoy the glory. It's a cushy number for McCracken and GB as far as some of the grassroots are concerned.

Rob is always eager to credit the local clubs when he's interviewed, making sure he acknowledges the grassroots gyms for producing the talent. But at the same time his confidence in what the GB programme adds to them rings through clearly.

'Their clubs have done a fantastic job to get them to this

stage,' he acknowledged, speaking in the run-up to the 2012 Olympic Games. 'We get the opportunity then to push them on and equip them for the world of international boxing and the Russians and the Cubans that are out there and that they've got to get past.'

Domestic boxing is different. You need to master the requisite style for international amateur scoring. You need to step up a level of performance, fitness and stamina. There is no competition in Britain to match the nature of a major international tournament, boxing bout after bout, day after day. It's gruelling. It's highly technical, too. The GB programme, under McCracken, sets about producing tournament boxers. 'The fittest group I've ever worked with,' concluded team doctor Mike Loosemore, who'd been with the British team for fifteen years.

McCracken made sure his team could never take it easy in their training sessions. They had three sessions in a typical day, shorter and sharper than you might expect but all designed to generate that fast, explosive amateur pace. Running, sprints or other devilish routines first thing in the morning, then their strength and conditioning, vital as GB had youngsters competing against the men and career amateurs from overseas. In the afternoon came their boxing session, with pads, bag work, sparring and more.

McCracken had been an international amateur himself and remembered fondly his days on the programme. He had always wanted to go to an Olympic Games then. Now he would take a team to one as head coach. He had regrets from his time on the squad and arrived as performance director with a vision of how he wanted to shape the set-up. 'I just thought I'd start afresh,' he said. 'I wanted to individualise it. When I was on the squad twenty-odd years ago I always thought it would be great if you could individualise the sport to the point where you'd have four or five boxers training in the gym and you'd have four or five coaches. Thankfully through the funding we're able to do that. So I changed it around. We stopped the large groups training together each day. Because I thought you can look more at the faults and the mistakes and the potential of boxers and iron out the problems quicker, or realise that they haven't got the potential, if you sit on them and individualise it as much as possible.'

Rob and the other coaches imparted a sense of how they wanted the GB team to box. There might be a philosophy for them, a template on how to get results. But all the boxers on this squad, while they could look around the gym at their decorated team-mates for inspiration, had their own style, and those who managed to stay on the programme had a coaching platform that willed them to express it in the ring. The boxers could not neglect their club coaches, the men who in so many ways made them what they had become. But neither could their respect and appreciation for McCracken be ignored.

Rob had created a rare alchemy in the GB gym. The boxers, not just the support staff, spoke of him in glowing terms. They wanted his approval, they wanted to fight for him. It made their gym a hard but happy camp. 'I think the key is as well that they have a good time here, that they have a laugh and a joke. They know that they can be relaxed here but also there's a time they've got to work hard. There's certain disciplines they've got to keep, weight-making and being very professional along those lines,' said Rob.

It was remarkable that he managed to infuse this sense of fun into the gym, when at the same time he established ruthless competition. The squad was never comfortable. With no clear number ones in most weight divisions, to push for selection for the major tournaments boxers had to continue to perform. It's a testament to their character, to the leadership within the squad living with one another in the nearby flats, that under such severe stresses the mood in the team could remain so upbeat.

The team had their targets for what they wanted to achieve in the amateur sport. The assumption for the men's team was that in years to come they would, some way, sooner or later, line up as professionals. But would they find anything in the pros to match the home from home they had in Sheffield? There was an innocence they lost when they left the amateurs. Rather than fighting for money, worrying about the business, with GB they fought for themselves, for the team, for their country and old-fashioned glory. Turn professional and the boxer is no longer just an athlete. He's a business and he's the boss of his own business. His trainer, his promoter, his manager, his lawyer, all come on to his payroll. The boxer has to pick the right guides to conduct him through the perilous, confusing world that is professional boxing.

The pro sport is riven with flaws. From uncompetitive or unfair matches to big fights failing to materialise. The sport has no real structure, no real season. There's no clear path to a title. Luck, influence and money churn up opportunities. The governance is chaotic, limited by geography; promoters can take their fights from one governing body to another depending on which jurisdiction best suits their interests at that time. Major

American promoters, the powerhouses of Golden Boy and Top Rank, like their smaller British counterparts, were committed to fostering their commercial rivalry, so much so that they couldn't bear to cooperate. Their Cold War meant the stars of either stable never met in the ring. The major contests, the best fighting the best, the hallmarks of boxing's past, occur on only the rarest occasions in the modern era. It follows a certain rationale but, though the policy suits some of the parts, it damages the whole.

So, too, does the proliferation of titles. Having a 'world' strap garnish a fight suits the television provider. It's convenient for selling an event. But the pros don't have a World champion the way the amateurs did. Historically there was once one world title per weight division. Now more sanctioning bodies have sprung up, shaking out to a state whereby you have four main respected belts, the alphabet soup of the WBC, the WBA, WBO and the IBF. It makes it hard to view a boxer as the bona fide number one until he has unified at least two of these belts. And that is an increasingly rare event. Of course, sanctioning fees have to be paid to those bodies each time one of their titles is contested; the political divides between promoters remain to make it hard for the best to meet the best. It becomes a self-feeding loop. There are too many titles, the general public don't know who the champions are, therefore too many players in the game can, for the right fee, make their fight into a title contest. The increasing number of belts in circulation devalues the importance of any single title. To make the hyper-inflation of titles even more ludicrous the individual sanctioning bodies realised they could bleed even more money out of the sport by having title variants for 'regular', 'interim' and 'super'

World champions at the same weight, at the same moment in time. Wladimir Klitschko could be fighting for the 'super' WBA heavyweight title, at the same time as Luis Ortiz held the 'interim' WBA heavyweight belt, while a 'regular' WBA heavyweight belt could appear for a couple of other boxers to fight for in Grozny, with no rationalisation for any of the different world titles. They get away with it because it suits too many of the market participants.

It's a wild, shambolic world but it rolls on. It's not so far removed from its historic roots. Boxing remains prizefighting. It may have been beyond a sport in its bareknuckle days but it had the glamour of an outlaw activity in the nineteenth century. When codified it assumed a prestige and significance hard to find in other sports. There was once a time when everyone could tell you who the heavyweight champion of the world was.

The heavyweight champion was an office that carried distinction. When the sport mattered to the general public, the man who held that title was important. Few sportsmen have had as great a social significance as Jack Johnson. He became the first black heavyweight champion, shattering the bar that stopped black Americans from competing with whites and he rammed the assumptions of racial superiority down the throats of his contemporary society. He was hated for it and hated for the freewheeling lifestyle that so widely expressed his disdain for other men's rules.

Two men stripped to the waist, facing once another in the ring. A stark, ancient image. Boxing is all about character. And the nature of the heavyweight champion said something about the character of his age. Jack Johnson broke through boundaries in the ring, through his actions and the life he led. Cavalier, flamboyant and dangerous. The next great champion did not follow in Johnson's lead. Joe Louis was a silent, awe-inspiring image. Unstoppable, though provided with plenty of easy opposition, too, he was instructed to watch his words and his behaviour. That made him a more palatable icon to the establishment of the time. His showdowns with Germany's Max Schmeling, before the war, became a symbolic contest between the two nations, one which America needed to win.

Floyd Patterson, an unwilling champion, could not cope with the pressure of expectation. He was a titlist acceptable to the establishment, expected to keep at bay Sonny Liston, a fearsomely strong fighter, out of prison, out for blood, unprepared to smooth over the concerns of his society and behave as they wanted him to behave. Patterson couldn't stand up to Liston. Cassius Clay, the man who would become Muhammad Ali, could.

But Ali was his own man. He became a symbol, rebellious in his youth, aggressive in the brand of Islam he followed, but he spoke for a generation when he refused to be drafted for the Vietnam War. It meant his defining contests were seen as psychic battles for the soul of his country, watched in awe by the rest of the world. Everyone who felt weak, who felt oppressed, could find an idol in Ali. He defeated the overwhelmingly powerful George Foreman and furious puncher Joe Frazier, men who would have been the greatest in any other era, in clashes that will long be remembered. He was a hero anyone could identify with, a hero everybody loved.

Perhaps Mike Tyson was the last great American heavyweight. So strong, so ferocious, so angry, so young when he first won a world title. He committed terrible crimes, won and wasted fortunes, went in and out of prison, a global superstar who finished with nothing. A symbol, too, of an age of excess.

But being a heavyweight great does not have to be a curse. Lennox Lewis, a Briton who boxed for Canada at the Olympic Games, unified three heavyweight belts in 1999. A cool, calculating pro, he used his long range to prise apart and put away his opposition. He was not loved in his time, his aloof manner perhaps a cause of that. To fans he seemed detached in a way that Tyson, so viscerally engaged in his passions, never was. But his cerebral approach to this bruising, bone-grinding business lay at the heart of his success. He left the sport off the back of a win, unhurt, sound in mind and body, and he left boxing a wealthy man. Considering the tragedies that befell so many of his predecessors, Lewis serves as a shining example.

For these men the Olympics was not the end goal, as it is for so many young boxers. Life is different at super-heavyweight. But the Games were a gateway to their great battles, their losses, their fortunes and their ruin. Lewis had an Olympic gold, the Games were the making of the young Ali, George Foreman, Joe Frazier and more. The Games set them on their path.

Modern boxing is smaller and tawdrier than the sport of old. But the romantic echoes of its great past still ring through it. Still allow for the right fighter and the right fight to capture the imagination. It can still inspire and so the sport carries the weight of its history heavily.

If you're a heavyweight you can't shrug off the past. Everyone was looking for the next great champ. When the time came for

Anthony Joshua to stride out to the Olympic ring, he would have to forget the footsteps in which he followed. He had to ignore the tradition in which his physical stature and good fortune had placed him.

Joshua felt like an ordinary boy from Watford. He'd worked hard. He'd had chances and he took them. He'd turned himself into a boxer. The next tournament wasn't about his potential. It was about winning.

The last loss rankled. Magomedrasul Medzhidov had been fighting at home, for his people, and he'd become World champion. Joshua had wanted that. To know that, on that day, he was the best at what he did. He'd believed he'd make it in Azerbaijan. 'I remember when I got to the final I thought, "Wow, this is real. I'm going to become the World champion." I had a great fight, I learned so much from that. I'd never boxed someone that strong. The guy had knocked out so many of his opponents and I could see why. He's a strong guy. I'd love to box him again,' said Anthony.

'It really tested me, my endurance, my heart, my chin, where I'm at technically. There was nowhere to hide in that ring in that fight. It was all or nothing. I really enjoyed it.

'Some people say I should have won it, some people say I should have lost, but in my heart I lost it and I put it in my past and I was focusing on the Olympics now. I don't dwell on things too much. But the World Championships took a lot out of me. That was so tough, with the training. We had about a week off, then it was straight back into the gym training for the Olympics. My body was going through so much at the time but I kept on pushing and the Olympics was here now. I was boxing in the Olympics.'

When he started out, Anthony Joshua never anticipated this. He never thought that he'd have fought across Britain, through Turkey, through Azerbaijan, suffered pain, dealt out punishment, lived through the pressure to come back home and compete in the great Games in his own city. When he started out, he couldn't have anticipated this.

In the months leading up to this tournament Joshua isolated himself. He lived like a warrior. The modern Olympics aren't so far removed from its ancient incarnation as we might like to presume. Its athletes still battle for the pride and prestige of their tribe.

'I try to represent the sport and youth as well,' he said, 'youth that are trying to make something in boxing. I try to represent them as well.' He was doing that, in where he'd taken his life, in how he conducted himself.

He was a big man and now he had great expectations to fulfil. When battling overseas, at least he'd been able to relish the relative obscurity. 'The World Championships, it was more about enjoying the fights,' he said. 'Azerbaijan was more about who has the will to win. That's what I loved about the Worlds.'

On the eve of the biggest tournament he'd experience, Joshua now had to ask himself whether his skill could match the hopes everybody else had raised for him.

The Big Show

For observers, let alone the men and women who would be taking part, the build-up to the Olympic Games reached a crescendo. In the weeks immediately prior to London 2012 negative stories engulfed the British media. Peculiar panics arose; that there weren't enough security personnel, so army leave was cancelled for soldiers to be marched into London. Missile launchers were apparently mounted atop blocks of flats, presumably in case of an aerial assault. Politicians issued dire warnings to stay out of the city centre, in case the transport system went into meltdown as a result of the volume of visitors.

Yet as soon as the Opening Ceremony began, with almost alarming speed all the fears, all the worries evaporated in a haze of unquestioning euphoria. No doubt any show that featured James Bond and the Queen parachuting into the Olympic Stadium would have that effect on England. By the time the British athletes processed in, the ceremony had all the hallmarks of a victory parade. Kitted out in Stella McCartney tracksuits trimmed with gold, as they marched in behind the Union flag ticker tape rained down on Team GB.

'Unbelievable' was the word that filtered along the boxers' ranks as they entered the stadium, lights flashing, tens of thousands cheering them there, millions watching on TV as all Team GB's athletes arrived.

The boxing team's little Welsh maestro Andrew Selby had never been so animated in front of a camera in his life. Wearing sunglasses, at night, he leapt into shot. Big Anthony Joshua strode behind him in similar gold-rimmed shades, beaming his smile into the nation's homes. The boxers, as you might expect, felt no great urge for solemnity, jumping about, showboating for the camera, letting their emotions run unchecked.

The boxing would take place at the ExCeL in London's Docklands. The job the local organising committee had done in fitting out the venue for the boxing tournament could not be faulted. Ten thousand seats had been erected round the ring, ranging far back, but there wasn't a bad view in the house. The low ceiling created a crucible of noise. The joyous spirit unleashed at the Opening Ceremony spilled into this arena. Normally at an Olympic Games the initial sessions are quiet, and, if not empty, certainly low key. Not so in London. The ExCeL was packed from the start and, such was the collective enthusiasm, when no GB competitor was in the ring they simply picked a boxer to root for. Mongolia and Thailand soon became surprise crowd hits, for no better reason than they came with a few fans who sang with gusto. For 10,000 happy Brits that was enough. But their love for anything GB drowned out all other sounds. Even a referee or a judge being announced from Great Britain prompted wild, delighted cheers, the merest hint of what was in store for the boxers.

Joshua didn't know what lay ahead of him. The Opening Ceremony was a taste of the euphoria about to be unleashed. He trained, was bussed to Queen Mary University and back. The corridors of their block in the Athletes' Village had a silent aura of professionalism.

London's Docklands were as close to home for Anthony Joshua as any other competitor. The big man shared a small room in the Village with the team captain, Thomas Stalker. The Liverpudlian expected to lead the way at this tournament. He had four reasons to expect every success: two European Championship silver medals, at two weights, a Commonwealth Games gold and a World Championship bronze medal. If he reached the semi-final of the Olympic Games he would become the first British boxer to win a medal at every major international amateur boxing competition. Taking a battling points win over India's Manoj Kumar, the GB Boxing team captain reached the quarter-final and was in line to become the most successful amateur boxer in his country's history. He had to win one more bout.

Mongolia had been a surprise hit at the Games. Why the Mongolian diaspora had descended on the ExCeL was unclear. A small knot of their manic supporters caught the attention of the rest of the crowd. It's a surreal Monday evening when 10,000 well-lubricated Brits chant 'Mon-go-li-a' in unison, with a knot of deliriously happy, traditionally dressed Mongolians dancing in the stands.

But the enthusiasm that team generated sounded an ominous note. Munkh-Erdene Uranchimeg was in his third

Olympic Games. In Athens in 2004 he hadn't won a medal. In Beijing in 2008 he hadn't won a medal. He had the chance now in London 2012. Against Thomas Stalker, the first time Britain boxed Mongolia at these Games.

There was something in the air about Mongolia. Not that they could shout down the locals. Yet they inspired Uranchimeg. His luck, his timing, was in. It was Stalker who found himself in a nightmare. He wanted it so badly, he was so determined, he was throwing one punch too many. After chucking his salvoes he left himself open for the Mongolian, also a southpaw, to thump over a right hook with enough force to jar Stalker's head. Uranchimeg wasn't matching the Englishman's volume, but he was landing clear blows, easy for the judges to score.

Stalker trudged back to his corner for the last round a point behind. In the third round against Manoj Kumar, his previous bout, Stalker's work rate had lapsed, and the Indian had come on, pushed him hard. Stalker had driven himself even harder than that in the first two rounds of this quarter-final. He was tiring.

The minute's break passed swiftly. He looked back over to Uranchimeg rising in the opposite corner. Stalker forced himself up on heavy legs. Took a slow step. The mounting panic sat sickly in his stomach. He choked it down and walked forward. He couldn't lose. Couldn't think. Couldn't hear the crowd. Ideas ran out. He had to fight.

Will carried him, both his hands drumming out tattoos on Uranchimeg. But the tension, the tiredness, dragged the strength from his blows. Like a bad dream, the Mongolian walked through them. Stalker finished combinations with straight right leads, he pushed them through, tried to push Uranchimeg back but still the Mongolian came on, always waiting, biding his time. But when Stalker wheeled awkwardly round him, Uranchimeg swung. His clear shots had the final say in their exchanges. Stalker looked for more, dug up the months, the years, of his training, pouring punches in, a haze of constant effort, so desperate was he to put some daylight between them.

The last round ended. Stalker thought he'd done enough. He was sure he'd done enough. In the stands McCracken believed the same. But the judges had the final round level. Uranchimeg retained his slender advantage. The Mongolian won 23–22.

Thomas Stalker's world caved in around him. His head dropped. Every expectation, every belief that he'd forged, evaporated. Already he was out of the ring, his hands on his hips, a towel round his neck, walking away, walking out with nothing.

The loss was a body blow to all the British boxers. That result ripped the heart and soul from the team. They all knew how hard Stalker had worked. They knew his principle. That at this level, on any given day, you can beat anyone. If you want it badly enough. They knew how much he wanted it. They'd seen him day in, day out, grinding his way through every session. He had poured as much sweat and blood on to their gym floor as any of them. He'd led by example, led in the way he'd fought through all their tournaments. 'He finds a way to win' was the mantra Stalker's coaches and team-mates so often repeated of him. They'd seen him succeed so many times, so many times against the odds, it became an article of faith to them all.

Now he had lost. And if Stalker could lose in London, so could any of his team-mates.

The one duty of a captain, which Stalker for once couldn't bear to carry out, was to face the media after that quarter-final. Dave Alloway, one of his cornermen, the man who had first passed the word to Stalker from the ring apron in Azerbaijan that he was an Olympian, stepped out from the changing room with jaw-jutting defiance. 'That was a captain's performance and he's the captain as long as he wants to be,' growled Alloway.

His words, the cast of his face, betrayed the pain felt in the team. Rob McCracken is not a man to be ruled by his emotions. He rarely revealed his feelings. Though the boxers were desperate for his approval, McCracken only gave it when merited. Rob didn't normally get carried away. He was rarely angered, never lost his temper. But the decision against Stalker left the GB performance director furious. He was adamant his captain had done enough, even if not by a vast margin. McCracken was certain Stalker deserved the win. He was appalled Thomas hadn't got it. It was not GB's policy to appeal decisions. Their boxers had suffered worse 'robberies' and GB had not appealed, unwilling to alienate judges from their boxers in future bouts. There was no basis for their protest, beyond outrage at the judges' view; they knew an appeal wouldn't get this result overturned. But McCracken filed it regardless, an expression of their anger.

It did no good, of course. AIBA's panel allowed GB's complaint to be considered but by one o'clock the following morning the appeal was dismissed. Stalker would not be reinstated. To them no argument could be made against the sport's subjective judging. Only a fault in the refereeing, deemed somehow to be a more objective measure, would persuade the review board to take action. It led to wider disquiet about the judging in the Olympic boxing tournament. It was not right, when so much work had gone in to getting this far, that so much could be decided by what, sometimes, appeared to be little more than luck.

'Even if I was one down going into the last, there's no way that that last round was level,' Stalker railed afterwards. 'There's no way. I just feel like I paid the price. One of the judges was a Cuban. He had me losing the last round by six points so in his eyes he never wanted me to be the winner anyway. It's so frustrating. I did show people I can fight.

'It wasn't the worst robbery but a win's a win. I feel like I should have won that fight. There was a Cuban and an Italian left in my weight category. I don't feel like I should have had them judging me. It comes down to politics. It's unfair. Because we were doing so well as well, we had five still in the semi-final stage.'

Both Joshua and his room-mate Stalker had been writing a diary from the ten-week training camp before the Games through the Olympic tournament itself. Joshua saw Stalker unable to complete his. He saw his captain unable even to look at that notebook. He could see his friend's inescapable anguish.

The pain in his voice made Thomas Stalker's thick Liverpool accent all the more raw. 'I never thought I weren't going to medal,' he rasped.

Luck had left Stalker. But not Anthony Joshua. The super-heavyweight's first bout had seen him drawn against Erislandy Savón. The Cuban's surname resonated with boxing history. He was a nephew of an amateur boxing legend, Felix Savón, a three-time Olympic champion. Joshua faced a defining moment. Get past the tricky Cuban and he wouldn't see the

Russian or Azeri hard men until the final, if they made it that far. Win that first bout and the tournament could open up for him. Win and a British super-heavyweight would have beaten a boxer named Savón. Win and Joshua would take a firm step on the fast track to stardom.

McCracken in his day had boxed in the same tournaments as the great Savón. 'He won them more often than not,' Rob chuckled. 'But this isn't Felix Savón,' he added quickly.

It was all set up for Joshua. But, of course, performing in the ring was all that mattered. GB were working hard to play down the expectation that weighed so heavily on their burgeoning new star. Such was the desire in the wider boxing world to see a new sensation born that many had simply factored in an inevitable victory for Anthony Joshua. The reality was anything but. Joshua had only had thirty-nine bouts. He was up against boxers who'd had hundreds. Being an international novice made the World silver medal already in his trophy cabinet all the more remarkable.

'Your luck sometimes runs out,' Joshua warned darkly before the start of the tournament. 'Like on a roulette machine, you have beginner's luck, you're winning. Then it comes down to strategy and hard work. I've had my luck now. I won't just try to depend on that. I'll depend on the work put in behind closed doors.'

Joshua made his declaration clear. He'd lived like a warrior-monk for the six months preceding the Games. He wanted to win. But he wanted to win it on the merit of his efforts, on his talent. With nothing left to chance.

Joshua had kept himself calm in Baku when he'd made his name. He'd kept himself focused on the tournament after his amazing victory over Roberto Cammarelle. Then he'd been able to focus on the competition, keep himself rooted. That was an expedition into enemy territory. In London it was far harder to shut out the world. The hype was at fever pitch. There was nowhere to shelter. He was penned in the Village, around the athletes. The Olympics were inescapable.

The athletes had their own route to the venue, their own reserved entry points. The changing room, the warm-up area behind the scenes was strictly cordoned off. Silent, partitioned by white walls. Joshua waited to make his entrance. Once again he stood in a gym. But this wasn't a real gym. This was a holding pen. Behind the scenes at the ExCeL he warmed up. Standing in too small a ring, as his coach scuttled round him, Joshua let his great fists smack into the pads. He looked big. His hands heavy. A touch slow.

'Every bout I was nervous for,' Joshua later growled. 'They're all the same. They've all got to get beat.'

Out of every venue at these well-supported Olympic Games, the boxing registered the highest decibel level. It was simply the loudest event at London 2012. 'How mad is that? Trust me,' he recalled. 'That was Spartan-like. You're locked away behind stage but you can hear the crowd roaring for blood. You're about to step out and fight in the arena. That was gladiator stuff. That was class.'

Forget about the crowd. He'd been drilled for this. Focus. Tunnel vision.

But he could not blot them out entirely. 'No one's there to see you lose,' he reminded himself. 'Embrace the support.'

Ten thousand waited for him to step out under the lights. Ten thousand already roaring. This was only on the other side of London to the Boston Arms in Tufnell Park, the tiny venue where Joshua had boxed his first bout. Now he was in the midst of something entirely different, set to perform at a whole new level. He was at an Olympics sooner than anyone had once believed possible, yet suddenly the world was expected of Anthony Joshua. 'More pressure, a lot more people with things to say. The experience I gained – don't get caught up in everyone else's pressure. People got more technical. I think it changed my game a bit. That I wanted to hit opponents without getting a single hit back. Which is impossible but I tried.'

His previous battles had had an exuberance about them. They'd been about fighting, about winning. Now the thought of losing was unbearable. He couldn't know what would happen out there. He tried to feed off the crowd, but they hadn't been able to help Captain Stalker.

You could not read in Joshua's face what he thought. His mind was in another place. He kept his eyes clear, staring straight ahead at the ring as he strode out into the wild cacophony of the arena.

This Savón cut a willowy figure at super-heavyweight. He'd come up from ninety-one kilos. He had the power to knock a man cold. But he was vulnerable, he could be unsettled, rushed, taken off his feet, too. Joshua, on paper, had a plan A and a plan B. He could box a bit, a touch of speed allied to his athleticism and now tremendous conditioning. That meant, if he wanted to, he could work with Savón, try to safely outpoint the Cuban. Should that fail, he had the power and the proven heart to go for broke and blaze through him. In theory.

As soon as the opening bell rang it sank in with horrible clarity that the script had not been pre-written. The Cuban team had not dominated the Worlds but they were the perennial superpower of amateur boxing. By London 2012 their boxers had peaked. Robeisy Ramírez and Roniel Iglesias had disappeared at the earliest stage of that tournament in Azerbaijan. At the Olympics the former had beaten the brilliant Andrew Selby to ultimately win gold, the latter had been just as magnificent in Stalker's division.

Erislandy Savón was on fire. Utterly switched on, he turned being a diminutive super-heavy to his advantage. He moved deftly across the canvas, expert technique countering big Anthony's efforts. Beautiful right hands glided over Joshua's jab, jolting his jaw. Savón positioned his feet masterfully. He struck off the back foot, his legs carried him clear. His flair, his speed, his shot selection, left Joshua lumbering, unable to take control.

If anything Joshua was caught between the two plans. Anxious to assert his strength and his power, he became a touch overeager. His patience had gone: he wanted to hit but he didn't want to go for broke and become too wild. His mind was half on fielding Savón's counters, half on attack. In the sweep of the action that left him stranded.

Joshua crept in on the Cuban. Anthony was having to push his shots forward, not finding the crisp connections that Savón enjoyed. But when the Briton's right hand boomed down, the impact still forced the Cuban aside. Joshua was getting through, growing into the fight, but he was in a desperately tight spot. He had not, however, missed Savón completely. The weight of his punches made that hard contact with the Cuban unmistakable.

The results flung up on the scoreboard showed the five

judges had seen more of the Cuban's output landing. But the system in amateur boxing wasn't about how one judge saw a round or a bout or even how one single judge compared the two boxers. Their role is simply to count punches landed. This was computer scoring, not the professional boxing system. Here there were no points for style. The computer reached the overall result by finding the three most similar scores, then averaging them. Yes, Savón may have had more points overall from all of the judges but in amateur boxing the outlying scores do not count. Across the rounds Joshua's three most similar scores were fractionally larger than Savón's. He edged it 17–16.

'I didn't have an outstanding performance for sure. I came back with the bitter taste of being defeated,' Savón reflected later. Speaking to me through a translator, he expressed his dissatisfaction with the score. 'I think he's a very good opponent but I don't think it was completely accurate,' he said.

Savón, though, was surprisingly effusive in his praise of his opponent. Separately, when I asked who was the best he'd faced, he stated simply, 'I would consider Joshua one of the most challenging boxers I've fought.'

Most observers of the Olympics had heard of Joshua, knew he was a World silver medallist, knew he was lined up as the 'next big thing'. But they weren't in Azerbaijan for the World Championships, hadn't seen him competing across Eastern Europe in minor tournaments. Only a few hundred had been in Bethnal Green's York Hall, Liverpool's Echo Arena or the leisure centre in Colchester for his national title triumphs. This bout against Savón was their first look at this great new hope and they saw just how well Savón handled him. Boxing fans swing from being recklessly sentimental to bitterly cynical in an instant. Joshua hadn't met their expectations. Suddenly he was doomed to be seen as a lucky man.

Joshua had got through, but he came out of the ring chastened, relieved to have got the win, knowing it had been a horribly near-run thing. His normally broad smile was a touch uneasy. He stood in front of the media, a bottle of water clutched in one big hand, a towel draped round his neck. His head nodded down as he traced a finger along the fence that separated him from the gathered journalists. Sheepish for a moment, he collected himself and looked up at the group in front of him.

'Even though it's your home crowd, when you're in there you're zoned in. It's different to what you see on the outside,' he said.

'We were both taking shots. In lower weights sometimes you take a shot and you don't see it. But in heavyweight you see your head flying all over the place. If you get hurt, you're going to go down.'

He would later add, 'I make things hard for myself or easy for myself in the ring. I didn't find him absolutely out of this world or anything like that. It's the world stage but I find them all the same. The same challenges I faced as an ABA champion fighting Dom Winrow or Abbas are the same problems I find facing Savón. They're just that different level. It's down to me. He was hard to pin down. I never expected him to stop and trade with me. I shut him down myself. I never big up the opponent or think that the opponent's better than me. There's always a way to beat an opponent.'

It stung Rob McCracken to see his star pupil dismissed for

benefiting from perceived hometown bias. 'We've been in the furthest places in the East battling for medals. The home support's always with the home fighters and so it should be,' Rob retorted. 'It's about time we had the home advantage and the home support but at the same time the judges will press the button if you're landing shots. It'll help spur the boxers on and it'll drive them and we really need it here. For sure, if it's a close, close bout, we'd hope that the support has spurred our boxer on in the last thirty seconds or the last round. But the Cuban, he's the boxer you don't want. You don't want to draw him. You want to meet him in the final because of his speed and his accuracy and basically how talented, how good he is.'

Redemption was on offer in Joshua's next bout. He would meet Zhang Zhilei, the large, impassive super-heavyweight from China who'd won a silver medal at the last Olympics. He was a serious operator, one whom Joshua had never boxed before.

Zhilei took up his southpaw stance. But Joshua was a fast learner, a 'sponge' as Paul Walmsley called him. He didn't repeat the mistakes of his first bout at the Games. He didn't rush himself, didn't lean forward. Joshua knew Zhilei wanted to counter him and wasn't about to oblige the Chinese veteran. Instead he stayed on the outside and turned his jab on to his stony-faced opponent. Zhilei had to bring his right up, just to pad away Joshua's lead.

Joshua tempted Zhilei in, cleaved at him with a left hook. The stand-off resumed, Joshua evading Zhilei's right hook, Zhilei escaping back before his opponent could apply more pressure. Though Zhilei had the guile you'd expect of an Olympic silver medallist, Joshua marshalled the bout. His jab lanced over, his left hook shook Zhilei's guard open, letting him slide in his straight right.

Zhilei's lead hook caught Joshua's jaw. The Briton rode it, patiently established his jab once more. Zhilei rose up again, his left cross hitting through, momentum swinging to the Chinese. But just as Joshua came under pressure, he dropped his straight right into Zhilei's chin, thumping him off his feet. A large man, Zhilei's back hit the ring boards with a crash.

After Zhilei rose and answered the standing count, Joshua put it on him, ratcheting the pressure up another degree, sneaking in another right hand. Mentally Joshua was in the ascendancy now: 'It knocks your confidence when you get knocked down so I thought I had him in a position where I had him wrapped up in my web.'

Joshua stayed clever. Let his opponent make the next move. Zhilei needed to go for it but his approach was restrained, by his counter-punching style, his habits and his disinclination to run on to Joshua's heavy fists. When he stepped in close, Zhilei flailed hastily with both hands. Joshua's lead pushed him back. When Anthony was nudged to the ropes, he let his right hand fly to keep his score. It finished tensely, Zhilei looking for more, finishing a combination with a right hook but that wasn't enough. Joshua had made sure of a 15–11 win.

That set Joshua up for a semi-final against the only man at the Olympics who was physically larger than Anthony himself. Ivan Dychko was just shy of six foot nine inches and, not unlike Zhilei, the shaven-headed Kazakh had the air of a movie villain. Yet Joshua had always had his doubts about him. I remembered speaking to Anthony in the GB gym, when they'd had the Kazakhs over for a training camp. 'He's got no bottle,'

Joshua confided of the super-heavyweight he'd been sparring with. Those sessions had been a significant personal marker for Anthony. In his early days on the squad he had found it hard. Dychko had hurt him in one sparring session. Then, months later, when they met again on a training camp, Anthony had battered him. 'It was nice,' he smiled. 'I could see the progression.

'The hard times didn't dishearten me. I just got to get better.'

Anthony knew that, for all Dychko's menace, he could beat the fight out of him. To do so, he would use the tool that had served him so well in his quarter-final, the simple jab. It was a skill of the next order now to outjab a taller man, and at six foot six himself it was a skill Joshua could have practised only rarely.

Dychko assayed his long one-two strike, dabbing at Joshua again with a lead. Joshua knocked him back with a hard jab and a harder cross. The Kazakh sent a fast right over from long range but Joshua answered with a well-judged left hook.

Slowly Joshua pounded pain into Dychko, keeping his upper body jerking, effective defensive movement. They traded fire at the start of the second round, an exchange Joshua was happy to make. It convinced Dychko to stay away from him. Joshua bobbed away from Dychko's far-reaching right, though the same shot caught him high.

No points separated them after the first two rounds but Joshua had wrapped his 'web' round Dychko. It was his fight, conforming to the pattern he wanted. Anthony's jab brought him in close, prompting a desperate hook as the Kazakh attempted to get himself clear. Joshua bloodied Dychko, persistent strikes damaging his nose. His left hook shifted the Kazakh to the side. He jabbed again, triggering Dychko to come back at him but again Joshua finished the dialogue with a left hook. A miss from Dychko left an opening for Joshua to come forward, three straight punches hitting home. A rear uppercut shook Dychko and Joshua's blows drove him back once more. In close again, a sudden left hook, rather than an uppercut, hurt Dychko. The tall Kazakh was left walking away, his nose bleeding freely, doomed to a 13–11 defeat.

Joshua marched up to the BBC camera after his semi-final win. 'I dedicate that to my captain Tom Stalker,' he declared. 'He's a legend. Unfortunately he didn't get the decision against the Mongolian. So that's for Tom.'

The dream for Joshua, though, had come true. He would box the super-heavyweight Olympic final in his hometown. There was no boxer left in his weight class like Erislandy Savón, none possessed of that all-round mobility and dynamism. But there was one left standing, the wiliest competitor in the division and one who had spent the past year plotting exactly how to beat Anthony Joshua. Roberto Cammarelle was back.

Azerbaijan's Magomedrasul Medzhidov, the last man to beat Joshua, had overcome the Russian Magomed Omarov to reach the semi-final and win an Olympic bronze medal. But there Italy's Cammarelle had defeated him to make sure of his place in the final.

Some teams came to London with a certain character. These groups of athletes trained together, sparred one another, learned from one another. They were shaped by coaches possessed of the same philosophy. The Ukrainians were tough, hard-headed, relentless, inspired by their brilliant lightweight Vasyl Lomachenko. The Cubans were fast, superbly skilled and confident in the virtuosity of their performance.

McCracken's boxers expressed themselves in their own styles but Rob had sketched out the philosophy that backed the British boxing team. 'Hit and move basically,' he said, 'but counter every time. You can't always hit and move. If you have to hold your feet for ten seconds, we teach them how to do that. How to be calm under fire and basically teach them all styles of boxing.'

The Italians were messy. They were not committed to the tenets of the 'sweet science'. They had come to win, but were prepared to find their own ways to do so. Some would spoil but Cammarelle had more refined methods. He wasn't an athlete galloping around the ring. A back injury had hampered his training for years. It reportedly prevented him from running – the foundation of most boxers' exercise regimes. The bodies of big men must withstand great forces. Wladimir Klitschko, the heavyweight champion of the world, had eliminated running from his training regime, relying more on swimming and sparring. When Cammarelle had met Joshua in Baku, he hadn't imposed himself physically on the bout. A touch fleshy, Cammarelle had tired. But by London 2012, like so many other competitors, the Italian copper had peaked. Trim, sharp, his feet didn't move much but there was a dexterity in his hands, in his counters, in his subtle body movements that could draw in his prey and punish them severely. A boxer who laid traps, exploited weaknesses, he had thrown back the years for these Games. Joshua couldn't rely solely on his physical prowess once again. If he did he would find himself in dire straits.

There was a film Anthony liked to watch, for motivation as much as anything else. *300* was a stylised version of an ancient

Spartan battle. It depicted a small detachment of warriors, vastly outnumbered, defending their homeland against wave after wave of enemies, soldiers and monsters. He was so taken with it his personal strength trainer had named a gut-busting circuit after the film. The movie ends with the Spartans surrounded, no hope of victory, but given the option of surrender. They choose to fight to the end. They chose to die rather than concede.

It was a silly film, with plenty of blood and thunderous battle cries. But it had a message that resonated – fight to the end. In his mind, for the months leading up to the Games, he had lived like a warrior, forsaking comforts, training for combat. Boxing is a controlled battle, it's play-fighting but serious play-fighting. For super-heavies the danger was immediate. The weight behind the punches of these men meant one mistake, one lapse and a super-heavy could be hurt, could be knocked down and out.

At stake wasn't just the risk of injury and damage. Win this last bout and the gates to superstardom could open. The over ninety-one-kilos final was on the last day of the Olympic Games. He would be one of Britain's last athletes going for a gold medal. The eyes of the nation would be on him.

Cammarelle marched in, unfazed by the surroundings. The corridor felt long as Joshua advanced down it, lights flashing along the dark walls on either side. He strived to keep his focus, concentrating on the ring up ahead. He stepped out into the bright arena, through the wall of sound. He did not acknowledge the crowd. Kept those eyes clear.

You can't tell the mind of another man. Did Roberto Cammarelle feel fear in the same way as Joshua? Cammarelle had won the last Olympic final in China, against the host nation's Zhang Zhilei, in Beijing, and he had done so with brutal clarity. He'd won at the Worlds at home in Italy, he'd campaigned all over the world, he knew Joshua intimately. What plan did he have lying in wait for the Londoner?

Joshua's jab descended on him, to sound him out. Cammarelle swayed his upper body back, the placement of his feet still keeping him in range. Both swung lead hooks through the air, until Joshua tried another tentative jab. Cammarelle, a southpaw, cuffed a lead right hook back at him. Anthony prodded him with a cross, moving Cammarelle around the ring, making the Italian come to him.

When Joshua strayed into a corner, Cammarelle's eyes never left their mark. He stole his moment, snapping a right hook across. The weight of the blow turned Joshua's jaw. Caught for an instant, he was pinned by the ropes on either side of him. The pain, the impacts, left him stranded for moment, hands and mind caught between defending and attacking. Cammarelle unleashed a merciless combination, shaking the Englishman's head some more.

That sudden moment of jeopardy meant the Italian seized the ascendancy in the bout. In the first round Anthony had harried his opponent with his long, range-finding jab. But he'd struggled to back that up with rights. The accuracy of Joshua's cross came on in the second round. It separated them for a moment before they tangled in a clinch. Joshua ducked Cammarelle's lead but the Italian hooked up with his left arm, drove the right hook over and mixed up his assaults, advancing behind sudden leads. He pushed Joshua off but his opponent thumped in his left hook, reaffirming his pride. Cammarelle nudged him towards a corner, his searching right piercing persistently through Anthony's guard.

Joshua's body was screaming as he traipsed back to the corner after the second round. Physically he was drained. He had trained for countless rounds, fought through so many, but now he was running on empty. Being out-thought wearied him. The unique stress of the moment, an Olympic final in London, had exhausted his reserves, that remarkable tension screwed his body unavoidably tight. It meant his limbs worked against their own movement. He slumped down on the stool in the blue corner. One of the coaches, Dave Alloway, told him, 'You're three points down.'

In amateur boxing, with one round left, that deficit is vast. Often in the last round the GB coaches would urge their boxers on by telling them a less favourable score than was really the case. Anthony didn't want to believe him but Dave insisted, 'No, Josh, I'm telling you.'

'No way,' he gasped.

He had only three minutes to change that. Everything he had worked for, everything he stood to gain, was sliding away from him.

The break evaporated disconcertingly fast. This was another turning point. He hadn't recovered, wasn't sure he was ready to go again. But prompted forward off the stool, he told himself, 'Keep pushing, keep pushing.' Fight to the end.

His legs burned. His limbs not functioning right, he had to fight through his limitations. Three points down, when you have to force it against a counter-puncher like Cammarelle, is a dark place to be. Joshua's options had suddenly narrowed. He didn't have a plan to counter the Italian's craft. But he flung himself into the teeth of the action. Committing himself to slug his way to victory if he had to.

'I just won't ever give up in there,' he said. 'Sometimes I wanted to stop but my mind was working and my arms were just flying around.'

He rushed Cammarelle as the latter edged away. The Italian ducked a mean Joshua right hand but the Briton stayed on him, a left hook connecting. Cammarelle used his wiles; to defend his lead he looked to tie Joshua up, preventing him from working. Joshua needed to fight his way out of those holds.

Joshua opened up on him, thumping hard, straight punches down the middle, the swelling roar of the crowd carrying him forward, carrying him on. He laboured through the pain, through the tiredness.

The bell sounded in the haze. The cue to stop fighting. Joshua himself looked curiously confident. He pumped a fist in the air as he prowled round the ring while the computer collated their scores. It may have been unfair that Joshua had been so far down after the second round, but it was impossible to tell if he had done enough to reverse so wide a deficit, despite the almighty efforts of his final round.

'I always leave it down to the judges. You can never guarantee a win until they've pulled your colour out in the corner,' he commented.

'I knew going into the third. I said, "You know, I'm not going to let this guy beat me in my head." When I went in, I put it all out there and I just gave it my best shot. I felt, you know what, I've got a chance here and I've got confidence. I said whatever happens from here I'm going to walk out with my head held high. Because I felt I gave it my best shot.'

Luck runs out. Chance had been cruel to some of his team-mates. But sometimes your luck holds. Joshua had levelled the main scores, 18–18. Officials milled about, knowing full well their organisation could ill afford to create a mess with the result of the super-heavyweight final. The scores went to countback, where they tot up the number of button presses from each of the judges, losing the highest and lowest scores. The countback was returned 56–53. To Joshua.

The row alongside me erupted. People launched themselves out of their seats. The decibel level in the arena shot off the scale, the crowd bellowed as one. My notebook went flying. I leapt up, charging off to do something, write something, I suppose. Joshua had done it. It might have been in doubt, but he came through. Ordained to be a champion.

The Homecoming

Anthony Joshua sat through his post-final press conference with the warm, weary satisfaction of a battle won. His gold medal capped a marvellous performance for the British boxing team. Joshua, Luke Campbell and Nicola Adams all had golds, the most outright Olympic boxing victories GB had had since 1908. (In that long-distant Olympics every medallist bar one was a Briton. Nowadays GB can only have one boxer in each division and they need to win their place through that intensely demanding qualifying process.) Adams was a historically significant figure: she became the first female Olympic boxing champion, beating multi-titled opponents in style along the way, always with a beaming smile on her face. Rightly, Nicola became the team's breakout star.

It was the best medal haul for the British boxing team overall since 1920, better even than 1956's golden generation of Terry Spinks and Dick McTaggart. In 1920 each nation could enter two boxers per weight class as well. It's impossible to deny the sport had evolved from those olden days, too. Factor in record-breaking World Championship performances for the team, its unprecedented European success, too, and this was unquestionably Britain's greatest ever boxing team.

'Everybody was so happy,' Nicola said. 'The coaches were happy, we were happy. We couldn't believe how well all the boxers had done. After we'd all finished, we felt like we were invincible.'

No great adventure should finish without a party. The GB boxers could not be faulted on that count. They had the Closing Ceremony to attend, an event slightly more bizarre than the Opening Ceremony but at least sweetened by the dulcet tones of both One Direction and the Spice Girls. The rest of the night was spent toasting their success in their accommodation, the GB block, their last night in the Olympic Village before they all shipped home. Some would go back to life as normal, for others nothing would be the same again. None of them knew what exactly waited for them on the other side.

Joshua, Campbell, Adams and performance director Rob McCracken would also receive MBEs at Buckingham Palace.

For Thomas Stalker it was a bitter homecoming. He had left Liverpool with the chance to become his country's most decorated amateur boxer. It had been years since he'd returned from a major without a medal. But now, after the most important competition of all, he came home empty-handed. His girlfriend and his daughters knew how much it meant. They cried, they sensed his misery. For them he had to put on a brave face, for them he had to be strong. But whenever he thought about it, he wanted to cry himself.

'To come so close to something and then not get it. It's heartbreaking,' he said. 'Everyone's gutted in Liverpool. It's like someone's died. It's driving me crazy because I can't stop thinking about it. Seeing Luke Campbell and Joshua get the gold medal, that was the highlight of my Olympic Games that. But I just wish that I was with them.'

As a team it was a resounding success. Stalker had led them in spirit and in action. Their Olympic Games were not made in that golden fortnight alone. It was forged over years, in the gym together, in Baku, fighting hard when they only had the support of one another. His attitude had led them through it. He had led them through it. But Stalker had only brought them to the finish line. He had not crossed it himself. That hurt him badly. He should have been proud of all he'd accomplished. But he could only feel the pain now of the final failure.

'I feel like I haven't done what I've wanted to do. As a team it's been brilliant. But when I come back to my home and my family, you haven't got your team with you then,' he said. 'Winning that medal would have done so much for me. Now I haven't done that, it's killed me. I'm so happy for all the lads and Nicola Adams, I'm proud of them all.

'People are going to forget about the fights. But that medal sticks with you the rest of your life. No matter where you go you're an Olympic medallist and that's what's killing me. That's what's hurting me more than anything.'

The medallists enjoyed more glorious homecomings. 'I didn't realise how much this was going to mean to so many people,' said Nicola Adams. Thousands turned out as she paraded through Leeds. Luke Campbell experienced something similar in Hull. Bronze medallist Anthony Ogogo had caught the imagination in Suffolk and had a parade of his own back home in Lowestoft. Weeks after the Games the medallists returned to London for the ultimate celebration:

GB athletes from every Olympic sport gathered in open-top buses to be driven through the heart of London. Hundreds of thousands packed the pavements on a route that stretched from St Paul's Cathedral to the Mall. It was a last chance for the public to grab their Union flags and cheer for Britain once again.

'I can't believe how many people turned out,' said Nicola. 'It's definitely a once in a lifetime experience. I wouldn't have missed that for nothing. And it didn't rain as well.'

But it marked the end, the final act, of their Olympic Games. 'You could really see how it gripped the nation,' she continued. 'I was a bit sad to see everything get back to normal. Even round London, round the Olympics, normally everybody's head's down, focused on where they need to go. People would actually stop and talk about what was going on in the Games. It even changed London for a little bit as well.

'It's over but I think everybody still wants to hold on to a little bit. I think it's that that's going to be the legacy.'

The Games, the event, the battle, had passed. Adams had her heart set on making further history at the next Olympics. The men on the team had a profound decision to make. Should they stay and do it all again in Rio de Janeiro? Or should they go?

Historically top amateurs have cashed in on their success, leveraging an Olympic medal for a lucrative deal as a professional prospect. In 2012 the landscape for these Olympians was different. Millions of loose pounds weren't floating out there, waiting to be funnelled to the nearest Olympian. For the lighter weights instant wealth was not there for the taking. That said, they were not without options.

This time the amateur game wasn't quite so willing to yield up its stars. The root of the British boxing team's success wasn't just the excellent athletes they had discovered. They had the funding to keep their Olympic prospects on full-time training in the build-up to London 2012, to the tune of £9.5 million from UK Sport over the four years. The five medals GB Boxing had won, from the funder's point of view, represented excellent value for money compared to other Olympic sports. Swimming, for instance, may have had the prestige and profile of a Formula One Olympic sport but in 2012 it chalked up only two medals, both bronze, to the tune of about £25 million from UK Sport.

Funding for the next Olympic cycle would be reallocated at the end of the year. Boxing, on its success, had a good claim for a greater share. But part of the funding application had to specify the athletes who would be built for Rio 2016. Boxing was unique in that it could lose its Olympic competitors not just to injury or form but to the hungry promoters of professional boxing.

AIBA didn't like that either. But the Olympics were an event the world governing body could utilise in the wider war they were waging. AIBA had made it quite clear that they believed boxing in all its forms should come under their banner. They had their World Series of Boxing, which tried to tempt amateurs into a quasi-professional league, with the added appeal of earning them more money on top of their regular funding while they retained their Olympic eligibility. For the 2013 season the World Series of Boxing had even managed to sign Vasyl Lomachenko, the Ukrainian who had won his second Olympic gold medal at London 2012, seemingly at a canter. Lomachenko was as top class a talent as there was in the sport. (In later years he did go down the traditional professional route, where he became a two-weight world champion more rapidly than anyone ever had before.) AIBA also planned eventually to launch their own brand of professional boxing, a direct challenge to the old pro game.

Their efforts to get their World Series up and running in America were faltering. Britain remained a key market for them. The country's boxing history would provide a legitimacy for the new format that cash-rich Kazakhstan, Azerbaijan and the like, for all their new money, could not. GB had also topped the boxing medal table at the Olympic Games. Britain was where the sport's new stars lay.

The upper reaches of AIBA knew well the strategic importance of Great Britain to their plans. When they first began to construct their World Series of Boxing, they had tried to get GB on board. Despite positive indications from the British association ultimately GB could not risk its funds, from the public coffers, in a commercial enterprise. They pulled out, sowing the seeds of enmity with AIBA, characterising themselves as an aloof, arrogant team, albeit one still more than capable of beating the old powers at their own game, but unwilling to participate in the 'AIBA family'.

But as conflict raged in the Olympic ring at the ExCeL, representatives of the World Series and AIBA met with Derek Mapp, the chair of the British Amateur Boxing Association, to open tentative discussions.

There were advantages for GB in returning to the AIBA fold. If their boxers turned professional they were lost to the amateurs for good. With the hybrid World Series, they had a simple cash incentive to keep their athletes in the Olympic movement for a little longer. The World Series would mean that GB boxers could earn more money, box like the pros but remain on the programme and stay eligible for Rio 2016. That gave World Series competitors a security conspicuously absent from the pro ranks. Professional boxers are prizefighters. And if they don't fight, whether through injury or their promoters failing to match them, they don't get paid.

For the GB back office keeping some seasoned Olympians also would serve a very valuable purpose. After the 2012 Games each Olympic sport in the UK had to get in that funding application for the next cycle by the end of November. That document would get them the lump sum for 2016 that would be portioned out to them over the coming years. When it came to athletic performance GB Boxing was in a happy position. The only part of the application where they might struggle was identifying the talent they'd still be able to call on. They didn't know who they'd still have in the gym by 2013, let alone 2016.

These two monumental tasks – seeing if they could pull together a World Series franchise and completing the funding application – fell to Matt Holt, the GB Boxing programme director.

The cycle kept on rolling. There was no opportunity to savour the team's triumphs at the London Games, no time to sit back and reflect on those achievements. The Games had finished in August. The World Series season would start in November and Britain would have to construct a franchise from scratch if they were going to take part. They had to move fast, far too fast for comfort, if it was going to happen. To add to the stress, any mistakes, in procedure, in policy, would leave the programme open to attack from opponents within the domestic sport.

'It's been busier in the two to three months since the Olympics than I have been at any other point since I've been involved in GB Boxing,' said Holt.

'It would have been nice to have a break but this is the job. Things are fast-moving, you've got to react to it. There wasn't time to really soak in some of the success that we had in London and you kind of move on to the next thing.

'Although it's immediately post-2012, no sooner do the closing speeches get made than you're already thinking about how you're going to prepare the team in four years' time. That cycle of continuity is really, really important. You don't take your foot off the gas and you utilise the time that you've got, which is the full four years, to the very best of the ability of the organisation so you don't waste any time.'

In truth they could have done with far more preparation time or with putting the groundwork in before London 2012 to be ready to cope with the turmoil after the Games. As it was, they had to scramble, evaluating from their squad who was willing and able to compete, factoring in the different weight divisions in the World Series and seeing what foreign boxers could be added to the franchise's roster, then seeing what could be done financially. They had to race against time and against professional promoters desirous of luring the stars away from the programme, but they assembled a team.

'Collectively there was a need to move fast. In terms of what the WSB franchise were able to offer the boxers. Getting the boxers into a room to provide them with the details of those offers, then obviously the boxers need time to think about it,' said Matt.

They were lucky, too, in having Rob McCracken in place. His methods had produced the goods at the Olympic Games and the tournaments building up to London 2012. With Carl Froch he had shown he could take a man to the very top of the professional game. AIBA, in their ambition to control the sport in all its forms, were taking the amateur code towards the pros. It nevertheless made McCracken, still banned from the corner because of the Froch connection, the man for the hour.

'We've won more medals in three years than we've won in about thirty, so,' he said with a shrug that spoke volumes, 'I got the right coaches in, I got the right team in place. We have a fantastic team, support staff, great boxing coaches, we also have great organisation and, most importantly, we have lots of talent.'

The programme got its rewards, too. When UK Sport's funding allocations for the next Olympic cycle were published at the end of the year, boxing received a 44 per cent increase to £13.8 million, more than Matt Holt had dared to hope for. In a further defence of the programme, the money would be released to GB Boxing on the condition that its governance structure was secured. The system looked set to last.

'I'm fully aware what boxing's like and I know that if you don't stay on top of it, things can go wrong pretty quickly,' McCracken cautioned. 'But I respect boxing, that's why I work hard at it, and I try to work as hard as I can to improve. My thing's about letting boxers fulfil their potential. If they win things along the way, fantastic. As long as they fulfil their potential, that's what it's about.'

Unlike most sports teams, with this one its success, failure and long-term future depended on its boxers and the power of their names. And three of GB Boxing's A-listers were notably absent from the World Series side's roster. Anthony Ogogo, an Olympic bronze medallist and as marketable as any young man, had lost none of his desire to conquer the world in whatever his next endeavour might be. But, as he put it simply, his heart wasn't in the WSB. He was considering offers from professional promoters. Hull's handsome Olympic gold medallist, Luke Campbell, maintained an enigmatic silence. It was often said of Campbell that he was the perfect amateur but that his style would not lend itself to the pros, that he'd be better suited to becoming a career amateur. But when Luke had been out of favour with the squad, down on his luck, injured, he had never lost faith in his ability to reach the pinnacle of his sport. He was not the kind of man to let stylistic quibbles hold him back from any decision he saw fit.

But for AIBA, the British Lionhearts and every pro promoter with any sort of money behind them there was one oh-so-precious commodity. A young Olympic super-heavyweight champion with a beaming smile.

Commodity is a loaded word, deliberately used. Professional boxing is a raw business. The fighters are thrown into the ring, expected to beat each other down, lumps of meat which, after the initial outlay, need to bleed money. Their skills and their struggle can be beautiful, their demeanour strangely noble, but behind them the business makes stark calculations. Riches are available to the brave, the brilliant and the wise, or at least the cunning. But disaster lurks more readily still for the unwary. A boxer leaving the safety of the amateurs has to be aware that he then becomes more than just an athlete. He's now a business and it's up to him to be the boss of that business.

Joshua could already sense how people related differently to him. 'After the Worlds I realised something had changed,' he said. He told himself, 'I'm going to go to the Olympics and I'm going to win it.' That prompted him to get an agent in place. 'So people had to go through him,' he explains. 'They had to gain his trust. I thought that already.'

To those in the hunt for Anthony Joshua's signature, he may have been the most alluring prize in boxing. But he was so much more than a commodity. I could never tell truly what was going on in that mind of his. That didn't mean he wasn't a thoughtful man. Quite the reverse. After the Olympics the boxing world was clamouring for the big man to declare his intentions.

Joshua made them wait.

Some words of Thomas Stalker sprang to mind. 'I've seen what everybody's been through,' he had said. 'You never think you're going to make it but you've got to keep working hard. Then you do see the rewards. In the end.'

Anthony Joshua could see the rewards. He had suffered and he'd worked and now, a young, powerful super-heavyweight, he could inherit the boxing world. He had the profile, appearing on television, in demand from every promoter in the sport. All the British pro boxing kingpins were interested. He hadn't escaped the notice of Golden Boy in the US or other major international promoters. He was a wanted man.

He had made it clear he would honour his contract with GB Boxing. That meant he'd stay amateur until March 2013, six months after receiving his Olympic medal in London. But pro boxing promoters had always been hovering round him, from his progress through his first national championship to his ascent to the Olympic podium. Insisting he was staying until March, Joshua hoped, would keep them at bay.

'With that side of things I think if you want to put yourself out there, you put yourself out there. You make it known that you want to make that decision. As of now I've made it pretty clear that I'm still an amateur,' he claimed. 'Promoters haven't hounded me personally. I've never had that. I don't know why.'

It's hard to tell with Joshua. He's not at all a dishonest man. He will talk frankly, if it's something he wishes to discuss. And if he doesn't want to talk about something, he won't. There's a dignity in that. It's one of the reasons he's so well respected in the sport. Along the way he's learned a valuable lesson, the hard way. In boxing you have to be on your guard. He has so much potential, so much ability and, as a big man, is in the fortunate position that he can gain from it. But he never wanted to be told by others who he was, cast by journalists, like me, as the boxer with a troubled past. He was determined to be himself.

'The only downside is that the advice continues to be the same. Be careful. Be clever. Don't do anything silly. I'm an ambassador for boxing, aren't I? And I'd really like to represent my sport the right way. You know how boxing is and how people look at fighting and stuff like that. My job is just as important as your job. We all represent boxing at the end of the day. So I just want to make sure I conduct myself properly,' he told me.

There's no training programme to prepare you for sudden fame. The Olympic gold, the new profile, meant Joshua was under a new level of scrutiny. He shrugged it off: 'Sometimes when I go down to the launderette the old lady recognises me and stuff like that.'

But the change was inevitable. Before the Olympic Games he was known in boxing. But he had more freedom of movement. He could go to the Haringey Box Cup, a tournament he'd boxed in as a novice. Plenty of people came up to him, to shake his hand, to pose for photos, and Joshua was happy to oblige. But he could relax and watch his clubmates box. He didn't mind talking and many of those who spoke to him already knew him from the club scene, from before he was famous.

After the Games, he was at a British World Series fixture in London. His agent was with him, his movements had to be choreographed. After the show he stood off in a corner of Earl's Court, a security guard restricting an area, while it was decided which exit to use. There was a group around him, they looked young, an entourage of sorts I supposed, and Anthony of course towered over them, a head, and shoulders, taller. He looked serious, hemmed in now. Not necessarily trapped. Inhibited, though.

A lot of money could be in his bank account, if he played it right. But I wondered if it would be less fun from now on. Hemmed in by fame, under the pressure of his status. He would have what all his team-mates wanted. But he got it so soon. His time to be young, the chance to be irresponsible, if only for a bit, had gone.

'First and foremost I'm always a fighter. You have to learn things you wouldn't have expected you had to learn. You just have to grow up a bit. Just educate yourself on certain things. I'm really glad to have found boxing because it's taught me a lot. It's made me make a lot of decisions. Being the boss of myself, or however you want to call it, from the start until the end,' he said.

'I'm always going to have to make decisions and be in control of my destiny. Everything will work out. Everything's going well. I just don't want to make any mistakes or rush anything.'

The anticipation for Joshua to turn professional was growing. It was the standard move: hand in your vest and headguard, cash in that gold medal for the lucrative purses of a heavyweight prizefighter. It's what was expected and the kind of money promoters would be throwing his way would make it hard to resist.

But something held Joshua back. The gym in Sheffield had proved as fine an academy for elite boxers as anywhere in the world. 'What's been happening now with GB, it's never failed me. So I don't feel any need to change a winning team. So there's no need to become big time and have someone massage my hands and feet while I'm sitting in the car. I'm fine. There's still a journey. There's still a long journey to go and we're winning at the minute so I'm happy. I'm happy where I am,' he said.

Divining his next move was like watching the Vatican for a puff of smoke. At times AIBA were full of hope that he'd sign up for the World Series of Boxing. A figure of his stature would give their nascent league the gravitas they craved. He made the right noises to please GB Boxing, saying he wanted to be an amateur World champion, that he wanted to dominate his bouts. The 2013 Worlds were in October, after the end of Joshua's current contract. GB signed their boxers for complete Olympic cycles, so to do the Worlds again Joshua would have to commit himself to Rio 2016. Among the pros Matchroom's representatives came out of a meeting with Joshua optimistic that the big man liked what he'd heard. An offer from Golden Boy was sitting on a shelf in his bedroom at home.

Still Joshua kept his own counsel. All things to all men maybe. You could see what you wanted to see in Anthony Joshua: signs of mastery, his athleticism, heart as well as a novice-like raw quality to his boxing, the hype currently exceeding his capabilities.

The programme had done an effective job shielding him from the world in the build-up to London. He could go up there and leave everything outside of his boxing behind. And Joshua had to develop in the ring. He was a work in progress. His first bout at London 2012 had been desperately close, but he'd got past the Cuban Erislandy Savón. He'd salvaged the final in the dying minutes of the bout. 'If I go to Rio, I would do it much better than I did in London,' he conceded. He had seen that in Roberto Cammarelle in the final. The Italian had beaten the local man in the Olympic final four years earlier and Joshua only just managed to handle him, digging out a countback victory in the nick of time. 'I think he was better at London 2012,' Joshua said of his rival. 'His experience, Olympic champion already. He's been there, he's done it. I think that's what benefited him.'

But herein was the clue to what the man from Watford was capable of. He'd had forty-three bouts. In the amateurs that made him an international novice. Yet he had found a way to beat the world's best, veterans of hundreds of contests. It may have been a damn near-run thing but Joshua had done it all, from scratch, in four years. He could and would improve. He had the chance to be great.

His choice now was not about selecting the most appealing financial package. It was about going where he could fulfil all that remarkable potential. In that sense GB could make a good case to keep him.

PART TWO

Why Fight

I was always a guest in their world. But I wanted to understand fighters. I'd had a vague idea I wanted to write boxing, years ago, when I was at university. Having read that sportswriting was the closest you could get to being a bum and getting paid for it, I figured that was the job for me. In an effort to understand the sport, I tried boxing myself. I got myself down the gym. It was a departure, something totally other than reading the Greek or the Latin I should have been studying. Boxing for me was a joyful, as well as a hurtful, experience, being in a place where I could try to be myself, spared the pressure of doing what was expected of me. In training I could haul myself round the Oxford University running track where Roger Bannister broke the four-minute mile. I got to try to punch people in the head. I took plenty of blows myself. I bled, I felt the pain. I felt fear. I felt free. I heard the sound, briefly, of a crowd shouting my name. Boxing, for the short time I did it, at the low level I did it, let me feel like someone bigger, someone better. Made me feel like I was getting something done. It was a strange kind of magic.

My coaches ultimately instructed me to give it up before I came up against someone who knew how to handle themselves and I contrived to get myself hurt. I had my last contest in 2006, two years before Anthony Joshua had even walked into Finchley Amateur Boxing Club. In only two years he would win the senior national title. With astonishing speed Joshua had learned how to box and shot to the very top of the sport, winning an Olympic gold medal in just four years. It was insane when you thought about it. He had gone from nothing to champion in next to no time. When I thought about how long it took me to string a few decent punches together, how I still hadn't mastered moving my head clear of a shot, it was mind-boggling to me that Joshua had managed to go so far, so quickly.

My attempt to box had not been successful, but nevertheless it was a great gift to me. It opened the door for me, to write in, to live in, a different world for a while. The sport helped me. It gave me a discipline, perhaps it gave me the muscle to sit down and write a book. Hauling yourself round the gym, up hills on freezing mornings, gets you in shape for boxing. But the physical is only one part of it. The sport gives you a peculiar determination.

One line always stayed with me from the experience. 'You can't be thick and be a boxer,' yelled the trainer Dave, whose voice rarely lowered from a yell, varying in pitch instead between a roar and insistent bark. He was right, of course. Soon I would discover he invariably was. To fight is to think. A high-octane game of move and counter-move, in which, if you make a mistake, you pay the price with pain.

I remember my first contest. Sitting ready and changed in a

dressing room, the wait on the day interminable. The afternoon and the evening stretched on, I couldn't think about anything else and then suddenly, all too quickly, it was time, time to go out. I couldn't delay it any longer and I was on a long walk to the ring.

The Oxford Union considers itself a distinguished institution. The debating chamber there has seen such personalities as Margaret Thatcher and Michael Jackson speaking in it, with the busts of wise old stone heads staring down on them. On this night it hosted the 'Town v Gown' boxing match, an opportunity for the local Oxford men to exercise their age-old enmity with the swollen scholars of the university and teach them a physical lesson in the sweet science.

I remember the wait in the changing room so clearly. The fear: I felt it real in my stomach. I had come this far, I was wearing the vest, I couldn't walk away. But that fear was a tangible thing. I remember Dave, the Oxford coach, laughing that people say they'd fight Mike Tyson for a million dollars. They wouldn't. Not if they had to wait in a changing room and actually think about what they were about to do. I was boxing someone as inexperienced as I was and it was all I could do to hold my jangling nerves together and propel myself out, down the corridor and into the ring.

Boxing brings something out of you when you watch it in a crowd, a latent bloodlust maybe or at least a rush of excitement, especially when you have a connection to one of the participants in the ring. Dense-packed, close to the ropes, the roar of a fight crowd creates a heady atmosphere.

Before I knew it I was walking slowly out in front of them, climbing up to the corner, a headguard clamped over my ears, fastened tight under my chin. I couldn't acknowledge the crowd, I could barely hear them. The bell ringing, all at once it was on.

The opponent came at me. I did all I knew to do. I jabbed my right. I remember it clearly still. I popped him hard and saw his body stutter, his movement disrupted by the shot. I saw him hurt. Two simple words burst into my mind. 'Kill him,' I thought, 'kill him.' I smacked him with the right again. I stepped forward, automatic, to stand in an orthodox stance and put more heft into my right, now a cross. I hit him again and again, I don't know how many times more. He careered back into the ropes, like he was trying to take a seat. A white towel, from his corner, was floating through the air, the referee was jumping between us. I hit him again, still going for him even as I was pulled away.

I stood in the centre of the ring, holding my fist in the air. I realised my coach Dave was shouting at me, telling me to get in a corner. Not understanding what he wanted instead I walked towards him. He shouted again, wanting me to go the other way. I hadn't even grasped I needed to be in a neutral corner so the referee could take up the count.

It didn't matter, though. The fight over. And it felt good.

The joy of winning, of hearing the cheers, coursed through me. At the same time, I was overcome with a wave of empathy, a sense of good feeling and fellowship for the opponent, whom moments earlier I had been desperate to smash unconscious. It's a curious game.

I trotted back to my corner. The other Oxford coach, Des, took out the gumshield from my mouth, tucked it into my vest. It was an oddly affecting gesture, like being taken into his confidence. 'We can do something with you,' he cackled.

While I basked in the warm afterglow of victory, I thought I could punch. I was confident there. But little did I realise I had so much more to learn. There was so much I didn't know. How to move, how to counter, how to defend. You can't just stand there lobbing punches. Hit and don't get hit, they always say. The art of boxing is the 'not getting hit' part. If you want to have style, you need to be able to defend. When you suddenly imagine yourself to be a knockout puncher and believe that any problem, if hit hard enough, will go away, you can neglect to learn the real skill of it.

I took a hard lesson in my second bout. I took an absolute pasting, that is. I thought I had been punching all right, on the bags, in sparring, in the gym. But in the ring, under the pressure of all those watching eyes, in the face of a live opponent, I couldn't get the punches off. I shuffled out to the centre of the canvas. I should have been able to move right. But I was rooted to the spot. No defence. Wide open. My opponent was shifting all around me, throwing punches easily, my head thudding from side to side beneath his fists. I tried to fight him off. Couldn't. Tried to move away. Couldn't escape. All I could do was take my licks. Stand and suffer.

I sat in the bar of the Oxford Union afterwards, dull to the pictures of whatever luminaries of times past hung on the wall in front of me. My upper lip was already swelling. My head ached. My pride was stung. But I felt dim. When I'd fought before, even when I trained or sparred, my body hummed with life. Now it was just flat, like I'd been doped. Only the sharp sensation of embarrassment managed to slice through all that, a hot kind of shame, to have been battered in front of everybody. That I felt acutely.

Starting out on small club shows, all amateur boxers would have had experiences similar to these in their early days. I merely had five bouts in total. Then the coaches advised me to pack it in. The sport may be called amateur boxing but the name is deceptive. The standard gets very high, very quickly. After ten bouts, if you're not good enough you can start getting hurt. After twenty bouts, the boxers who make it that far are serious, committed, and they're planning on going places in boxing. It's a dangerous sea if you swim too far out of your depth. Yet Anthony Joshua would win the senior national championships in just eighteen bouts. It was almost unfathomable to me.

The coach was not only right, he was looking out for me. I had to get back to real life. Study for exams, get through them, get out of the Oxford bubble, get a job. Be normal. And you can't do that when you're legging it up hills at dawn, hauling your carcass round the track or spending your evenings punching bags, punching people, banging through press-ups, sit-ups, holding the dreaded plank position. It was time to get back to reality.

Boxing for me opened a door to a new world. The sport left me convinced that boxing matters. Its dangers can't be ignored. There is an ugliness to it, in wrong decisions, in the damage, in the bad deals. But there is a beauty to the sport. The true grace you see under pressure, the refining simplicity of punch and counter-punch. Two fighters moving in and out, judging their distance, selecting their shots. It's easy to forget the benefits of boxing, too. There are rewards for some – at the ultra-elite level of this sport those rewards can be vast. Boxing, I believe, can do good. Sitting down with Dr Mike Loosemore, really the leading medical expert in the sport, for a coffee, a decade later, in the dreary aftermath of the Rio Olympics I plucked up the courage to ask how comfortable he felt in boxing as a doctor. The risk of real accident, he cautioned, was rare. 'The health benefits far outweigh any physical downside,' he reckoned. Putting it simply, 'If you're going to go in the ring and you're not fit, you're going to get hit and when you get hit, it hurts.' The sport forces a fighter to get exceptionally fit.

But there was more to boxing than keeping people in peak physical condition. 'All of society now is based on how many pieces of paper you can get and how many exams you can get,' Mike said. 'Two hundred years ago that wouldn't perhaps have been so useful. If we were physically strong and we were brave and we could fight with our hands or fight in an open combat situation, we would have been extremely valuable to society and we would have been well rewarded.'

In the modern age, he continued, 'It's very difficult to get standing within your peer group. By boxing, by showing physical courage in front of your peer group and by standing against people who are your own weight, your own age, your own experience, in a one-to-one situation, nobody else is there to help you. It's not like a team game, you're on your own and if you get hit it hurts. That shows physical courage. It gives you a lot of standing within your peer group. And if you have standing within your peer group, you don't have to do other things to get standing. You don't have to do criminal stuff, you don't have to vandalise things, because you have that standing.

'It helps give people who are looking for direction something they can do and be good at.'

People who box experience that sensation. Having something of their own. Those who coach or volunteer in the sport can observe first-hand what it does for people. But it can be a closed world, one misunderstood or scorned by outsiders. It was refreshing therefore to sit in a fifth-floor office in Portcullis House, talking to a politician, MP Charlotte Leslie, the chair of the All Party Parliamentary Group for Boxing, about the potential, the myriad possibilities locked in this sport.

'What do human beings need to be happy? They need a sense of identity – who am I? A sense of purpose – what am I here for? And a sense of community – who am I with? And if kids are not given that through mainstream society, through school, they feel ostracised, they'll find that somewhere else. So if a gang says, "You are for this and you are with us", they go there and I think that's one of the pulls of extremism,' she said. 'But that's exactly what boxing clubs provide. So for kids who haven't got any of those things, the boxing club is there. They are themselves, they are a boxer. They are there to be part of the club, win competitions or just become a better boxer, and their community is their boxing club.

'It gives them all those things that perhaps they haven't had in their lives. Boxing clubs provide them with identity, community and purpose.'

Boxing is a sport of extremes. It's not for everyone, it won't appeal to all of us but that, I thought, was precisely the point. Boxing could, occasionally, reach the people who needed it most.

The sport took me places I never thought I'd go. Gritty gyms in the inner city, to a ringside seat in Las Vegas, to walking through vast casinos in the Far East, stadia in Azerbaijan and Kazakhstan, not to mention an Olympics in my home city. Dabbling in the sport myself, I had learned a little. That, for instance, you didn't have to be a natural, but you must acquire the skill. You have to keep showing up. I'd found out some things about myself. I got to know both victory and defeat. I could fight, in my way. I thought, too, I'd acquired more of an idea of what I was talking about.

But I hadn't won the one that mattered. It left me asking myself why I hadn't dug a little deeper. Why hadn't I worked a little harder? Did that say something about me? Was I a choker? I managed to keep on showing up to sessions and plodding through them, but I found it so hard to keep myself in that red zone of suffering, where real character is revealed, where true advances are made. I could only imagine what it took to make it in boxing, to keep driving yourself into that place, the heartbreaking pain of constant work. I could imagine it. I couldn't do it. And it left me in awe of those who could.

The Choice

All I'd had was a glimpse of the sport. A hint of what it could do for you. However, as a writer I was privileged to watch a group of young people, through endless work, through a faith in themselves in dark times and good, transform. They made themselves into what they became. A leader, like Thomas Stalker, an artist like Luke Campbell. A champion like Anthony Joshua. Each of them were all of those things.

They spent hours alone. Running, training, thinking. They spent years together. Driving each other on. Helping each other, giving support and encouragement because there was no one else who could. There was no one, outside of their team, who knew what they were going through. None of them had had it easy. They had all failed at some point. Some failed time and time again until they got what they wanted. Others won and continued to win, until at the moment of truth they fell short. But they still rallied. Liverpool, Hull or Watford – where they came from didn't create them. They chose who they became. When they failed, when they suffered, they showed their class, they showed their character. To come back. To keep pushing. To believe.

When Anthony Joshua had stepped out of the ring after the Olympic final, he was greeted by Audley Harrison and Lennox Lewis, two former super-heavyweight gold medallists. Audley had turned professional, to great fanfare in Britain. Self-promoted, his career had had no competitive architecture. Relatively old when he left the amateurs, he regressed. He lost every serious fight he had, yet he broadcasted an evangelical faith in himself. It got him to big fights. Got him vast paydays. But boxing is unforgiving. He became a laughing stock. He was repeatedly knocked out.

In Lennox Lewis, Joshua stood in front of the last great heavyweight king. A calm, calculating figure in the ring, Lewis had entered two Olympic Games. He had suffered shock defeats as a professional but he corrected them. He had the nights in Vegas, he was the archetype of a champ.

They were the embodiments of the two paths that stood ahead of Joshua. Anthony, in his abilities, had the raw material. He had the status that came from the Olympic super-heavyweight gold medal which hung heavy round his neck. He could cash that in now. He could chase the money, take the path of least risk, for the highest reward.

But would he then become all that he could be? To realise his potential, he had to go where he could flourish as a boxer. He had to make his skill, his sport his goal, not the vast rewards he stood to reap from it. He could choose to become rich. Or to become great. Instead of simply taking the highest financial option available to him he had to consider what would be best for his boxing.

Yet by the start of July 2013, Joshua was still in the GB gym. He had, of course, been offered a new contract to stay on the

Olympic programme but it remained unsigned. But nor had he signed with anybody else.

An operation on his foot had healed and Anthony got back to his training with renewed vigour. There were voices all around him, as there would be surrounding any man in his position. The Sheffield gym had changed slightly. The Olympic ring had been moved in. Joshua's image adorned the wall, along with the team's other London 2012 medallists. But when the door shut here it closed off the outside world. In his time here, with a smile on his face, Anthony could focus, remind himself that the boxing had to be his all-consuming goal.

'All of a sudden you have access to people like good trainers and people in America want to chat to you. Lennox Lewis wants to talk to you. Audley Harrison wants to talk to you. It's like, "Wow, this is great." Then all of a sudden you're on the phone till twelve at night and you're too tired to wake up for training in the morning,' he admitted.

'It wasn't hard to stay focused, just making sure you always put your boxing first.'

Despite tempting offers to experience other gyms, he was drawn back to the centre in Sheffield. While considering his future options, he looked happy enough working out in the gym, even though now he was in the unaccustomed role of sparring partner. While Joshua was undecided, Joe Joyce, the man he had beaten in the 2011 London ABAs, would go to the 2013 European Championships. In the Olympic ring set up in their gym, Joshua and Frazer Clarke, another super-heavy pushed down the pecking order, rotated in and out against Joyce. Rob McCracken leaned on the ring apron, quietly directing different roles, isolating one technique for them to work on, before changing it to an open spar.

Joshua was sharp. Even in this more relaxed session you could see the explosive power he was whipping up into his hook. He was thinking about his feet, trying to get that balance right. 'Balance,' as Luke Campbell said, 'is everything in a boxing ring.' As a boxer Joshua was developing. He was spot on with his assessment of himself. 'A lot of what used to get me through with my boxing was fitness, was brute strength,' he said. 'Now a lot of it comes down to how my technique is. Am I slipping shots, counter-attacks? I'm boxing a bit more now. Back then it was "you give me one, I'm going to give you three. You give me two, I'll give you five." Just a battle of who's the strongest. If I still have the fitter and stronger element and have the technique, I'm already levels ahead.'

As had become his custom he stayed on after the session, doing his neck and wrist exercises, heaving his bulk up into chin-ups. He spent a long time doing it. 'They always tell me to take it easy,' he reflected. 'There is a danger of overtraining but, come on – Mayweather, Mayweather's the lead boxer of my generation. He's all about hard work.'

Floyd Mayweather: brash, dangerous, cruel, the pre-eminent boxer of the modern age. But he wasn't the only fighter on Joshua's mind. A studious type, when it came to boxing he was watching Sugar Ray Leonard, Aaron Pryor, Muhammad Ali. Watching the greats. He was looking at their footwork, building his own foundation.

'If I stay dedicated and give up my twenties, thirties and so on and just dedicate it to boxing, I will do well,' he said. 'If I just take it for granted, I won't progress. If I stay dedicated to the sport I think good things will come.'

Joshua was a precocious talent. In just four years, from walking into the gym in Finchley, he had reached the summit of the sport, winning an incredible Olympic gold, in just forty-three bouts. He was working on his skills, maintaining that physicality, his confidence growing. How much further could he go? That would all depend on him, on his ambition and his effort.

'There's still work to do,' he promised.

New Beginnings

'You still feel exactly the same going into a pro ring as you would an amateur ring. You've still got the same emotions. You've still got the same nerves. It's the same psychologically.' Luke Campbell, like Joshua, had won gold at London 2012. Everything for him had changed. Hull, his hometown, loved Luke Campbell. The masses had turned out in force for his professional debut. On 13 July 2013 Craven Park Stadium, the home of Hull Kingston Rovers rugby league team, was an incredible sight. As the hands of the clock edged towards midnight 7,000 people milled about the pitch, in full voice.

Luke had his own changing room. He held those nerves in check. He had faced a crowd before, but never one like this. This was his own.

A short walk down the corridor. He stepped into the cool air. He stepped into the noise. The roar was all around him. Seven thousand people were all around him. They left their seats in the stands to spread across the ground, all the way to the open-air ring in the centre of the pitch. Luke stood among them as the music and the lights ripped through the night. He walked forward, his expression locked, almost mournful. He broke into a gentle jog. He kept his eyes on the ring ahead of him, not breaking his stare even as arms reached out on either side of him, not to push or jostle him, just to touch his passing shoulder.

He progressed to the ring, the crowd parting for him, an ascension, a ceremony now more than a sporting event. For a prospect going into what was, after all, only his first professional fight this had no precedent. I'd never seen anything like it. My pen bounced off the page of my notebook. I could feel the excitement.

Luke was Hull's. He had gone out. Gone round the world. Conquered it. Now he was back and the wild crowd bellowed its approval.

The volume of sound reached a crescendo as Luke put a spindly leg through the ropes. Then he stood to his full height. His legs may still have been stick-thin but his body had filled out during his absence from the ring. In 2012 he had been a bantamweight, now he was nine stone nine pounds, a lightweight. Muscle knotted his shoulders, stood out in his midriff. He wasn't fighting in an amateur vest any more. He held his arms aloft, raising another thrilled cheer from the stadium. He'd been a youth last time I'd seen him. Now he was a man.

Across the ring from him was Andy Harris, a new journeyman who'd gone six rounds with Thomas Stalker in Liverpool up at light welterweight. In theory, therefore, he should have been capable of giving Campbell an argument. Not in practice.

Not a soul there wanted to see Harris do well. That can drain the fight out of anyone. Mike Bromby, Campbell's childhood coach, was in his corner for this first professional fight. He sent Luke out. Harris, overeager, rushed forward to meet him.

The fight itself was a blur. Campbell boxed as though he'd never been away. As fast and slick-sharp as ever, he leapt back as Harris flew at him. At the same time instinctively Campbell snapped his lead right hook across. The blow caught Harris high on the temple and already he was falling in the opening seconds of the bout. His hands and knees hit the canvas. The referee barked the mandatory count into his face. Campbell manoeuvred round him, pressed in. Those hooks chopped across and he bundled Harris down once more.

Harris rose, reeled away. Campbell's cross staggered him into the ropes and he sensed the finish. Reckless, in a way he would never have boxed in the amateurs, Campbell flung himself forward. He threw everything off either hand at Harris, shuddering his prey against the ropes and the referee was between them, waving it off after one minute and twenty-eight seconds.

Campbell raised those fists in the air again, unleashing the final act of the ritual, letting the crowd exult in the sacrifice they'd wanted.

Would Campbell translate to the pros? Stripped to the waist, knocking people down and out, he hadn't missed a beat.

'I train to hit someone and not get hit back. It's a game plan I like to stick to when I'm in the ring,' he smiled.

Anthony Joshua watched it all from the crowd. He had spent a year on the sidelines. It was a long, long time to wait. 'A lion's always patient before it goes in for the kill,' he'd once said cheerfully to me. But when it came to that fateful choice, where next to go, whether to stay amateur or turn professional, as the months ticked by the wait looked less and less calculated, more like a level of indecision worthy of Hamlet.

The GB gym in Sheffield held a special place in his heart. In many ways the programme had made him. The coaches were some of the best around; they'd done a great job with him. They'd prepared him for the Cubans, the Russians and the Kazakhs who prowled the amateur boxing world. There was an emotional bond that kept him in Sheffield, kept him a part of that team, a bond Joshua did not want to break.

But the money was in professional boxing and the numbers being thrown at him were impressive. Joshua had done well to resist signing up for the craziest sum lobbed at him in the immediate aftermath of the Games. He fielded the offers from the pros but took seriously what was out there in the amateurs. He hadn't joined the British Lionhearts in the World Series of Boxing, though many of his team-mates had. He wasn't going to commit himself to anything hastily. But he watched them closely. He liked the way they presented their matches, dressing up the events better than any lower-level pro show. He loved representing his country. The Lionhearts would allow him to stay in the GB set-up, earn a bit more cash and keep him on the Olympic circuit.

Would Joshua's talents remain on the same trajectory without the cutting-edge facilities of the programme in Sheffield? The GB set-up might have been more professional than a pro gym but the wider sport offered a sharp reminder as to why it was called amateur boxing. In the UK amateur boxing was doing its best to tear itself apart.

The GB programme had structural enemies. It sat above the Home Nations but elements in Scotland and England had never forgotten the old days, when they used to be in charge. GB's wealth of resources was envied. The Board of the Amateur Boxing Association of England had banned WSB boxers from their national championships, on spurious 'medical grounds', a move easily interpreted as a spiteful dig at GB. It was unclear what it was going to achieve, other than anger the international governing body for the sport as a whole. The next strike from the 'blazers' took aim at the chairman of GB Boxing, Derek Mapp. What Mapp had done wrong was unclear. He was highly regarded within the programme. He'd backed the boxers when they had troubles outside the ring. Mapp wasn't in the job for money; he actually appeared to care. When Joshua was sitting ringside at the Lionhearts, Mapp, with no regard for either his less than spritely limbs or the smart suit he wore, clambered over seats to catch up with him. Discussions around Joshua's contract for the next cycle had been going on in the background. Mapp was making the point that he wanted to talk directly to Anthony. It was a nice gesture. It showed he cared about the programme.

But Amateur Boxing Scotland wanted more influence. They moved to oust Mapp from his position and support from certain influential quarters in England ensured that this was carried through. The internal politicking so outraged UK Sport that it threatened to divert GB Boxing's funding through a new vehicle unless order was restored. AIBA, the world governing body, didn't like the direction all this was heading in and saw it as good a reason as any to withdraw their financial backing of the British Lionhearts. Just like that, after only one season, the franchise ceased to exist.

The English ABA wasn't just at war with GB, it was at war with itself. Its efforts to resolve its own governance issues reached such a crisis point that it could have plunged itself into bankruptcy. The very future of amateur boxing in England was beginning to look distinctly uncertain.

And AIBA hadn't forgotten the slight the ABA's Board had directed at its favoured World Series boxers. For breaching its rules, AIBA suspended the English federation temporarily. While that suspension was in place, English boxers couldn't even compete internationally. A year on from the Olympics, with participation and positivity about the sport generally on the rise, instead of a legacy being built, chaos reigned. It was not a state of affairs designed to appeal to a thoughtful man like Anthony Joshua.

There are many things to like about amateur boxing and without doubt one of its most appealing qualities is its clear competition structure. At the Worlds in October 2013, the best amateurs would gather in Almaty, Kazakhstan. They'd fight through to the end and the last man standing would be the champion. Simple. It made sense. There would be some innovations, too, with computer scoring axed, the headguards were off, and in came a professional-style, 10–9, 10–8 system for scoring the rounds. This was to pave the way for AIBA's own version of pro boxing, the APB, that they would launch in 2014. The game had changed. Joshua, Campbell and the rest made up the last generation of true amateur boxers. Now the others had left that world behind, Joshua had to consider whether he should follow them.

The standard boxing equation read that Joshua was currently at the top in the amateur world. A loss could damage his earning potential and so it was too great a risk not to turn pro. It wasn't a calculation I'd necessarily make. For a start Joshua was good enough to win the Worlds, even out in Kazakhstan, in emphatic style. The Commonwealth Games in the UK in 2014 would be a huge event and were he to stay on all the way to the next Olympics he would only be twenty-six after his second Games: young, especially for a heavyweight. His skills would have vastly improved by then. Professional boxing is no light undertaking. No one really trusts promoters. Fighters might lose their winnings or scramble their brains, yet promoters manage to emerge unscathed, physically of course, financially more often than not.

If he was going to venture into professional boxing, he'd have to be on his guard, in the ring, but even more so in the world outside the ropes. Joshua summed it up: 'Boxing's full of desperate people, I think. But that's the same with anything. I've got some good people that I know help me with my boxing at the minute and they're the people that I take advice from and we communicate. I don't really need advice from a stranger. I've got the people I trust in place.'

Joshua had eight different contracts before him. He was dealing the cards that would dictate his new life. All the major players in the sport had made their offers. The options were there. He had to ask himself what he wanted. Who did he want to be?

The state of play within the professional sport was murkier than even the amateurs. Pro boxing had an entirely different structure. For a start there were the four respected 'world' titles and no official way to get to them. The claims of rival champions were set against each other, although they were all too rarely actually forced to fight each other. Everything was disputed. Increasingly it was the champions who made the titles. How respected the boxer was, how accepted he was, invested kudos in the belt he wore. For all the unfettered capitalism that drives the prizefighting business, there remained this egalitarian streak. Winning the belief of the fans would make a champion. Yes, Joshua had won the Olympics. But he wanted to be the heavyweight champion of the world. He would turn over.

'While I was making my decisions WSB was thriving, the Lionhearts were doing so well. It was like, "Wow, I could be part of this." And then recently WSB have pulled out. It's just APB and APB, it's not solid, it's not solid just yet. It's a trial and error period. You know what, I thought to myself this professional game is the way forward for me as this APB is, like, a halfway step to becoming professional. So I'd rather do it the full way and become number one as a professional fighter.'

Joshua ruled out the contracts that would have kept him amateur and on Rob McCracken's GB team. 'Obviously, Rob, he wanted me to stay as an amateur and I think a lot of the coaches did there. The advice was where I could get in the next four years and where I could be after that.

'But I was adamant. I knew what I wanted to do. That's what I like about GB. They're always on the other end of the phone for me. So I can call them any time, even though I've turned pro and they wanted me to stay amateur. If I said I'm in a bit of trouble, I need some advice on this situation, they'll be more than willing to pick up the phone to me. That's how I left it with them. And I let them all know about my decision, about

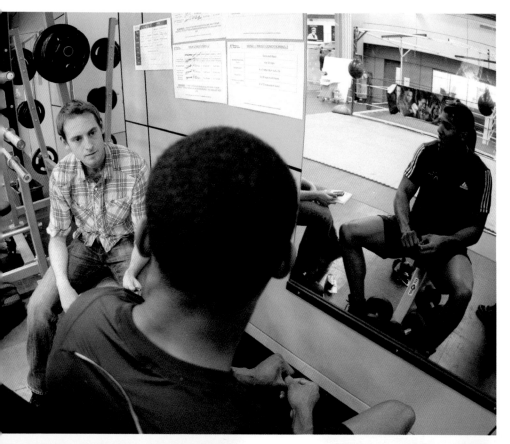

Top: At the GB Boxing gym in the English Institute of Sport in Sheffield the author in conversation with Joshua, as he prepares for the 2011 World Championships.

Bottom left: Dominic Winrow congratulates Anthony Joshua as he becomes the ABA senior champion for the first time.

Bottom right: After suffering a defeat at the European Championships, Joshua clips his head into a harness and exercises his neck with heavy weights.

Top: Focused on his opponent, Anthony Joshua steps into the ring at York Hall, Bethnal Green as he enters the final of the 2010 ABA national championships.

Left: At the Heydar Aliyev Stadium, Baku Anthony Joshua celebrates his breakthrough, reaching the final of the 2011 World Championships.

Top: Joshua poses with the first GB boxers to qualify for the 2012 Olympic Games, including Luke Campbell (right) and Thomas Stalker (second from right).

Middle: Joshua deposits Chinese Olympic silver medallist Zhang Zhilei on the deck.

Bottom: Joshua connects with his jab as he edges out slick Cuban Erislandy Savón in his first contest at London 2012.

Top: After a tense wait, the decision in the super-heavyweight final at London 2012 goes to Anthony Joshua.

Bottom: At a deafeningly loud ExCeL Arena Joshua claims Olympic gold.

Top: Joshua and fellow gold medallist Nicola Adams parade in an open-top bus through the heart of London.

Bottom: Outside Buckingham Palace Joshua presents his MBE.

Top: Anthony Joshua joins forces with promoter Eddie Hearn for his professional career.

Bottom left: In Joshua's pro debut Emanuele Leo feels the weight of a right cross.

Bottom right: Joshua hones his technique on the pads with trainer Tony Sims.

Top: On his way to winning the British heavyweight title Joshua sends Dillian Whyte flying.

Bottom left: Joshua lands a pinpoint right to stun IBF champion Charles Martin.

Bottom right: Ticker tape rains down on Joshua and his team at the O2 Arena.

Top left: Joshua grinds down stubborn American challenger Dominic Breazeale in his first world title defence.

Top right: The IBF champion fells Eric Molina and stands over his victim.

Bottom: Joshua listens to his crowd at the Manchester Arena as former world champion Wladimir Klitschko calls him out.

not coming back to camp. Before I left, the last week, I let them know. I think that was the best thing to do. Deep down I think they know it was a big decision. But I think they just know the professional game is very tough.'

Promoters are hugely significant in a fighter's career. They stage the events, putting together the shows that prospects will appear on. They deal with the most crucial component of a young fighter's career: which television company will broadcast those bills. Eddie Hearn had taken the reins at Matchroom Sport, his father, Barry's company which was quickly expanding to become the largest promotional house in the UK at the time. He enjoyed an exclusive contract with television juggernaut Sky Sports. Frank Warren, the other major promoter in Britain, had founded a specialist boxing TV channel of his own, BoxNation.

Promoters tend to choose the opponents to carefully build up their prized prospects, with the help of their matchmaker. They make those deals as they look to boost their man's reputation and support base while guiding him along the path, ideally to rich titles, as well as taking a view on how far and how quickly to push their fighters. A good promoter can be the architect of a successful fighter's career.

Typically they feed journeymen to a prospect for their first ten or so pro fights, before gradually finding more testing opposition and steering that prospect on to the next level. A promoter's business model optimally prompts them to look for the least risky (and therefore a less exciting) contest but for the most reward.

Equally, some of the most spectacularly acrimonious fallouts in boxing have been between fighter and promoter.

That the boxer gets the money he deserves matters. After all, he's the one who's doing the fighting. The promoter will ultimately need to bring in the big fights. A boxer does not want to be locked into a deal with someone who he fears is making the wrong decisions or failing to deliver.

A hot prospect will be offered a signing-on fee and paid a purse for each prizefight. How many fights a year he'll have, how many rounds each of those will be scheduled for, how many years the arrangement will last, are all different elements of the deal. A boxer will ideally have his own manager to represent his interests and a trainer to help him plot out his career. They'll take a percentage of what the promoter pays the boxer.

A boxing impresario ought to get his fighter on to good bills, in front of lively ticket-buying crowds, broadcast on a well-viewed television channel, boxing against opponents of different styles, from whom he can learn something and still look good against.

Anthony Joshua, a super-heavyweight gold medallist at a highly successful Olympic Games in his home city, was a tremendous prospect and could expect offers worth hundreds of thousands of pounds. He had a lot to gain. But that meant that if he took the wrong option there was a lot to lose.

He had met with Eddie Hearn's Matchroom first, the promoter who had already taken a fair few of Anthony's team-mates on to his books. The Watford man had a whole world to explore and Matchroom's wasn't the biggest offer that had been made to him.

Hearn struck him as laid-back. The promoter wasn't overly keen, didn't phone Joshua all the time. But he was confident. 'I want you to be comfortable signing with me' was Hearn's approach. He believed Matchroom would be right for Joshua, even as he went out to look at his other options. 'We're comfortable with that,' said Hearn. 'See what's out there for you and I'm sure you'll come back to us.'

Joshua did the rounds. 'I went round and did my homework,' he remembered. He could have followed GB's Anthony Ogogo to the USA and sought an American promoter. Heavyweight boxing was booming in Germany. The Klitschko brothers, Wladimir and Vitali, who between them held every shard of the world crown, packed out football stadia every time they laced on a pair of gloves. 'Boxing's a small circle so when you speak to one promoter, someone sees you. I think more promoters started bringing their offers forward. Major players did make their offers. Matchroom's finances were good, really good. There are some rich guys in America, who don't know much about boxing, just want to be involved in your career and throw big heaps of money at you. When you break it down over a long period of time, it doesn't add up. Their American contracts are five years, six years, and stuff. It's a long time to tie yourself in. So it didn't add up for me. The numbers were great. If I signed today and I was just in it for the money, I would probably be in America and not making my debut for another two years because they'd still be waiting for TV deals.

'America? I'm English. I don't really have no business out there. The contract wasn't what I was interested in. Europe? Once again, I'm English so I want to be here. And then Matchroom Sport have got the boxing sewn up right now. I narrowed it down. I met Eddie first and I met Eddie last. So I did a big circle.'

He came back to Matchroom. Hearn was getting his fighters out regularly. He had an exclusive deal with Sky. While the broadcaster was by no means the only show in town, they had one of the slickest operations and a long and impressive history with boxing. They would love Joshua on board. A few days before the first anniversary of the Olympic Opening Ceremony Joshua sat before his last contract. His pen scratched along the paper. 'Simple,' he said. 'All the thinking had been done. So it's just crack on. Get the ball rolling.

'No emotion, no nothing.'

This was another choice. Like when he started in the sport, when he chose to live the life he needed, when he chose to take up his levels of performance. Once again he chose a new life. He had to prepare his body, his abilities and his skill to take him where he wanted to be.

His first fight was sealed for 5 October 2013 at the London 02, a show effectively in honour of Joshua, one he decided to dub 'carpe diem', Latin for 'seize the day'. 'This is set up. As soon as I signed we've got a date and we've got about three more dates lined up and that's what I needed, to be active as well as paid,' he said.

'Short-term is this year. Let's get this year out of the way. Let's get a few wins wrapped up. Let's get used to no headguard, no vest. Let's get used to some real, hardcore boxing fans. Then next year I'll set a new goal, it'll be 2014. Get this year out the way, injury-free, focused, dedicated, a new level of fitness, and then I'll be ready for 2014. I know my long-term goal but I'm going to focus on the short term at the minute. Because I've got a long way to go.'

'My goals,' he added. 'We all know what the long term is. That goes without saying.'

He was now Britain's great heavyweight hope. His predecessors, Audley Harrison and Lennox Lewis, cast their long shadows over him. Would Joshua be the next heavily hyped big man to turn out a bust? Or could he make good on the raw potential he undoubtedly possessed? If, from scratch, he could win the Olympics in four years' time, how far might he progress in professional boxing in a commensurate time?

The buzz in the press was palpable, even if it was a tentative, very British strain of optimism. There had been disappointments in the recent past. But Joshua might just be the man to deliver the biggest prize of all.

'People are positive but I've got to prove it now. You know what I mean. That's the next stage. It's got to be positive all the way through. I've just got to keep on winning. I feel sharp. I'm learning a lot. So get the first one out the way. You're going to feel nerves and so on and so forth. Keep my head down, embrace the crowd and just box on my own ability,' he said.

'I tried on some ten-ounce gloves,' he continued, adding, maybe with enthusiasm, maybe with a degree of trepidation, 'you could break down a brick wall with those.'

Joshua wasn't likely to learn much from the soft touches he'd be fed in the early stage of his career. Nor are sports fans known for their patience. How long they'd tolerate Joshua bowling over journeymen, paying his dues to get to a significant fight, remained to be seen. But that was the standard professional apprenticeship all the great champions had undergone. In a sport where you're not allowed to lose, that is the structure you get saddled with. Even then the path to a world title does not run smoothly, even if in the modern age any one weight division does have about four of them. You don't *have* to fight for the British belt. Amir Khan didn't feel the need and he became a world champion a couple of times over. For Lennox Lewis it was a key fight in his development. It's up to your promoter to move you, to judge how to match you, how to step you up, to cultivate your world ranking with the different sanctioning bodies. If the boxer is in a good position, popular enough to make a major fight worthwhile, then the promoter has to choose which title to go for, work out how to prevent his man from being dodged or find him a champ he can beat. It ain't tennis.

'I think Lennox was the best British fighter we've had,' Joshua said. 'I want to try and be named as one of the best British fighters as well. And with that obviously putting my name alongside Lennox says world champion. That's what I mean. World championship belts are one thing. But I'm interested in becoming the best fighter. I could chill out, not train, dream of becoming a word champion and just go in and fight. I know I need to focus on my training, improving, getting fitter, getting all the wins. All the championship belts, they just fall into place. As long as I'm getting the hard work done here, that all falls into place. I can't be dreaming about it and not working for it. So my main thing is becoming a great fighter. Then I think everything's going to fall into place. So that's it. Just keep on training hard.'

Joshua had to be aware, whether he liked it or not, that he was now more than just an athlete. He no longer had the security of the GB programme; he was out in the unforgiving world of the pros, with many an eye turning on him and seeing someone who could be a source of a great deal of money. Fevered paranoia often felt like a reasonable state of mind in which to approach this new sport. He was out there and, if he was going to succeed, he would have to look after himself.

'I really wanted to emulate the Olympic system and take it to the professional ranks. You've seen me fight, you know I've been in some tough fights. I just need to be sure as a professional, over twelve rounds, if it does get tough, I'm going to be a hundred per cent ready. So that's what took time. I feel I'm ready to take that leap.

'I've got to make sure training's ticked, living correct's ticked, winning's ticked, and all of those great, great things, of becoming an icon, becoming a legend, becoming a brand, they come secondary. My main focus is becoming the best athlete I can be.'

It was a step into the unknown. Nothing was guaranteed. He had the ability but it couldn't assure him success, let alone happiness. But he'd carved out this chance for himself. Now it was indeed a case of 'carpe diem'.

All of us, sooner or later, grow up. We don't all sign off our youth with the stroke of a pen. But whether we grasp it fully or not, at some point we walk out into a world where there's no authority out there to guide you. No one has a better idea which way to go than you yourself. All of a sudden you're a man and the path is yours.

The stakes may have been high, the dramas impressive, the perils great, but Joshua still faced the same task that confronts us all. To find your way out there, you ask yourself, 'Who am I?' and then try to come up with an answer you can live with. His real task wasn't to hold himself out there, up above, and persuade the world that he was not a reincarnation of Audley Harrison. Nor was it to make them believe he could be the next Lennox Lewis. He had to try to be Anthony Joshua. Whoever that might turn out to be.

'I'm the next Anthony Joshua. I'm just me,' he smiled. 'Can I live?

'Can I live? I just like to fight. I'm not trying to be . . . I'm not trying to be like anybody else. Those guys are inspirational. I look up to them. But it's my time. It's my era now. It's a different time. A different era, with different fighters, different people. So just let me live. Let me be me.

'That's all I can say on that, really.'

The Evolution of a Champion

Anthony Joshua strode from the ring, back through the stands at the O2 Arena in Greenwich. Trailing after him were his corner team, a group of friends and a troop of journalists. In the crowds on either side he recognised faces, from home, from Sheffield. He reached out a glove to bump a fist or just nodded with a broad smile. The procession moved with him as he made his way to the quiet corridor backstage at the O2. He had completed his first professional fight. It had taken him two minutes and forty-seven seconds.

Joshua had wanted to do something different with that first prizefight. His opponent, Emanuele Leo, hadn't fought any recognisable names. But shipped over from Italy, Leo did bring a precious document, an 8–0 unbeaten record. He wasn't quite the usual journeyman, the type of boxer charged with giving a prospect more of a workout than a fight.

Joshua was jittery in the ring under the lights at the O2. There's no doubt there were nerves there.

His cousin Ben, who'd taken him to the Finchley boxing club all those years ago, was making his debut on the same bill.

'Do I need to bring my wraps along with me?' Anthony had anxiously asked him beforehand, wondering about the bandages his cornerman would wrap round his fists and wrists to secure them beneath his gloves. Joshua even put his shorts on back to front by mistake before making his entrance. Fortunately that went unnoticed.

'It's like you're going into battle,' Joshua said later. 'This is the pros now. You've got to step it up a level. I can't live off what I'd done.'

In action Anthony rushed his work, his jab reached for the Italian's body, not quite measuring the distance. What if he wandered on to a right? Would this golden opportunity disappear from his grasp? This was heavyweight boxing, a large opponent heaving his weight behind a punch was dangerous for anyone, even an Olympic champ. But Joshua's long right touched Leo. With a backhand uppercut he stood the Italian up. He hammered that right down the middle. Leo, reeling, reached for the safety of a clinch. Joshua's attack was hectic but he was still too strong for Leo. He landed a stiff one-two. The Italian couldn't turn him away. Joshua slugged him with a big right. Leo sank, and a final right to the jaw put him away. He may have been out of the ring for over a year but Joshua fought on instinct. 'I can't remember . . . I just hit him, it's natural,' he said. 'You need to tuck up, counter, don't just go for it. Because that's how easy it is to lose and I don't want to lose.'

He had time now to digest where he was. 'I want to make something out of it,' he declared. 'I want respect, I want to compete with the guys that can box, that are there to win as well.

'I just want respect out of boxing.'

Big Olympic gold medallists have failed to convince before. A pro needs to look dangerous, to bring people along with him. Anthony Joshua did just that when he stamped his authority on his second fight when he met Paul Butlin in Sheffield. The Rutlander was a more typical journeyman; he lost more than he won but knew his way around a boxing ring. Butlin typically could handle himself. But Joshua targeted his chin with supreme force. His left hook snaked round Butlin's guard, rocking his defence apart. At once Joshua's right slammed full into his head. The straight cross hammered him down into the canvas, opening up a severe cut over his left eye. Butlin staggered up, the referee cruelly letting him continue. Joshua harried him to the ropes, looking for a cold finish. A hook visibly hurt Butlin's body. He listed to the side, wincing through the sheet of blood. His arms dropped, leaving him open. This time the referee spared him from the finishing blow.

The gentlemanly world of international amateur boxing was behind Joshua. This was a blood sport and its fans liked what they saw.

'Regardless of whether or not I'm the main attraction, in my mind I've still got to feel like I'm the main man. I've got to put on a performance. I've got a point to prove and I think that's how every fighter feels, from a junior to a senior,' Anthony said. 'A fight's still a fight, whether you're on the undercard or the main attraction. In the fighter's heart it's all or nothing.'

He returned to London, to York Hall in Bethnal Green, the small, much-loved boxing venue where he had won his first senior amateur title. This time around, in November 2013, he had a prime slot on Sky Sports, on a bill featuring one of their

Prizefighter tournaments, a three-round elimination competition for pros. It was a heavyweight version of that competition, and this particular edition of the tournament proved a draining, dispiriting spectacle, even to watch. The *Prizefighter* contained ageing pugs, out-of-shape journeymen who battled it out for the cash payout. The shell of James Toney, a once great middleweight, was among them. He had no business being there. The competition was ultimately won by Michael Sprott, a former European champion who would lose inside a round to Joshua in Liverpool little over a year later. The fate of Toney, labouring, washed up far from his American homeland, losing a three-round semi-final in the East End of London, was a cautionary tale. You can reach the summits of this sport, but if you have an appetite for self-destruction, boxing will just as readily spit you all the way back to the bottom.

York Hall was rich in symbolism. Standing with the broadcast team was Larry Holmes, one of history's great heavyweights even if he would always be in the shadow of his predecessor, and eventual victim, Muhammad Ali.

Sitting ringside, too, was Michael Watson. Injured terribly when he fought Chris Eubank in 1991, it was a miracle the Londoner survived. He fought his way out of a coma, partially paralysed. There was an immense dignity about him. In his person you could see the shades of this endeavour, the dark dangers that lurked within boxing and the character of the men who faced them.

Not that Joshua could spare much thought for the symbolic figures around him. To fight he had to blot out the hall outside the ring. He did that effectively enough, barrelling into Hrvoje Kisicek. The Croat import regrouped, rushed him, jabbing the body, pressing in close to escape the discomforts of being stuck at long range. Joshua knocked him away with a left hook. Early, still in the first round, Kisicek's work became ragged, his balance off. Joshua towered over him. He teed off with hooks to the body and head. Kisicek's attack in response was feeble. This was a mismatch.

Kisicek landed an ineffectual left. It bounced off Joshua and he fired a cross right back at the Croat. His left hit, the right hand came over again and the following left was unnecessary. Kisicek went down. He made it upright still, only for Joshua to lay into him. He pummelled the Croat into the ropes, so intent on ending it that he shrugged the referee off his shoulder as he tried to break them up. Joshua kept on, drilling his prey into strands – a finisher's mindset – before eventually the referee interceded.

Joshua then had the surreal experience of stepping down from the ring into a debrief with Larry Holmes. 'Do not rush. Do not run before you can walk' were the great man's words of advice.

The fast clip of Joshua's early career took a pause when he picked up a hand injury but in February 2014 he could begin a nationwide tour. The first stop was the Motorpoint Arena in Cardiff. He was given a local man, Dorian Darch, as an opponent. With a 7–2 winning record, Darch would be sure to come at him, lobbing punches.

Darch had a go, even slugged a decent right across. The Welshman, however, squinted beneath the weight of Joshua's right hand. Boxers rarely show pain but Darch had to screw up his face as he bustled forward; you could tell he was hurt. Joshua caught him momentarily on the ropes and flung down punches with both hands, trapping him there. Darch escaped with a left hook, squirming out of trouble.

Up off his stool first for the second round, Joshua found his rhythm. The punches began to flow. He slotted them round Darch's outstretched arms. They hit the mark and pounded the last vestiges of resistance out of the Welshman. A final left hook and his legs shuddered beneath him, wobbling him away. The fight was over.

Joshua, surprisingly, was frustrated with himself. 'It's hard to find your rhythm in the first four minutes of a fight,' he sighed, with a kind of Luke Campbell-like perfectionism. 'I didn't get to build into what I had planned. But it's onwards and upwards.

'I'm going to go around now, go to different places, see different things and experience different atmospheres.

'My story will unfold in time.'

A month later, with Cardiff behind him, Joshua was in Glasgow inside a modern exhibition centre on the banks of the River Clyde, a 10,000-seat venue dressed for a world title fight. Joshua was the supporting act to local hero Ricky Burns and he played his part. A countering left hook sent his opponent, Hector Avila, rolling along the canvas, unable to answer the referee's count of ten. But what had mattered was the way the crowd received Joshua. He was a long way from London. The 10,000 Scots may have been there for Burns, their champion, but they streamed out of the bars and into their seats in the hall to see the big man arrive. A great roar filled the arena, an extraordinary sight as Joshua marched to the ring with a tartan strip on his shorts and the Proclaimers' '500 Miles' booming over the sound system. 'It was close to the Olympic final you know,' Joshua grinned, referring to the fervent atmosphere.

His reputation, and his popularity, was growing fast. In May 2014 he got a glimpse of what was possible. Carl Froch's rematch with George Groves, fuelled by the mutual antipathy, filled Wembley Stadium with 80,000 baying fans. It was a vast undertaking and Joshua took a slot on the undercard. It was still daylight when he fought and the stands weren't yet full. But with that number of people in such a large stadium, even with the roof open, their cheers, even mere chatter, rumbled round the arena, creating a rolling wall of sound.

'I tried keeping my head on my shoulders. It is different. It is real different. That's the first time I boxed outside, even as an amateur, in my career,' he said. 'There are a lot of mental skills you need to prepare for as well.'

Joshua stepped to the scratch opposite a fighter he happened to know well. Matt Legg was not a distinguished boxer. He'd won more than he'd lost but had the dubious distinction of being the man who lost to the terribly faded James Toney at York Hall the previous year. Legg had started out training with Ricky English, Joshua's first ever coach, and the man from Watford had in fact followed his stop-start career. 'I've got a lot of respect for him as a man, as an opponent, too,' the Olympian said.

Beforehand a bemused Legg had smiled, 'Who'd have thought we'd fight each other at Wembley Stadium?'

Joshua had, of course, far outstripped him. He was developing, improving. 'My hunger and my determination got me through a lot of my career. I'm at a stage now where I want to start applying head movement and slipping punches, coming back,' he said. 'I feel confident defending shots now. Sometimes you box a bit out of range because the game is to hit and not get hit. Sometimes that makes me tend to box well out of range and try and fall in to hit my opponent. But I feel a bit more comfortable in range, in distance. Defending, then boom, boom. That's mentally where I'm at now. I just need to try to transfer that into the ring.'

Legg rushed across the ring to greet Joshua with an attack. He even tagged him with a left hook. The punch disrupted Joshua for a split second but he soon set about his cruel work. He shot a right-hand uppercut directly through Legg's guard. It crumpled him to the canvas, knocked out in less than half a round.

Only then could Joshua direct his attention to the distant crowd arranged across the vast stadium around him. This was a place he could get used to. He'd have to accept the burden of that pressure, to be the future champion everyone wanted him to be. 'Now I don't need to shut down. I just need to enjoy it. Walk with my shoulders back. Look at all this great support British boxing has got,' he said.

Joshua was now ready to step up beyond the journeyman opponents. A couple of veterans were handed to him in Liverpool and Manchester. He manhandled them. Next up, back at the Echo Arena in Liverpool, was Matt Skelton. The grizzled 'Bedford Bear' was getting on, forty-seven years old, a mauling veteran who was still violent enough to rough up, perhaps even beat lesser calibre prospects. The thinking was that he had the wiles to get inside and mess Joshua around, at least for a short time. Skelton had the knack of clinging to a boxer's chest, leaning on him, clubbing him down, tiring him out.

Joshua had no truck with such methods. He met him on the inside and slung him out. Skelton just couldn't deal with his strength. Joshua broke him down. His backhand hooked in, the uppercut struck again. A right hit home and Skelton fell. He struggled up to meet Joshua, who leapt on him, his left hook cracking across. He swiped his right to the body and Skelton slid down the ropes, his eye already swollen closed. The referee stepped in to end it.

'What you're seeing is the evolution of the next heavyweight champion of the world,' beamed promoter Eddie Hearn.

It is standard practice for promoters to make bold claims about their fighters. But with Joshua his words had a ring of truth about them. He was only seven fights into his professional career, but he had won every one inside the distance, clearing them all out within a mere eleven rounds in total. When the Hearns looked at him, you sensed they saw a hundred million pound payout down the line, if the plan came to fruition. At least Anthony, the man throwing and fielding the punches, ought to make some money out of it, too.

The Englishman did, however, receive an endorsement of much greater weight. He'd been emailing the heavyweight champion of the world. Wladimir Klitschko, whom he considered 'the ultimate professional', invited him over to spar.

Klitschko, the holder of the WBO, WBA and IBF titles, three of the four major world championships, was preparing for a stern challenge against Bulgaria's Kubrat Pulev. He based his training camp in a picturesque hunting lodge in Stanglwirt in the Austrian Tyrol. He pared down his work. A six foot seven inch behemoth, he no longer put in miles running but instead swam for his cardiovascular training and sparred round after round for conditioning and to maintain his mastery of the technical fundamentals of the sport. Klitschko tended to bring rising prospects in for sparring. He could take a good look at them, see their weaknesses and, in case they did fight in future, use the sparring to let them know who was the boss between the ropes. But the deal went two ways. In return Joshua would get twenty rounds of precious sparring with the champ.

'The main thing I look for when I'm training is peace. I know we talk about the fame and finance and stuff, but you've got to keep that gladiator spirit. You're in the mountains, you're zoned out and the only thing you can think of is boxing . . . I went out there on my own, handled business. I had to push myself after training, do my own thing. It was great.

'The way he's got his camp set up – it's just very particular to becoming a champ and staying there. It's very basic. But very effective.'

That was Klitschko's own style. He'd stripped his art down to basics. Jab, jab, jab again, bring in the heavy cross or a crisp uppercut, the footwork essential, judging distance with that jab. Thinking clearly, thinking calmly. 'He lives a simple life and trains hard. He's not trying to go around like he's the best heavyweight in the world. He proves that to himself. He's not trying to flash his money. He knows what he's got, he knows who he is,' the Briton said.

Joshua impressed the champ during that training camp. Klitschko recalled: 'Definitely you could feel his athleticism. So he's very athletic and I think we were pretty competitive in the sparring, both. We respect each other but both competitive.

'There was dominance from each of us. It's not like I was

more dominant than him or he was more dominant than I. It was pretty equal.'

Joshua's own confidence was flourishing. In September 2014 he boxed at the Manchester Arena against Konstantin Airich, a stolid Hamburg-based Kazakh. Up in the ring, under the lights, Anthony was relaxed. He let his fists fly fast. His hands drifted low, a reminder of the old habits of his inexperienced past. Nevertheless, that recklessness had an air of cavalier spirit about it. He all but laughed off the odd glancing blow the Kazakh swung through. Smiling, he toyed with the dumpy Airich, keeping his prey on the end of his long jab. The bout went into the third round, the longest Joshua had been extended as a pro, though on this occasion it seemed due more to a whim than the particular efforts of his opponent.

'Training's gruesome. Fighting should be the easy part. Fighting should be the enjoyable part,' he said afterwards. 'These guys aren't in my league. I'm just having fun with it, trying to get the rounds.'

Almost too relaxed, he shrugged himself awake, and let the heavy shots go. That right cross of his seared through Airich's guard. Joshua repeated the shot to stagger the Kazakh towards the ropes. Airich couldn't keep him off. Joshua beat him down to one knee, and finishing the assault he swiped a final, vicious uppercut at the crouching figure. Airich could have sought the solace of the canvas. Instead he tottered up. Regretting the decision immediately, he jerked his body back. Joshua moved then with ominous speed. His right cannoned into Airich. Joshua turned his body counter-clockwise, to charge up his left, unleashed it, and, twisting his weight behind the punch, launched it fully into Airich's face. That was enough to stop the fight.

'Since the age of eighteen I've worked hard. I haven't changed overnight. I've always gone in to win, even when I was less experienced as an amateur. I always had that desire to get in and hurt them, outmuscle them,' Anthony said. 'These guys are there to take what I've been working on for the last seven years. I won't let that happen.

'I'm not going to let these guys get in the way of my dream.'

It's a cruel game, the hurt business. But Joshua had torn through his early tests. A year on from his pro debut he could return to the O2 in Greenwich to headline a show staged in his honour. As an opponent, Denis Bakhtov was the next rung up the ladder from the likes of Konstantin Airich. In his forty-seven-fight career Bakhtov had lost only nine times. A sturdy operator, the Russian was more than a sacrifice being offered up to Joshua's burgeoning reputation. Bakhtov believed that against him Joshua would have to prove whether or not he could be a champion. On paper this was a real fight.

There may have been a world title eliminator on the bill but Joshua was, for the first time, the headline act. To confirm the occasion he was afforded all the ritualised trappings that go with a big fight. On the Monday before Saturday's fight night a boxing ring was set up on the floor of a shopping centre in Watford. A healthy crowd clustered round it to see the big man. You're doing well when folk turn out merely to watch you train, let alone fight. Joshua arrived with his retinue. He took a turn round the outside of the cordoned-off area, posing for pictures, bumping fists with children before he stopped to tape his hands.

He was now a public figure. He'd have to get used to a new level of scrutiny. 'I've done it for four years,' he shrugged, 'when no one cared, only guys like you who were really into boxing. No one really cared about what I was doing. All of a sudden people are judging me, saying they know my career better than I know it, when I was the one who had the vision in the first place. All of a sudden people know "AJ's" career or know me better than I know myself.

'So I just don't really take to all the hype because I'll never forget when no one cared about what I was doing. A small hall in Dagenham to this doesn't really mean much to me. Because it can all go like that.'

Inside the ring for the public workout he jumped rope, getting those feet up off the canvas, knees high. And the aficionados watched. Would those feet be fast enough to carry him where he needed to go? Trainer Tony Sims took him through his rounds on the pads. Joshua's right streaked into a mitt with a healthy crack. He stepped in close to work compact combinations. The sound of those repeated shots on the pads was percussive, like the drumbeat of his own applause. There are so many qualities a prospective champion needs to succeed. He must have an array of shots at his disposal, guile in action, ringcraft, as it's known. He needs to be able to defend himself under pressure, think clearly, have a solid chin – one that can withstand the weight of a heavyweight punch. And, above all, he requires the elements that make a crowd stand and cheer – the heart and stomach for a fight. We admire those qualities, not because we necessarily have them, but because we want to see people who can push themselves beyond their imposed limits. If only for twelve rounds, we want to see someone like that fighting for us. That's the thing about watching your champion win. If only for a moment you feel like a king, too.

* * *

Bakhtov scarcely made it out of the first round. A wrathful Joshua fell on him from the start. The taller man with longer reach, it would have favoured him to trade on those advantages. Instead he marched into the Russian's territory and met him on the inside. He broke him there and, like a military force turned into a rout, Bakhtov had no weapons to reply to him. Bleeding, shaken, the onslaught shocked him to such an extent that all he could do was fall back on his own resilience and hope that would be enough. He held himself in there for the first round. Even then his stance, rocking, looked ready to fold beneath him.

'He's dangerous, you know. I had him up against the ropes and I could feel that he was tucking up, even when he looked hurt, and he was trying to swing,' Anthony said. 'I could definitely feel that he was capable of trading on the inside.'

But Joshua came out for the second round just as hungrily. A huge right hurled the Russian back. Joshua doubled it, letting that punch burst against Bakhtov's defences. The referee pulled Joshua off him for a moment but, losing confidence in his own decision, waved him on again. A sharp left hook cracked open Bakhtov's guard and that cross stabbed down to finish it.

Once the roar of the crowd had melted away, down a deserted corridor off the main arena floor, in a quiet backroom, Joshua settled into a chair. It was late and this was his final duty of fight week, the last press conference. He had won an

'International' belt from the WBC. He laid the strap out on the desk in front of him. It was an ersatz title. It made him a champion of nothing in particular but, crucially, it did bolster his place in the heavyweight rankings. It was that first step on the road to the world title.

'I need to turn this into the real one,' he said.

* * *

I remember one of their old coaches, Paul, saying of the British team, 'You want them to win so much.' And you do. You want to see in them the things you want for yourself. Success. Happiness. They would suffer, though. That's what they'd chosen. That's boxing. Finding some contentment in life matters, but maybe none of them would be satisfied if they didn't try, didn't strive for that ultimate win.

Joshua had done something special as an amateur. It could all go off the rails in the pros. Cautionary tales were legion. But if he made the right choices it just might go spectacularly right. He'd put himself in that position. Now it was up to him to decide what to do with his chance.

I remembered Anthony looming over me at the press conference after he'd won his Olympic gold.

'I did that for you, John,' he said with mock seriousness.

My mind went blank. When you spend enough time watching people fight, too much time without seeing natural light, you begin to think the whole human drama laid out before you is being carried out for your benefit. Which is ridiculous. But I found myself blinking as big Anthony articulated what I secretly hoped. After spending two weeks confined inside the hangar-like ExCeL, subsisting mainly on pies from concessions within the arena, cabin fever had set in. I had lost some sense of perspective.

My brain eventually clicked into gear. Joshua had beaten Italy's super-heavyweight Cammarelle again and over the last couple of years I'd made clear my delight in seeing the Italian team suffer losses. Anthony was referring to my ongoing feud with a small, elderly Italian journalist that had stretched across continents and Olympic qualification tournaments. (He stole my seat in Azerbaijan – it's a long story.)

The ride following Joshua from his early amateur bouts in gritty venues in London to the Worlds in Baku and the great Olympic Games, to now enjoying a ringside seat for his progress through the professional ranks had been epic. It had been a lot of fun, too. Anthony had always been easy to get along with and always seemed to appreciate those who had been there from the beginning.

His future sparring partner Frazer Clarke remembered their first encounter. It was on a club show, years ago, one of the crucial victories that helped Joshua up the domestic rankings. 'I'd never heard of him, never seen him,' Frazer jovially recalled. 'I wasn't scheduled to box him. I was supposed to be boxing some other kid. My trainer said, "The lad's pulled out last minute. I've got some replacement from Finchley." I was thinking, whoever, I'm not bothered.'

His attitude changed somewhat at the weigh-in ahead of the contest. 'On the scales a big shadow came over behind me,' Frazer laughed. He turned round and saw Joshua for the first time. 'It looked like Zeus himself had been carved and he was standing there. I thought, "Oh God, I'm in for a bit of a tough night here."

'It's quite nice to look back on now. When people talk about him, I say, "I boxed him, you know."'

Then he added, 'I think he changed the way everyone went about their business in GB, seeing the way he trains and the way he ups his level. I think everyone upped their game a bit. When he went on to win the gold medal he changed the game. For me, he definitely gives you something to look up to. I've seen it first-hand.'

Joshua is in the inspiration business. These boxers created opportunities for themselves, and they took them. They started out with their hands, their bodies and their wits and they made themselves into what they wanted to be. In their lives, against the odds, they've already shown how to be successful. They didn't all become gold medallists. They won't all become champions. But they tried.

And if you can watch someone and start to believe in them, start to believe in what they can be, it's not such a great step to start believing in yourself and what you might do, one day.

The Modern Heavyweight

In professional boxing pain is constant. It is the currency boxers trade in. They dole it out, they accept it from opponents, from sparring partners, from themselves. They force themselves through that unrelenting training and it leaves them all, the good ones especially, hurting.

Joshua got a quick fight in before the end of 2014. He stopped by Liverpool once more, this time to hammer the luckless Michael Sprott inside a round. A likeable man from Reading, Sprott had once been the British champion. But that was ten years ago. His career had ticked on but his ambition had begun to trickle away. He started to lose, regularly. He became better known for being one of heavyweight champion Wladimir Klitschko's sparring partners. This sport is unforgiving and, as Sprott aged, the wars of his career caught up with him. His speed and his timing were deserting him. He couldn't punch the way he used to or stand up to the blows he once could. Joshua was too much for him. Their bout had been scheduled for ten rounds with three judges scoring. That was much too optimistic.

Sprott tried to chip away at him with jabs, prodding his left at Joshua's body, hooking in his lead. It didn't take Anthony long. He lined up a right cross. He noted at once that the hit, not even clean, forced Sprott to step back. Joshua saw his man hurt and pressed in. Cross after cross shot through, catching Sprott clearly. Joshua hit him into the ropes, let a combination fly, a flurry of hooks tattooing against Sprott's fleshy body. Joshua teed off with a few more savage shots to the head and Sprott was trapped in the rigging, getting hurt. These were thunderous punches bouncing off his temple. The referee had to end it. It only lasted eighty-six seconds.

Joshua's own words at the beginning of his professional career could serve as a caution for him. 'Sometimes you become a victim of your own power. When you're knocking everyone out, you believe you can do it to anyone,' he had said, thinking of David Price's downfall. 'When you get hit by a big shot it takes a lot out of you. Sometimes it doesn't hurt as much but your blood starts boiling and then you lose your composure, start getting frustrated. You're trying to hurt him. You want to get him out of there as well before he gets you out of there. He caught you with one of those shots; you think, potentially this guy could knock me out if I get caught by one of them again.'

The Sprott fight rounded off a busy year for Joshua, but when he took time to relax pain caught up with him. A persistent ache in his back disrupted him. For all that work, even if he made it look easy in the ring, Joshua was paying the price. 'I think as a heavyweight there's so much ground and pound. To be elite you put your body through so much that you have to adjust. When I watch fighting, I watch Sugar Ray Leonard, I watch Mayweather and all those guys. Remember they're like welterweights so a lot of my idols are a lot lighter than me, so when I'm trying to train like them it puts my body through twice as much pain. I've just got to try and alter what I'm watching and try to make it suit a heavyweight frame.'

Joshua was diagnosed with a stress fracture of the back, not a major injury but the kind that could have kept him out for half a year. 'You call it a stress fracture from overuse. It's just that I've been grafting since I started boxing, just non-stop graft. Then the back gave way and that was it,' he explained.

He couldn't fight, couldn't train as normal, but he did not become despondent. His sense of mission remained strong. He knew his purpose: to blast his way up the heavyweight rankings. Although he was sidelined, his mindset was in the right place. He just had to turn his attentions to his own body. There was work to be done. While he was powerful, even he had a physical weakness. It was something he'd endeavour to eliminate.

'Everything to do with recovery is about pain, is about core work, massaging, not a luxury massage, but very, very painful deep-tissue massages. Everything was based around sports anyway so even when I was doing recovery work I wasn't just lounging around waiting for it to get better. There's a lot of therapy you can do to improve yourself and then I learned a lot about my own condition, where I'm weak in the body,' he said. 'As a seventeen-stone heavyweight, I practise to generate power every day. Power is not something we're lacking so it's just conditioning certain areas.'

The reconstruction project began. 'Cut your legs off and your arms and what you've got left is your trunk, so I've strengthened up this area. Basic core and glutes, they support a lot of the back area, because we generate a lot of power through there, so I need to strengthen that area,' he said.

His training became increasingly high-tech. He found an altitude chamber to work in, Ultra G trousers (which mitigate gravity to take the weight off the legs), to run in, throwing in some ultrasound therapy, too. With a nod to old-school training, he smiled, 'Technology in the modern day is brilliant, so I might as well use it.'

He was travelling to different gyms to avail himself of different facilities for his strength and conditioning and his boxing. He'd taken on professional trainer Tony Sims, an experienced coach who worked with many of Matchroom's star fighters in a small, private gym in the Essex countryside. His strength coach was Jamie Reynolds, who took him through dynamic conditioning routines, far removed from the old-school training methods so typical in the sport. He used a nutritionist, Mark Ellison, who worked with GB Boxing as well as handling Manchester United and other high-profile clients. Joshua still sought out his one-time amateur rivals and now friends Joe Joyce and Frazer Clarke as sparring partners. Rob McCracken remained a trusted source of advice. Eddie Hearn, his promoter, was of course a constant. Anthony would bring in his own publicist, Andy Bell, to work in tandem with his promotional and management companies. A circle of close friends and family, among them David Ghansa and his cousin Ben Ileyemi, were part of his team for events. The enterprise was all driven by his sense of mission and singular focus. The training was key. Get the process right and the results would follow. Joshua broke it down stage by stage, session by session. He worked himself hard.

'There's times I felt close to death. Serious. My heart's too thick. I'm not even chatting shit. Sometimes my heart is too thick because I get pushed in the gym. It's all good. I've stopped feeling the pain. I don't go to the gym worrying about the pain but how I can get my training session right. If I get it right then it's a short session because there's nothing to correct. But if we keep on getting shit wrong, it's like, do it again, do it again, do it again, until it gets right. So I need to go into the gym with a mindset of how can I get today perfect.'

It was a case of perfecting his technique and keeping those big hits coming. Forced to stay out of the ring, during his absence he still studied how to knock a man out, how to enhance the brutal efficiency he brought to his job. It wasn't just power. 'Balance,' he said. 'Everything's balance. Not too much pressure over your front, not too much pressure on your back, get your feet in and when you're in range you jab, you follow up, bang, just let it go naturally. So just balance. As long as you've got the balance right you're always in a position to throw punches. So your opponent might not have his feet right and then all of a sudden he's swung a wild shot, spun off. We're ready: boom, boom, they don't see it coming. As long as you're balanced, you're always in a position to throw strong, heavy punches.'

For years now he had lived boxing. To become a natural fighter, or what looks like a natural, he had to practise his techniques over and over again so that they became instinctive. 'They've always been trying to teach me the basics and I've only started to understand now. It's taken a while and I'm slowly starting trying to perfect these things,' he said. Not that he'd been making major changes. 'Because everything's worked that we've been doing. It's not worth scrapping everything we've been doing. What I've changed is my attitude. Because I used to go into the boxing gym to get fit, hit the bag. When I'm going in there now, I'm already fit. It's about how I can be technically good, work on my defence, counter, inside, so it's all about my technique now, not fitness. My attitude's changed,' he reiterated.

I caught up with Anthony in Newcastle in early 2015. He'd been out of action for four months and was now testing the water again, far from London, all the way in the north of England, against a quiet American, Jason Gavern. Unexpectedly, the visitor oozed respect for Joshua. They weighed in on a raised platform in a side room at a Hilton hotel. Joshua is a big name, even in the north, and a crowd packed into the chamber to see him take to the stage. Gavern declined to engage in the usual pre-fight histrionics so familiar to the sport. 'The whole pantomime of boxing', as Anthony had noted with a shake of the head. Here in Newcastle they completed the obligatory head-to-head pose but Gavern indulged in none of the eyeballing, preening or general machismo that is customary in these situations. Just a journeyman, off his ranch in Florida, ready to test out how good a prospect Anthony Joshua really was.

'I take two things from it. I think that's just his character, so respect to him, and then the other is that he could come out trying to take my head off in the fight. You can't really think that he's going to come out and let me beat him up in the fight. Even if he is the nice guy,' Joshua smiled.

Gavern had recently lost to Deontay Wilder, the Alabama heavyweight who in his very next fight won the WBC world title. Against Wilder, Gavern had retired on his stool at the start of the fifth round. 'Styles make fights,' Joshua cautioned, an oft-repeated mantra but one which still rang true. Different fighters cope with one another in different ways; a different approach can yield different results. The Gavern fight would still be used to compare Joshua to Wilder, a reigning heavyweight titlist. There was undoubtedly ambition in Joshua. He did want a quick ending, even if his outlook was tempered by realism. 'Me and Deontay are two completely different animals. If I was to get him out in two, it doesn't mean I'm going to beat Deontay tomorrow. You know what I mean.

'If I could stop him, so be it. If not, there's nothing wrong with getting rounds under my belt,' he added, albeit with no great enthusiasm.

He continued with more fervour. 'These guys can be beaten but the only way he'll beat me is if I'm off my game and I fall into that trickery and I let him fool me. But I understand there's two sides of the coin and I understand that he could just come out swinging haymakers at me.'

I sat alongside him on the edge of the platform where they'd had the weigh-in. We faced outwards as we spoke. The stage had been cleared of the scales and the other fighters on the bill, but the room was still packed. A crowd waited a few yards ahead of us, on the other side of a short metal barrier that penned them back. Or was it fencing us in? The mass of expectant faces were all turned towards Joshua, hanging on his every answer. It unnerved me, making me hesitate as I asked my questions. But this, I supposed, must be Anthony's perspective, always with an audience, always observed. When you're big, everybody sees you.

He was taking it in his stride. 'I'm here to gain something from my fights,' he continued. 'I actually want to get some experience and build my way up and become a proper champion. Do you know what I mean?

'Gavern should be there to give me some rounds. He's wild, man. If he catches you at heavyweight, ten-ounce gloves, you never know,' Joshua mused. 'So I've just got make sure I'm on my A game. It's not about beating Gavern, it's how I look doing it. If I can look good, work on the inside, slip a few shots. It's about looking good doing it. I know a couple of enemies in the heavyweight division might be watching as well.'

For someone at such an early stage of his professional career it was strange to think that already he had enemies, those who were looking with envious eyes at the attention he was getting, the money he was starting to make, his exalted place as near enough the main attraction on the televised shows. Bigger fights were coming. 'It just needs, as they say, people who can hit back, people who are going to stay there, test my endurance, test my skills, test my will. First ten fighters, like every professional, is always like a building-up stage and now I've gone past that. I'm in my eleventh so we go to the next stage and then nothing crazy, no championships belts,' he said. 'It's a blessing.'

He was unhurried, strikingly so for a man who, in twenty-four hours, would go before the crowd at the Metro Radio Arena to box on national television. I'd be sleeping, praying or at least nervously pacing round a hotel room. He lingered, walking straight up to the line of onlookers, who you could tell were British sports fans. They'd formed an orderly queue and Joshua proceeded along the line, signing autographs, posing for selfies. It wasn't an obligation; there was no promoter or press agent lurking at his shoulder prompting him to do it. He chose to do it. This tour of Britain was a chance for him to make new fans, a fist bump here, a picture there, one smile and a handshake at a time. He was wise enough to know that giving them some of his time, even when he couldn't really afford it, would be appreciated.

The American's schemes would not derail Joshua's plan. Gavern didn't enter the ring the following day throwing bombs. Drafted in at little notice, he did have one tactic. He spoiled. Gavern kept clear of Joshua's jab at first. He tried to bound in with a left, then a right. But an easy left from Joshua looped round, caught him. He pushed him back with a straight right. He was picking Gavern off early in the first round and he ducked forward. He ducked under the shots to grab Joshua in a clinch.

Anthony tracked after him, unhurried, shaking out his arms to loosen up. He lashed in his cross, jolted Gavern with a double jab. It was clear Gavern couldn't stay on the outside, he couldn't stay on the end of those punches. He kept ducking in, clinging desperately close to Joshua, believing he was safer on the inside.

In the second round Joshua did not at first set a fast pace, cantering back as Gavern winged a right hook at his body. Anthony came in with a straight one-two angling down. He scooped up his left, hard, cuffing Gavern off his feet.

Joshua stayed on him, sensing the journeyman's trouble. He scraped across a wide left hook, triggered more rights and Gavern wilted beneath that pressure, falling down to the canvas a second time, cringing from further left hooks.

The American geed up the crowd, clambering slowly to his feet only to pump his fist in the air, a gesture of ill-considered defiance. Vicious hooks in close spun Gavern away as the bell rang to end the second round. Gavern simply whooped aloud as he marched back to his corner, his apparent enthusiasm masking his pain.

Soon enough, in the third round, Joshua clubbed him back into a corner, hitting in the right, then the left. The shots dropped Gavern yet again. The American's knees struck the deck and he simply clung on to Joshua's leg, for a moment like a supplicant begging for mercy. There was none, of course.

Only then did Gavern put his weight behind a wild haymaker. It sailed wide, falling short. Joshua licked his lips and cracked his prey with his left hook once again. Then he clipped him with that left to bomb in with a right, sending Gavern down a fourth time, a left swiping at him as he fell.

He didn't consider it a cheap shot, even if Gavern had been touching down. 'Even if I did, I must have grazed his head because I didn't feel I was pounding anyone's head, just a tussle,' Joshua shrugged.

Gavern lay flat on his back as the referee took up the count. At eight the American rolled over on to one knee, grabbing the ropes with his gloved hands. He couldn't, or (sensibly) wouldn't, haul himself off the canvas in time. He stayed with his back turned to the referee as the official stood over him to wave both arms in the air, signalling the contest, such as it was, was over.

'I'm just trying to build up momentum again against Jason Gavern. I knew he was going to be a tricky customer. It's hard to show everything in three rounds against someone who's kind of awkward,' a frustrated Joshua said afterwards. 'But as the rounds started going on, I started finding my rhythm and trying to get that left uppercut in and left hook to the head, and sooner or later started catching and I knew I was going to break him down.'

Sitting on a couch in a cramped changing room at the back of the Metro Arena, Anthony held court. It had not been a perfect performance, but it would do. 'I'm not going to beat myself up. Normally I do that, but, looking at it, I've done all right. I handled business. I got him out of there, I made light work of it, three rounds. I can put it behind me. I can't dwell on it. I would have loved to have gone out there and peppered him, left, right, centre, worked him on the inside, but he's an awkward customer. That's what these fighters are there to do, there to be awkward, and it's not just about beating them, it's more to me about how I beat them. So I look at it as, how can I improve? It gives me something to work on.'

He was not back to his best although he was loose. His back had not troubled him. And, after all, he had taken care of Gavern more quickly than Wilder had managed. 'He was in there with Deontay Wilder before he fought for the WBC belt. He retired on his stool, Jason Gavern retired on his stool in the fifth round,' Joshua reflected. 'To go in there and hit him with a few shots, not knock him out but chop him down and make him quit in the ring does speak volumes. That the power's there, the accuracy was coming. I think moving forward mainly my back was good. I made easy work of Jason Gavern and we can move on now.'

I trudged back to my hotel through the centre of Newcastle. It was late on a cold night but the streets were busy. A long, rowdy queue stretched out from Greggs the bakers. Despite the chill the men wore only T-shirts with no coats, the women even less. For two o'clock it's a loud, cheerful place. The roadshow would continue, the next stop, in four weeks, would be Birmingham in the Midlands. As I threaded my way along the pavement, I mulled over Joshua's parting words. 'How good would it be for you guys if I was heavyweight champion of the world? We'd really have something to talk about then.'

Through the Gate

Kevin Johnson is a strange man. Nicknamed 'the Kingpin', bedecked with gold chains, wearing sunglasses both indoors and out, Johnson looked more like a music mogul or a promoter than a prizefighter himself. He was due to fight Joshua in January 2015, a fight which was postponed due to the latter's back injury. At a press conference before the cancellation the fast-talking American had for some reason picked up a child. It was unclear who the child actually belonged to (the kid wasn't Johnson's) and for some reason sat him on his knee while everyone tried to carry on with the press conference as normal.

'I'm telling you, I'm going to get you,' Johnson hollered with increasing fervour.

He had challenged for a world title in the past, he'd gone the distance with Vitali Klitschko some years back and proved his toughness. More recently he'd gone the full twelve rounds with both Dereck Chisora and Tyson Fury. But he gave the appearance of purpose when his date with Joshua had to be rescheduled. He refused to take the fight earlier in the year, so that he could have the full time to prepare, promising darkly that the world would see something from Kevin Johnson that it had never seen before.

He did, however, stop by Birmingham's Barclaycard Arena to confront Joshua after his final tune-up bout. Anthony picked up the twelfth inside-the-distance victory of his professional career to find Johnson, adorned with a baseball cap and flashes of jewellery, ushered into the ring to face him. Johnson was short, squat but broad around the chest, his arms thick. He had been training.

'I got the antidote,' the American barked as the Birmingham crowd jeered him.

'Who are ya? Who are ya?' the British fans chanted over and over.

'What I got is what I got and I know exactly what I need to do to stop this guy,' Johnson would drawl. 'It's easy, it's going to be very easy because of one thing I never had to do it. I've got it now.'

He declined to specify what that one thing was.

Joshua shifted a touch on his feet, still in his fight shorts, with his gloves laced over his fists. Unsmiling, he looked down at his next victim. Half graciously he announced to the crowd, 'May the best man win. But I'm sure everyone in here knows who the best man is out of me and him.'

Whether it hurt Johnson's pride was unclear, but earlier in the evening Joshua had subjected Raphael Zumbano Love to a more literal put-down. The Brazilian looked a big man. He had managed to last into the tenth round with highly rated contender Charles Martin three months before. But that was about his only eye-catching credential. He was not equipped to challenge Anthony Joshua. Zumbano knelt to pray on the ring canvas before the first bell rang to get the fight underway.

His long hair bounced up and down as he steered clear of Joshua's jabs. He lobbed a tired jab back at him. Joshua tapped a left hook to the head. The same shot hit the body. Love shook his head.

'There were times I was hitting him and I turned my knuckles down, so I could really hurt him when I'm punching with the backhand-left-hook-backhand. I thought, you know what, I could step up and knock this guy out. I thought Zumbano's a tough character. He didn't show any chinks in his armour so I hit him. He laughed it off. I thought, "Okay, cool," ' Joshua said.

Only in the second round Zumbano stiffened beneath another left hook. The Brazilian tried another jab. It was too slow, a mere invitation to Joshua. Last time out in Newcastle Anthony's timing had been out, his aim a touch off. Not so here in Birmingham. He saw the opening again. His right cross bombed straight into Zumbano's jaw, an instinctive shot, arrow-straight. It sent him flying. Joshua pulled his right arm back along the line of the punch, a smooth, simple one-punch hit. Zumbano crashed back-first on to the canvas. He wasn't getting up from that. Joshua had his finishing arm held up, cocked, already a celebration.

'The good thing is it shows I've got the power, the accuracy, to knock guys out and it shows that hard work's paying off.'

This was the final major arena of Joshua's tour of the UK, before he returned to London where he would go straight into his next fight in just three weeks' time. In Birmingham the crowd could get close to him and he was popular here. He was mobbed once more on his way back to the changing room.

Once Kevin Johnson had been ushered away from him, Joshua was quite relaxed about facing off with his next opponent. 'I never give it in the first place but I'm used to people talking a lot of shit. That's boxing,' he shrugged. 'Bringing back boxing the way it should be, old-school boxing, music in between rounds, Kevin Johnson getting in the ring trash-talking. I felt good enough to let Kevin lace them up, I would have waited in the ring and I would have fought him there and then.'

'He's got a point to prove and I really enjoyed that because in only a couple of weeks we're going to be able to put his thoughts and expectations to rest,' he added. 'Tyson used to stand in the ring after a fight and he would be hyped up, talking about how he would decapitate opponents not superior to himself.'

Zumbano wasn't up to much; he was target practice. But it was good practice for Joshua. He wanted a tall body to hit, he got it. 'Just slowly becoming more of a rounded fighter, inside work, jabbing. The second thing is just that. It's not my fault but we've had a lot of short opponents and Zumbano was fairly tall so that gave me the opportunity to practise my balance and practise counters as well because I'm punching the same height rather than punching down. Where normally fighters are trying to counter me, I put myself in a position to counter Zumbano,' he said, appraising his brief exertions of the evening. 'I would say it's trickier fighting a shorter opponent, due to the fact that you're more vulnerable. That's what can happen. It's that simple, trust me. As a heavyweight you're tall, you throw a lazy jab, a short heavyweight can close his eyes and' – Joshua clapped his right fist into an open palm with a crack – 'swing a right hand over and that's what I've got to defend. So I find it pretty comfortable fighting taller opponents.'

Kevin Johnson wasn't a straightforward style. He was short, defensive and awkward. Joshua had not been tested yet and this 'gatekeeper' was there to pose him problems. Gatekeepers were another type of opponent. For the journeymen he'd faced so far, their job was to get through the bout so they could fight again a week later. A boxer like Kevin Johnson had once been world class, a one-time contender. Those days were past, even if the American didn't want to admit it. But for those boxers who wanted to progress into the world top ten or burnish their credentials for a title shot, they had to beat a gatekeeper. Joshua could therefore not afford to lose.

'The good thing about Johnson is that I don't think we've got no fear of each other,' Joshua said. 'He's been in with Klitschko and these men, so I don't really think that my name rings any bells for him either, which puts two fearless fighters in the ring. As I said in there, may the best man win. By the sounds of things the UK and the Birmingham fans were shouting for me so I think they already know what the outcome's going to be.'

Joshua was sitting behind a flimsy desk in a quiet side room for a press conference at the Barclaycard Arena. The journalists sat on fold-out chairs, as if they were in a school classroom paying attention to a hushed lesson on the next stage of the fighter's career. 'If you look at all walks in life, you always have to stick to your strategy and be confident about it. And there's always an ultimate goal and right now it's a fuzzy picture because we're trying things, different opponent types, styles, and I think we'll soon find out whether our strategy's worked or not. But right now it seems to be working so I don't understand why people would want to change that when something's working perfectly. I think the hard work is slowly starting to pay off as a professional,' he mused.

Men who were supposed to last rounds with him, he was taking out. He was already a media favourite, popular with crowds turning out to see his fights and the multitudes tuning in to watch him on TV. But with that attention came pressure, to move more quickly and box in a higher class of opposition. 'For sure, feet are on the ground, reach for the stars,' Joshua nodded. 'I seem to have a bit of expectation now but it doesn't make me crumble, it makes me strive for greatness. I want to achieve the goals and expectations that even my family, my close friends and people who supported me are putting on my shoulders. It's great I've got something to look forward to. That's what life's about, when you wake up with a purpose.'

Joshua was determined. He did have vision, even though he knew he was completing the apprenticeship phase of his career. He was building the foundation for the next stage. 'History repeats itself, whether I'm going to get knocked out by Johnson that ends my career or I go on to be one of the greats like Larry Holmes or Ali and so on. Not many people can mention Ali's first eleven opponents, do you know what I mean? But they are the things that define them to put on great shows like the Thrilla in Manila, Rumble in the Jungle. Without these opponents you're never going to get to that level. If I go on to do great things people will say, "You know what, he done really well and he done it right."'

Admittedly he then added, 'If I get knocked out and I get put too far, they'll say, "You know what, I told you he weren't ready."'

Of course, whether Johnson was the man to do that was another question. The two fighters came face-to-face again just a few weeks later in London in the final days before their contest. From the way Johnson spoke you'd have thought he was a one-man wrecking machine. But his fighting style was hardly destructive. He bobbed his upper body forward and back, keeping in a defensive shell. He'd prance forward with a jab to frustrate an attack and, although he was on a losing run by the time he met Joshua, no one, not even Vitali Klitschko had stopped him inside twelve rounds before. He surely could not halt the march of Joshua, but could he be awkward enough to be a stumbling block? Wily enough to move Joshua around, make him look short of ideas, maybe expose him as a novice professional? There was enough for a kernel of doubt, which Johnson cultivated, preaching, with messianic passion, his own faith in himself.

'This is going to be the best heavyweight fight that has been seen – I counted – in the last thirteen years exactly. Guaranteed,' Johnson declared. 'I've been boxing eighteen years and never in eighteen years have I been training the way I'm training now.'

In the same breath he assured promoter Eddie Hearn that, once he'd taken care of Joshua, he'd gladly step in and fulfil the rest of Joshua's contract. 'Thank you' was Hearn's quiet response.

The American continued loudly. 'I wrote a book. I dropped the book three days ago. I wanted to drop the book the day before this fight. Because the book is actually going to tell you why I'm going to beat him.'

Working himself up, he spoke feverishly: 'You mean to tell me I'm going to let this clown mess up my book and what I'm going to do. Shit. I beg to differ. That's guaranteed. That's how much I know for a fact I'm going to win.'

He turned back to Hearn. 'As a matter of fact I'm going to get you the special hardback copy, too,' he murmured.

'Thank you,' the promoter said once again.

Johnson was not finished. He mulled over the nature of power. 'Who dictates and says that a person has power? What makes a person powerful? What do you look at to say this guy is a knockout artist? To me he has no power,' Johnson said, somewhat startlingly. 'Power is generated from a clever, artistic fighter letting it loose through a punch.

'I don't need my hands up. He don't have power. He's not going to hurt me,' Johnson continued. 'I don't want to make a statement by outboxing him, which is so easy to do. I don't want to do that. I want to stop this kid because that not only makes a statement, it actually solidifies what I just invested back into my career, one hundred per cent dedication. I have everything I should have had.'

Was there method in Johnson's words? Was he going to try to remove the most effective part of Joshua's game and take on his strength? Joshua shrugged. 'He's been training. It doesn't matter, he could train for months for a fight but I never take my foot off the gas. You know that.'

But he could only ponder what the peculiar difficulties of Johnson would be and what shape their contest would take. 'Because he's a veteran, he's got that ability to control the pace of a fight,' Joshua noted. 'It'll be interesting to see him control, if he does, the first half, then round after round coach will be telling me this is what he's going to do, do this and then we'll start seeing it work.

'After the rounds gone with Johnson we'll start breaking him down, too. Whether he controls the pace, I'm going to find a gap over those ten rounds and punish him for any of his mistakes. I don't really care if he comes steaming out. I'm definitely fit enough to go at a Riddick Bowe–Holyfield pace and if he wants to go nice and slow, I'm definitely controlled and patient enough.'

He remained controlled before the bout, too, reflecting impassively on the American's pre-fight boasts. Speaking to me after a final press conference, before being whisked away for a final sparring session, he reflected on coming across Johnson in Klitschko's training camp and now having to confront him. 'He is just the same, where he was very loud, very brash. He's from America. Very confident, that's what I expect and that's what he's like,' Joshua said without apparent relish. His dispassion was telling. He was keeping himself level, keeping any emotion grounded. 'I'll take pleasure in defeating a world champion. I can't really look at Johnson and take pleasure in defeating someone like that because he's not the best in the world, is he? I can't really get too frustrated or too carried away with someone like Johnson. I've just got to keep my head on my shoulders and get him out the way. That's what I always say, treat him like any opponent,' Joshua said firmly.

But the American continued the psy-ops. At the weigh-in Johnson tried to stare him down. Barrel-chested, if much the shorter man, he glowered up at Joshua. Johnson's head, shaped like a cannon ball, looked slightly flattened. It meant his features appeared squashed, as though he were squinting as he tried to stare out the Englishman. Johnson raised a palm and pressed it to Joshua's chest, presumably to take the measure of his heartbeat. The American nodded, as though he were satisfied with what he found. Joshua kept his hands clasped behind his back, staring down without expression as Johnson shifted beneath his gaze.

The congenial atmosphere of the weigh-in was a world removed from the O2 Arena the following night. It was an important show for Matchroom, Joshua's promotional outfit, and for broadcaster Sky Sports. It was their first Box Office event to feature Joshua as a key selling point. This was a pay-per-view card. It cost viewers an extra £16.99 to watch. Thus these shows were subject to some controversy. While a great fight is admittedly hard to resist, this card at the end of May 2015 did not have a singularly compelling main event. A world welterweight title fight that would pit Frankie Gavin against Kell Brook topped the bill, with good fights featuring lesser known British fighters further down the pecking order as well as two further world title clashes. But for Sky and Matchroom, Anthony Joshua's name and popularity were the most effective tools to sell this as a pay-per-view.

The night was brutal. Two of Anthony's stablemates at the Matchroom gym, John Ryder and Kevin Mitchell, were sharing his changing room. Both men came back to Anthony's dressing room battered and defeated after their fights. Ryder had been boxing for the British middleweight title he so craved. In the ascendancy against Nick Blackwell, a sudden right hook caught him. A rapid left and further flurry followed up. Stunned, Ryder backed off. Disorientated by the blow, he couldn't choose whether to go into a clinch to ride out the onslaught or back up away out of range. All the while Blackwell, with blood pouring from his nose, ploughed forward, hammering in more hurtful punches to halt Ryder. John, caught in a fog of his own confusion, was stopped inside seven rounds.

Mitchell was a mercurial if wayward talent. He should have been a world champion, he had the ability. But living dissolutely, drinking too much, had seen him squander the best years of his career. He had found discipline, too late, with trainer Tony Sims. Tonight at the O2 this would be his last world title fight. He lost. It was, however, a thriller against Jorge Linares, the Venezuelan who held the WBC lightweight title. A huge swelling sprouted out of the side of Mitchell's head. A long, ugly cut opened and bled freely. Under huge pressure, almost succumbing, the Londoner burst off the ropes, throwing everything he had at Linares. A stirring effort but Mitchell was in bad shape as he went into the tenth round. The champion finally battered the fight out of him, knocking him to his knees and out of the contest.

The ending would haunt his trainer Tony Sims, Joshua's cornerman. Sims had been in countless high-profile fights. But it was this one that would play on his mind. 'Where that cut was bad, when the referee came over to me, I just wish I'd have said to him let the doctor have a look at this, rather than sending him out for that tenth round,' Sims said, much later on. If the bout had been halted due to an accidental injury, one not caused by a punch, then whoever was leading according to the judges in the rounds completed so far would win the contest. It was up to the referee to bring in the doctor to judge the severity of a cut. But maybe a word from the trainer could have guided the official, perhaps nudged him in the right direction. 'It's the little tiny mistakes. Because he was ahead on points, if it had gone to the scorecards . . . Little things like

that, when you're up at a high level, they play in the back of
your mind,' Sims continued. It was a tiny point. As a trainer it
was not his call to make, he couldn't force the bout to go to the
cards. But it troubled him. The pressure in these fights was that
intense. It's funny how the smallest of details linger. Amid all
the drama, it seems, so much can hinge on these, the finest of
margins. The slightest of actions can change everything.

Joshua could see the damaged faces of Mitchell and Ryder
as he prepared to go out to the arena himself, all passing by
him in a whirl. 'It's boxing. You've got one coming back, like
well done, then Mitchell's had a tough fight, so that's boxing
for you, anything can happen,' Anthony said. In 'the fight
mentality' you take it in your stride. 'But when you look back
at it, it's unbelievable,' he added.

The swell of noise from the crowd, whipped up to a frenzy
after Mitchell's battling defeat, swept Joshua to the ring. The
smell of blood was in their nostrils all right. 'Everyone wants
to come out and see us boys in action. We're local boys, we're
grinding away in the gym and they want to come and see what
we're about. Boxing's a sport where your manhood gets tested.
They just want to see what we're all about. We're just in the
gym, tucked away from all this stuff, and we get to come and
see eighteen thousand people cheering, supporting us, and our
duty is to go out there and put on an explosive performance
and that's what it's all about really,' he went on.

In the ring, finally opposite Johnson, Anthony was ready to
fight. 'I've got a duty to do,' he said later. 'It's nothing personal.
It's just business. It was just another fight.'

For the opening minute of the contest Joshua did indeed
manage to resist the siren call of the crowd. He didn't charge,

he didn't rush. He jabbed. He punched out a one-two, left-right combination. Johnson, at first keeping his hands low, arms relaxed as he'd said he would, sidled clear. The American sent his left to Anthony's body. Joshua hooked in his lead as his opponent attacked. Now Johnson brought up his gloves, to catch the punches coming his way. Joshua jolted him with a right cross, a hard, scoring blow. Johnson and the crowd registered it. Attacking him with more vigour, Anthony hit the body, not an easy shot to land on a smaller man. He had the quicker hands, throwing them crisply and already bringing them back to his guard. Johnson assayed a foot shuffle as he tracked along the ropes. He banged his fists into those gloves, failing to break through Anthony's defence. Defiant maybe but a sign he was already feeling the punches coming his way.

'That wasn't aggressive, that was calculated,' Joshua said later. But he detected a flaw in Johnson's jab. 'I could see he was a bit lazy with where he replaced it so that's when I countered him with the right. From then I just kind of followed up.'

Joshua snapped his attack up another gear. He slammed in a cross, setting up a left hook. Johnson, stunned, leapt at him with a hook. But Anthony marched inexorably through him. A right, a left hook and another right flung Johnson down. He took a knee; one arm on the ropes the American pulled himself upright. He beat that count but Anthony was on him immediately. A blurring flurry of heavy punches tossed Johnson halfway through the ropes. Anthony battered him down into the canvas as the bell rang repeatedly to end the first round.

The referee and his cornerman helped a shell-shocked Johnson up, hefting him into his corner and on to his stool. No one had done this to Kevin Johnson before, manhandled him with such ease. It was like Joshua was lobbing a ragdoll across the ring. Johnson couldn't resist the attack; he could barely keep his footing beneath the onslaught.

As Johnson, still dazed, trudged over to meet him, Joshua came out for the second round with the same intensity. His left hook bombed across, opening Johnson for a right that shook him badly. Joshua lined up a long one-two. He hammered at him, blasting that vaunted defence apart. Johnson cowered on the ropes, trying to tilt himself away from the punches. But his feet wouldn't move. That happens when you're hurt. A right thundered through, a left hook flung Johnson away and the referee, Ian John-Lewis, at last threw himself bodily between them, sparing the American further suffering in only the second round.

Joshua was exultant. 'This is what it's all about,' he cried out to the delirious crowd.

Equally giddy, his promoter Eddie Hearn took to the microphone. 'That was devastating,' he gasped. 'Eighteen thousand people were here tonight. What they witnessed was the future heavyweight champion of the world.

'He's a great man, he's a great fighter and he's Great British.'

The roar of the crowd echoed all around him, a thunderous, furious racket and those fans loved every word of it.

An Educated Gamble

'I just want to become a bit more devastating.'

Backstage the adrenalin had evaporated. Joshua was more circumspect about swatting Johnson aside. He shrugged off the achievement. 'If he does test me, then I've got problems,' Anthony said dismissively. 'He's not Wladimir Klitschko so I'm not really worried about him.'

He analysed his own efforts. 'You just can't hold back the excitement. I feel like I'm developing as well so I'm getting more comfortable, like parrying shots and defending, so I'm a bit more comfortable in the ring and as I'm starting to develop I start to enjoy my fighting more,' Joshua said. 'I knew that if he thought he could hit me with the jab, he'd think he could beat me. So I made sure I was wary of his best punch, and that was his jab, and I made sure I made my jab better than his. So when I started hitting him back with the jab I could already see that I was getting my range.'

The crowd had thrilled at the ending, even if Joshua wasn't so impressed with his own handiwork. 'It weren't the best finish but, because we've been fighting back-to-back, I think my inside work could have been better,' he said. 'I was trying to use more angles but I didn't want to explode too much because I didn't want to get "old-manned" – him tuck up and then six rounds later I punch myself out and he's still there, you know. When you're fighting all these things are going through your head, stuff like that.'

He rattled off a long list of British rivals, happy to accommodate any of them with a fight. He was untroubled by whoever it might be. 'I don't mind. It's not about who I face next, it's about my own self-development,' he said. 'Wherever I go . . . I've got to conquer my own self. How far can I push Anthony Joshua? I have no interest in these other opponents, no interest in conquering America. All I worry about is myself and how I can better myself, and if bettering myself takes me to be the best in the world in my division, let's go there. Let's take it there. That's what boxing's about. This is a test. This is a test. They just want to see how far Anthony Joshua can go before someone pushes his button. And I think it's going to be a long time before that happens.

'For me what I want to do next is get in the gym.'

Joshua would retreat to the gym, to continue his journey of self-discovery on the bags, on the pads, in the training and out on the hard runs on the track. It was a matter of limits. How far he could push his, whether he could extend his endurance. Whether he could maintain the dread monotony, the zen-like focus a boxer needs to excel. 'Routine, in an intelligent man, is a sign of ambition.' The line from W. H. Auden seemed appropriate; Joshua could dedicate the summer months of 2015 to the familiar pattern of his work.

The next foe was summoned from Scotland. Gary Cornish

was even taller than Joshua and the heavier man. He rarely spoke and had somehow acquired a 21–0 unbeaten record, boxing no one of note in his four-year professional career. Based in Inverness, in the north of Scotland, it was a mystery how he even managed to get sparring partners. The taciturn Scot did little to shed further light on the matter. He wasn't even sure if there were any other heavyweights in Scotland. 'I think there's only one, to be honest,' he pondered. 'So we don't really get sparring up there. We've got to ship them in or travel away.'

So how would he beat someone like Anthony Joshua? Someone with genuine power and increasing poise. Someone who could boast a glittering amateur record in quick time and was gaining more experience day after day.

'Just prepare like I prepare for any other fight,' Cornish offered. 'We'll find sparring partners that replicate his style and we'll be ready.'

It sounded optimistic. But Cornish contended, 'Eddie Hearn's put people in front of him and he's beat them. Tommy Gilmour's put people in front of me and I've beat them. So we can only beat the people in front of us.'

The Scotsman's argument was that they weren't so different. But Cornish's professional run had not been stellar so far and Joshua had the pedigree. Anthony held an Olympic gold medal, a World silver, too, while Cornish had had a mere nine bouts as an amateur. 'I've been making up for it in the pros. There wasn't many amateur fights out there for me but we've had twenty-one pro fights and Tommy has got them all shapes, all different sizes for me to learn. We've been doing our apprenticeship in the pros.'

Given how destructive Joshua had been, the devastating style of the knockouts he'd scored, didn't Cornish think twice about taking this fight? Didn't he hesitate? He did not elaborate, but in a firm, clipped tone simply said, 'Not at all.' With that our interview, such as it was, was done.

Joshua was far kinder to Cornish than my own assessment of him. 'He's very fit, he moves a lot and he's got a very good double jab and he throws a hooking right hand,' he said. 'Throws good jabs, he moves well for a big guy. But I can't tell you everything about Cornish because it's so different when you're the man in there on the night.'

On the British heavyweight scene Anthony Joshua was a most wanted man. So many were so desperate to beat him. 'They know if they beat me, because I've built up this little hype train together, I get derailed and they jump on, so I think that gives them that bit more ambition.'

But he added, 'You know my mentality. Unless they're world champion, I can't show them too much respect. I have to go in there with the mentality that they will be defeated. He's live, he's tall, he's game, he's undefeated.'

This fight would be for the vacant Commonwealth heavyweight title, the first significant belt on offer in Joshua's professional career. For him it was an advance up the ladder, moving through the different levels of the sport just as he had done as an amateur boxer. Joshua saw it as a key step towards the British title, a belt held in higher regard than the Commonwealth title. 'That's what I need. I don't want it but I need it, I need that British title. I need it all really. But I need these belts right now to get respect amongst people in the industry,' he said. 'I need that belt so it's, "You know what, he's starting to arrive on the scene."'

He went on, 'The Commonwealth and the British is like the ABA and GB Championship level, so I'm just arriving on the scene and that's important, really important.'

Two days before the fight Joshua is in a room high up within the O2. Windows in the wall overlook the arena floor. It gives some scope of the size of the venue, how many people can stream in, how far the small ring will be from these upper tiers. The last press conference has just taken place and some chairs are pulled up in front of Joshua so a few journalists can cluster round him, a kind of debrief after the main session for the cameras. The following Saturday would not only be the Englishman's Commonwealth title fight but, later that same night, over in America, Floyd Mayweather would be having his final fight in Las Vegas before passing into retirement. Floyd may have been prone to ostentatious displays of cash and jewellery, as well as bragging about his wealth, but regardless of that he was the finest fighter of his era. However, he was signing off with a low-key bout against Andre Berto, a man no one, probably not even Berto himself, considered a match for Mayweather. The demand for that fight, even if it would be Mayweather's last, was not high. It raised the intriguing possibility that at the O2 Joshua would sell more tickets and attract a bigger crowd at the live gate than Mayweather's in Las Vegas.

'It's mad, isn't it?' Anthony laughed. 'It's his last fight and it's not even a big draw. Mayweather, he hasn't got a fanbase. People go to watch him lose. That's not really a fanbase, unless it's like a mega, mega event, like a global event. I don't know if he has that core any more. They can't relate. He's distanced himself from the public so much, with the money and stuff, so

I think people don't go to watch him win and just have a good night out.

'I don't know, that's just my opinion. I think we've done more tickets than them,' he laughed mischievously.

Joshua's crowd had taken to him. They bellowed into the night, creating a wall of noise that Gary Cornish had to walk through. His entrance music was switched on to try to make some headway for him. The Scotsman had come with a lone bagpiper to escort him to the ring, an instrument that did nothing to cut through the sound around him. The crowd harangued him with shouts of 'Who are ya?' from all sides. Once he had run that gauntlet Joshua appeared on the entryway behind him. The boos switched to huge cheers, reverberating all through the mass of bodies that stretched round the arena.

'It is a serious atmosphere to deal with,' Joshua admitted. 'There's no turning back once you're there.'

Backing Anthony up were the two coaches from his Finchley amateur boxing club, Sean Murphy and John Oliver. They marched in after him, one of them carrying his WBC International strap aloft. 'You can't forget where you come from,' Joshua said. 'It was only the other day, seven years ago, that I walked in the gym and they started training me up to Olympic level, then the Olympic team took me to the professionals. Keep those people close and that's why they're still with me now on the journey.'

He had moved fast, his record now 13–0, but he had come far. Thirteen thousand people now roared Joshua on. As the announcer introduced the fighters to the arena, Cornish stiffly held an arm up to the crowd. The pale Scot was stony-faced. The opening bell set them on one another. Joshua was quick.

He blocked a lead left, jabbed back. He landed his lead to the body. Cornish tried a left hook but could not find the connection. 'He came out straightaway with a solid jab. I could see in his eyes, I think he thought, "I've got nothing to lose here." He could be dangerous,' Joshua said.

Whatever Joshua saw in those eyes – it could have been fear, fury or desperation – it didn't matter. He lined up a right-left, hard punches. The cry of 'England' (broken up into three syllables, of course, En-ger-land) was in his ears. Joshua put his weight behind another cross. The shot levelled Cornish. All of this inside only the first round. Cornish clambered up, finding his feet briefly. But Joshua was on him. A right missed but his hands were flying. Standing right by him, almost too close, Joshua managed to hook his left through the Scot's guard, punching with just the arm but hard enough to floor Cornish once and for all, winning by knockout in ninety-seven seconds.

'I managed to catch him with a flush shot luckily early on and put him away. I think it's just complementing all the training. You know when you've had a good training camp. I think we just had a good training camp and it paid off,' Anthony reflected. 'You can never predict it. You can never predict a round, can you?

'To do it in one, I'm not complaining but it would have been good to have gone a few more. It's good for the people who came out to watch as well.'

Whether the Briton had just about done more tickets than Floyd Mayweather that night over in Las Vegas was a moot point, though under repeated questioning his promoter Eddie Hearn finally relented to the media, conceding, 'Okay I'll say it, AJ outsold Mayweather.'

What Joshua had done was take control of the crowd, take control of himself and take control of his opponent. He would now do the same with his career.

Too often successful fighters lose fortunes. Boxing is an unscrupulous trade. There are managers to be paid, promoters gleefully taking their cut, whose interests don't necessarily align with those of the men they claim to represent. Boxers spend their lives training in the gym and rarely do they have the education to be at ease with contracts, their business dealings and the financial side of their careers.

Joshua admitted that an education was something he'd lost in pursuit of his dream. 'You're giving up so much of yourself. I would love to get back and just focus on developing my own mindset. No regrets, but I'm aware of it, definitely aware of it. There's some intelligent people out there. I want to sit down with these intelligent people. That's where boxing takes you,' he said. 'I don't want to be the dumb guy in the corner that doesn't have nothing to say.

'I want to engage and that comes with knowledge so that's what I feel I need to just enhance.'

He continued, 'Remember as boxers we sacrifice our education to become the best we can physically. So you're put in these situations of dealing with the public, face-to-face. That's why some people can just flip and just start getting angry because they don't know how to handle situations.'

He had gone into his professional career eager to take a broader view. 'There's a life outside of boxing. Even though I box, box, box, I just try and keep an entrepreneur's mind frame because it keeps your mind active, it keeps you creative,' he'd told me. 'If it was just boxing I'd become a bit dull. You've got to have a bit more about you.'

Joshua was applying his shrewd approach to tackling the business of boxing. He was examining the financial side of his enterprise and decided to take his own affairs in hand. The normal set-up for a boxer was to take the fights his promoter gave him, to give his manager, if he had one, their cut and hope for the best. With a major promoter, a high public profile and competing in big events, additional commercial deals might eventually be offered to the boxer. But once Joshua decided to turn professional he saw there was another side to his career, beyond solely the fights. There is the business of being a personality, handling his broadening fame and separate commercial deals. Since the Olympics he had been represented by major talent agencies. Their job was to identify the value in his image and take on a broader remit beyond the sport, one that wouldn't necessarily always coincide with his promoter's activity. An agency, however, still takes a significant percentage. In 2015 Joshua went a step further. He set up his own management group, with his uncle Seyi, who'd been alongside him from the beginning of his career and a young but clearly competent commercial manager, Freddie Cunningham. It was Anthony's idea to address this task himself. 'He had the confidence to say, I'll take you on as part of my business,' Freddie pointed out.

It was a big call. 'He's one of the hottest UK, potentially global, talents there is at the moment. To set up your own company when you've got the likes of Wasserman wanting to represent you, and they're massive, huge companies and hugely successful in what they do. But they're not necessarily right for Anthony because he wants to be so involved,' Cunningham continued.

Now Joshua would be making the decisions. It was a bold move to put himself in command, but a good example for other boxers. They didn't have to just take what was given. They could take charge.

His management group was tasked with bringing in brands that weren't typically associated with boxing, and in tandem attracting a new audience to the sport. They found success, bringing in the likes of Lucozade, Beats, Under Armour. Fashion, music and fitness companies which hadn't been involved in boxing recently but wanted to be linked to Anthony Joshua. With his promoter Joshua also insisted on quality undercard bouts ahead of his fights. As far as he was concerned his events should be shows. 'Our constant remit is to show him to a wider audience,' Freddie explained. 'We want to get them into it, we want to get them more involved in it and understand it more and start following his career and start following all his fights. That's the goal, to get as many eyes on boxing and Anthony as possible. Already I think there's a fanbase coming to the O2 that I think is slightly different, who maybe are coming to their first fights. To have a great undercard and then Anthony as well, it's just showcasing the sport really well.'

Cautionary tales abound in boxing. The major promoters tend to emerge from their scrapes with money. The men who did the fighting, some of them did make fortunes, but too many lost out. It's painful to think what some could have had, and to hear what others lost. Evander Holyfield notoriously squandered a fortune that ran into hundreds of millions, just one of many high-profile examples.

'He's seen the mistakes that have been made, he doesn't want to make the same mistakes. Always wants to be in control of his money, maximise his money, make sure he's got stable companies,' Freddie said. 'They lose all their money and Anthony's so aware of that and reads so much about it all . . . He doesn't want to be that guy.'

There are many grim endings to boxing stories. But there was a vision for Joshua's to end happily. For his team to conduct his business through the right processes, to build long-term relationships with other companies, for his career then to continue after he'd finished competing himself.

There were dangers; there always would be in boxing, especially among the heavyweights. That was part of the risk and the reward. 'Heavyweight boxing, it's a massive sport and you've got the chance to be one of the biggest sportsmen in the world. It's hard to build outside of the sport but it's possible. People have done it in the past and they've gone right to the top and they've been the biggest guys they could be,' Cunningham mused. 'People do like knockouts. Heavyweight boxing, isn't it? It's the uncertainty, the unknown. You genuinely don't know what can happen.'

That was the dream, though, a far distant one at this point. Anthony Joshua had a long way to go. To reach it, he would have to last through the hard, enduring battle of a professional boxing career. But, Freddie noted, 'There's an end goal with it all. It's all focused, there's an objective and there's a target at the end of it. It's going to take a lot of work and there are so many different factors but at least we've got a strategy we can work towards and there's an end goal in it all.

'Hopefully we'll get there.'

Joshua took another bold decision, too. For his next fight he would for the first time headline a pay-per-view event. It was a risky financial manoeuvre. Of course, success would be highly lucrative and catapult him into big time and big money events. But stepping up too soon could prove costly. If his profile wasn't ready for it, if the event failed at the box office, it could stymie his progression.

But there were indicators to go on, like the speed of ticket sales for the Gary Cornish fight and the viewing figures he had enjoyed so far, that going on pay-per-view would be an educated gamble. And Joshua and his team had just the right opponent in mind.

The Whyte Stuff

The enmity between Anthony Joshua and Dillian Whyte had festered. Their grudge had grown bitterly personal over the years since their amateur contest. Boxers win and lose. It's the natural way of things in the sport. But they don't normally retain a hatred for one another. Where then, I wondered, did such spite come from?

'You were the one who interviewed me –' Anthony told me when I asked at a press conference. The crowd of journalists in the room swivelled to face me as I sat awkwardly among them. Joshua continued, '– when you asked about the remarks that Dillian had made about me and I just gave you my opinion.'

So apparently I started it . . .

Dillian Whyte seethed. Reading an article I'd written, a feature on Anthony Joshua in the magazine *Boxing News*, that familiar anger surged through him. He wanted to lash out. Specifically, he wanted to lash out at Joshua.

Whyte had never forgotten his amateur victory over the future Olympic champion. But for him that win had been more curse than blessing. It's all he was known for, being one of only three men to beat Joshua. It had also brought greater scrutiny on him. Once his background as a kickboxer had been unearthed he'd had his amateur card rescinded. It forced him to turn professional. He went over, though, without the backing of a major promoter. He toiled along the small-hall circuit, boxing at many grim venues – the Coronet Theatre in Elephant and Castle, the Olympia in Liverpool and the Troxy in Limehouse, the dives, frankly, of professional boxing. All the while Joshua was in the English Institute of Sport, the pristine home of GB Boxing, becoming the number one super-heavyweight in the country and earning fame, acclaim and his Olympic gold medal.

Whyte could only look on enviously. He might have beaten Joshua. But it wasn't him being touted as the future heavyweight champion of the world. 'He won an Olympic gold and they gave him the right fights, the right publicity, he's knocking out the guys in good fashion,' Whyte recounted. 'Fair play to him. I mean, I've come up the hard way. I fought on small shows and sold thousands and thousands of pounds' worth of tickets to get fights. I've gone through my ups and downs and stuff so he's had a slightly easier road than what I have.'

Whyte's career stalled abruptly when he failed a drug test. His argument that he tested positive due to inadvertent use, because the substance was in an over-the-counter nutritional supplement he bought, was accepted by UK Anti-Doping. But whether deliberate or not, an athlete is responsible for what is found in his body. Whyte was banned from boxing for two years. His hostility towards Joshua could only fester.

'That's never going to be forgotten about,' he said gruffly of his suspension. 'It's happened. My case is online for anybody who wants to view it. So there's no point defending it any more.'

The Brixton man kept himself as active as he could during his two-year exile. He went round gyms, getting the best sparring he could. With other younger fighters he made his way out to Wladimir Klitschko's training base in Stanglwirt, Austria.

His time there coincided with Anthony Joshua's. The pair spoke. They seemed to put their differences aside at least while they were out there. Then they settled on a truce of sorts, even a peace. 'When we was in camp he acted a certain way, sorry for the stuff. He acted a certain way so I was, like, you know what, that's cool, that's old,' Whyte said. That détente, though, proved only temporary.

The article I'd written had struck a raw nerve, making Whyte all the more furious as he served out his ban from professional boxing. The two were constantly being linked on social media. Thinking I was debunking the rivalry, I simply detailed how, while Joshua had gone all the way and won an Olympic gold medal, Whyte had not even won the ABA Championships in England. Joshua had kicked up a stir in the professional ranks as he blazed through his run of knockouts, all the while Whyte had been banned from the pros for his positive test.

Joshua had chuckled dismissively when, at the very beginning of his professional career, I had questioned him about Mr Whyte. 'I don't know how him and his promoter have managed to talk this up into people's heads. I don't know. I don't really watch Dillian Whyte,' he had said. 'Dillian Whyte just needs to chill. All this hype, when we fight and he loses, what's he going to say then?'

I pointed out Joshua had in fact only had two contests when

he'd boxed Whyte. 'He's going on like I was a champion amateur at the time. I was, like, come on, man. Take it easy. You didn't compete against the best me, and I'm still not the best me. I don't know why he talks about it like me and him had some big rivalry as amateurs. It was far from that,' Joshua said. Perhaps most galling for Whyte was that Joshua didn't seem to consider him on the same level. 'He's getting kicked out of the amateurs, getting kicked out of the professionals and then he's talking all this stuff that he wants to compete with me. Be professional about your career,' Anthony went on.

'He's not a professional type of character.'

My copy was perhaps more damning of Whyte's track record but, whatever the case, the words threw him into a rage when he read them. 'When I came back he started talking all this stuff like, I don't know, like he took my kindness for weakness. So I had to go back to how I was with him. Don't be fake. If you don't like me, tell me you don't like me. I'm cool with that. I can work with you if I don't like you. But don't pretend that we're cool and then say stuff behind my back. That's just snaky. That's the stuff scumbags do,' Whyte said bitterly.

Whyte turned his ire on Joshua. With a view to matching them later in the year, promoter Eddie Hearn found a place for Whyte on the undercard of the Gary Cornish fight. Although Whyte was due to box someone else entirely, a small American, Brian Minto, who shouldn't have been much of a threat to him, he paid his actual opponent little mind. At the final press conference before the bill, Whyte rounded on Joshua, lambasting him as a 'good behaving punk' among other choice insults. Anthony held his tongue then; he had to get through and win the Commonwealth title. But with relish he signed on to fight Whyte in December 2015 for the vacant British heavyweight title, at the O2 once again.

The British title has a special appeal to boxers. In a world where there are multiple world titles, countless minor international or intercontinental belts, there is only one Lonsdale Belt. With an ornate design, for many Brits it is the most beautiful title out there. Great British fighters, like Lennox Lewis, had fought for that belt in key contests. Joshua wanted to follow in those footsteps. 'We want to go that route,' Anthony said. 'I'm still on the road so we're getting there.'

It was to his greater personal satisfaction that this title fight came with a score to settle. 'People will still want to see me get beat. People like the bad guy. There's not far in between, I don't think, good and bad. There's not far in between. You've still got to win. That's what people are going to remember. That's what matters. It seems that way in my sport. People only care about whether you win.'

Whyte maintained the myth that GB boxers like Joshua had somehow had it easy. He, after all, had needed to fight his way on to the international amateur squad. Once there he'd had to up his training to brutal levels and battle his way through tournaments across Europe, Turkey and Azerbaijan. Not to mention actually winning an Olympic gold medal and delivering the performances asked of him as a professional. Nothing about that had been easy. Joshua had earned it. In contrast, just by stoking their rivalry to fever pitch, Whyte had carried himself straight to this title fight and if he won, with Joshua cast down he would simply occupy his place in the British boxing firmament. Victory would whisk Whyte straight to a new level of fame, while Joshua's career would take a hefty setback. He wanted what Anthony had and, simply put, a win would give it to him. This was Dillian Whyte's chance.

'You want to take what they have. It's not hate or anything like that. It's just that this man's in my way. I need to get to that level and get beyond that level. My drive is just to get past him,' Whyte said. 'I've been fighting for a long time. I haven't been beaten up by anybody or been outgunned or dominated by anybody in life as well as in the ring. So I'm not going to let one guy, because everybody's hyping him or because he's muscular, he's knocked everybody out, come and dominate me. No way. No way. It's never going to happen.'

Whyte was a hard man. 'A lot of people I grew up with are either dead or in prison or strung out on drugs or something, though. A lot of friends I grew up with are either dead or doing life sentences for murder and stuff like that. I'm just grateful that I got into kickboxing to keep myself out of trouble. From there I went into boxing,' he said. 'Then I found that I liked it. Then years later I found my dad and my granddad actually boxed bareknuckles and didn't tell me.'

He gave every indication he was going to stand his ground. 'I was very heavy-handed from when I was a kid as well. Listen, kids at school are ruthless. They don't care,' he continued. 'Bullies used to pick on me until I started trying to knock them out. Then that changed quickly.

'I've always loved fighting so I've been fighting since forever . . . I did it the other way round. A lot of people start boxing technically. I did it the other way round. I started fighting. Now I'm grasping more the technical side. I started boxing by being strong.'

The psychology of a fighter is a delicate thing. Surprisingly so. Anthony's offhand dismissal of Whyte had hurt his pride and triggered a new round of spite. But Joshua had changed completely from when he boxed his amateur contest with Whyte. Physically he was a different animal. After seven years of unremitting, heavy-duty training he looked different. He had a different quality of power. He had refined the quality of his boxing immeasurably, almost unrecognisably, so that in the intervening years he had managed to win the Olympic Games, not to mention the national amateur championships. Yet Whyte still had that win over him. Did it make a difference? Did it create a crucial, if tiny, fissure in Anthony's self-belief, knowing that Whyte had the beating of him once, even if it was all those years ago? Would Whyte for his part still see the same raw amateur he had boxed before? Would that leave Whyte with little doubt that he would win? Normally it was Joshua's confidence that was cast-iron. But in this fight Whyte's belief that he was the better man was, by this stage, almost an article of faith.

Joshua couldn't believe his opponent was taking so much from three amateur rounds that had faded into a now far distant past. 'Deep, deep down I don't think he is. Deep, deep, deep down. He can take a little bit but I don't think it's everything to him,' Joshua mused. 'So I think deep, deep, deep down he's not taking too much away from it. Because I think you really have to look at the progress, and development and body shape, the mentality. As you said, I had an intense amateur career. Even though it was short, it was quite quick and intense and then the pros. I've been working at it since 2008 so I think he'll take that into account as well.'

There was a grudging understanding from Joshua, at least, of Whyte's mindset. 'I think with boxing you get to show yourself as a character and I think he comes across as a very confident person. I don't know whether that's through what he's achieved. As you said, he had a short amateur career and not so many fights as a pro. I think it's him as a person.'

Whyte's term 'good behaving punk' stayed with me. He meant it as an insult. But I didn't think it really so offensive. It was almost an acknowledgement that there were different sides to Anthony's character. Joshua was tough. When it was on, when it was time to fight, it was on. But outside the ring the Watford man was a benign presence, someone who made time for people, treated them with respect. If he was a gentle giant until the chime of that first bell, he was one you didn't want to cross. He conducted himself according to the different contexts he came across in his life. He adapted and thrived. Whyte was brash, loud, quick to anger and quick to fight. He refused to allow Joshua any complexity or nuance to his character. These different sides to Anthony's personality, rather than seeing them as complexities Whyte simply dismissed as false. Heavyweights were meant to fit a certain template: a vicious Mike Tyson in his prime hardly given to self-doubt or understatement; a Frank Bruno, big, strong but undermined by his own thoughts; a Muhammad Ali, brash, cocky, but with the physical gifts to back it up. Nuance here was rarely allowed. 'It's one or the other in boxing,' Anthony pondered later. But he added, 'It's a good path and it's a good indication for you to build your character . . . You've got a good grounding in boxing to show your character to the people and just be natural with it. I mean, this is your chance to announce yourself on the stage.

'When you're in front of the camera so many times, your true character always comes out. I'm not a false person, I just am what I am, I take it as it comes and then people are either going to like you or not. If you're a bad person people will pick up on that. When they see you so many times in the media and you're a good person people pick up on that, and I'm just being myself and people seem to get along with me. It's nothing special. It just is what it is.'

He'd been told before, in fact by Paul Smith, a former world title challenger and quality television pundit, 'Most people, they're good guys trying to be bad . . . You're a bad guy trying to be good.' That sounded an apt description. Anthony could laugh. 'I love fighting,' he said simply. 'I enjoy it.'

But the fissures between Joshua and Whyte ran deep. From north and south London, from different communities. The bad blood between them was undeniable and their anger was raw.

Whyte, however, would get away from their home city for this fight. He kept his links with Wladimir Klitschko's camp and had been taken on by the old champion's own trainer, Johnathon Banks. Whyte was sure this would give him a new dimension. At thirty-three, Banks was unusually young for a trainer. An active heavyweight, he had been a fixture in the Klitschko gym and on the champion's undercards, although his boxing career meandered, going nowhere. But he was learning. He was the heir to Manny Steward, mentored by the great trainer of the modern era. After the sad death of Steward, Banks was the man applying the precision engineering in Klitschko's training camps. Whyte was a brawler; at heart he just wanted to slug it out. But Banks could be the man to refine him. Add some finesse. And make him a much more dangerous man.

'Welcome to big-time boxing,' Klitschko told Whyte when he entered the camp in Austria. 'Up here it's a whole next level.'

'I'm changing my style. I'm blending both styles together. For me it's good because I can see how it's going to benefit me. It's been great working with him. Johnathon's all about technique,' Whyte said, his easy Jamaican lilt strongly discernible in his voice.

He was learning from Wladimir Klitschko himself. 'His approach to fights, how he trains, what he does, how he gets ready, where is he mentally. He said a few things to me as well: "You need to control your emotions. You control your emotions and you can win this fight,"' Whyte explained. 'He said little things to me that have been inspirations for me.'

Joshua, in contrast, kept close to his roots. Ever since he had turned professional he had maintained a good relationship with GB Boxing. After his gold medal heroics they always considered him part of 'the GB family'. Joshua would always be welcome in their gym. He split his time training in the Matchroom gym and at the Olympic team's facility. Anthony was the perfect poster boy for the programme, happy to front a campaign to recruit new talent at no cost. He sparred with the Olympic hopefuls. It helped them. It was no accident that Frazer Clarke and Joe Joyce were developing into two of the best amateur super-heavyweights in the world. They were ambitious and had the speed of top-level international boxers. Clarke's technical skills were as good as any young heavyweight and Joyce was solid and relentless in style. Like a wall coming at you, a clubbing attacker, he could set a pace that few managed to live with. Curiously, these were men who had boxed Joshua as amateurs; now they were friends who trained together.

'It's my second home,' he said of the set-up in Sheffield. 'I wouldn't change it for the world either because of the routine. I'm around hungry fighters.'

It helped him technically, rotating in a different sparring partner every few rounds. 'They're so quick for five rounds, they're doing WSB now so they're basically professionals anyway. I'm sparring like three people, two people, it was really hard for me to adapt and that's the privilege. That's why I don't take it for granted going up there because they are basically like top-end professionals,' Anthony said. 'Even outside of the gym, having that affiliation with GB still, that's why I kind of try and conduct myself properly. Because I still would do anything for GB. They're a big organisation, Lottery-funded, so it's a publicly funded gym. So I do represent myself properly in that sense and going up there, some of the boys haven't won belts. That's what I'm saying, some of the boys aren't world champions or Olympic champions but they train like champions.'

For the GB boxers they got to have the reigning Olympic super-heavyweight champion on hand to work out with. 'How's that not going to develop you?' smiled coach Rob McCracken. 'You bring them on. It's got to be good for them, three or four rounds and they're out and that's what they need. Eight rounds is not going to help them but three or four rounds they get out, it's great for them and it's a huge benefit.'

McCracken, a mentor figure, had a real bond with Joshua. He would join him professionally and work his corner for future title fights. Rob was not a man prone to overexuberance.

At the heart of one of the biggest fights in recent British history, I remembered seeing Rob leaning on the corner post, looking almost bored as Carl Froch had his hand raised in victory after his rematch with George Groves. Once when I pressed him for recollections of the night, it wasn't Froch's glorious, almost career-defining, finishing blow that he recalled. Deadpan, when pressed for memories of that particular evening he preferred to tell of his travails trying to reclaim his car from the car park. As performance director of Great Britain's Olympic squad McCracken was under acute pressure, especially as the Games drew near. He managed a multi-million-pound programme that expected results. Yet these pressures never seemed to get to him. He always appeared unruffled, calculated, above all pragmatic. Throughout McCracken was determined to get the best for his boxers. 'Nothing's left to chance, we're very thorough. The level of detail is second to none,' he said with quiet, unshakeable confidence. 'Give them everything we can to try and help them succeed. That's what it's all about.'

A large picture of Joshua had joined those of Britain's other Olympic medallists adorning the walls of the GB gym. Anthony himself trained beneath those images. It meant a lot to the next generation of hopefuls following in his footsteps. 'AJ,' McCracken continued in his laconic tone, 'you know, he is what he is. He's a great role model, he's a tremendous human being. It's great for them to look up to people like that but also think, "You know what, I could do it. They've done it, I can do it."

'It has a knock-on effect. The others believe they can do it.'

Joshua needed to train with single-minded purpose, in the

same way that for Dillian Whyte taking Anthony down was the be-all and end-all. 'I hear him talking about fighting Fury and fighting Deontay Wilder. Me, I'm not even looking at that. I'm just looking at fighting him, getting the job done and whatever comes after comes after. I'm looking at 12 December and nothing past that,' Whyte said. 'All I'm focusing on is eleven o'clock on 12 December and that's it.'

Joshua wondered if he represented the limit of Whyte's ambition. But he recognised that if he did, if this was it for Whyte, all the more reason for him to exercise caution with this particular antagonist. 'He's got his eye on the prize. That's a dangerous fighter. Someone who wants to beat *you*, that's a dangerous fighter, and I'm not looking above that. But I definitely would like to go on and achieve more than beating Dillian Whyte. So I've got to really focus on that, get him out of the way so I can continue down the yellow brick road.

'My ambition's a bit higher than Dillian Whyte. But I've got to focus on that fight. Trust me, I understand the deal with that boy. And then I can move on to what I'm trying to do.'

The Brawl

Standing between Joshua and Dillian Whyte was not a comfortable place to be. With two days left before they were due to box, the clock was ticking down. The longer they spent in each other's company the more they bristled with hostility. Whyte spoke with barely contained ferocity. During their final press conference he wanted to attack Joshua there and then, or at least wait until he was leaving the hotel and get him in the car park outside. And Whyte assured Anthony with cold fury that, whatever happened in their title fight, for him it wouldn't be over. This feud cut the Brixton man deep.

Eddie Hearn said, 'There was a moment in the press conference when Dillian was saying, "I'm telling you after this fight, whatever happens, I'll find you." He was going to stand up, I think. Once that happens . . .'

Hearn had to stand between them as they faced off for the cameras. Whyte, with a broad grin, still spoke quietly to Joshua, while Anthony, his jaw tight, talked back through a thin smile. Hearn shifted uncomfortably trying to manoeuvre them apart. There was nothing he could have done, though, if two men that big and that strong had laid hands on each other.

'In the head-to-heads you look at the size of those guys and it only takes a push or a shove and it just snowballs into a cyclone of trouble and security, and the next thing you know someone's on the floor. We don't need that,' Eddie said. 'When you feel like there's going to be some trouble, I'll just step in. But that's with the light weights. Today I went, "Okay, guys. Yup?" And I went like that and no one moved. But I can't do anything. If they don't want to move, they ain't going to move.

'After a minute when you're listening to what they're saying, you know. I've been around confrontations where it has kicked off and I know what it takes to kick off. Things are getting said that, I'm thinking, it's going to go now. We have to stop this or everybody get ready.'

Joshua looked down on Whyte, listened to how his latest antagonist spoke to him. He contained himself but could only think one thing. That he was going to knock Dillian Whyte out.

'Shows the type of person he is. Brute. Rough and ready background. That's what boxing needs, it needs characters like that,' Joshua said moments later. But he added firmly, 'Talk is cheap. Talk is definitely cheap. All jokes aside, talk is cheap. He can say all these things. But I'm sure I'll be fine.'

Whyte, however, crowed, 'I've been in his head for a long time. I've been in his head for a long, long time. Since October 2009 I've been in his head and he's admitted that to me, face-to-face, in Austria.'

Joshua seemed ready. 'His strength is the fact that he's beaten me once and he thinks he can do it again. Probably he feels that with the Klitschko camp he thinks that he's a powerhouse,' he said of Whyte. 'But I'm going to go out there with the same attitudes, same ambitions and end it potentially in the same style.'

He maintained, 'There's not the edge where I'm going to go out there and swing for the trees', a pledge, though, that he would not keep.

Two days before fight night Joshua had dismissed Michael Buffer offhand when the announcer offered to flip a coin to decide who should ringwalk first. Since they would be fighting for the vacant British title, there was no champion to enter second. Joshua just gave Whyte the second entrance, the one normally reserved for the champion. He shrugged off the pomp and circumstance, itching to get started. Buffer timidly pocketed the coin.

On Saturday night Joshua stood under the lights, waiting impatiently for Whyte. He stood in the centre of the ring, staring out into the crowd. He wore dark shorts and a vest-like top without sleeves. He shook out his sinewy arms, ready to hit, ready to hurt.

'That was a different thing for him there. Dillian Whyte done the right thing there. He drew everything out of him that he could. He was totally wound up,' his cornerman Tony Sims would say afterwards. 'As the bell went he was like one of them dolls that you wind up and there's no stopping him.'

Whyte took his time processing to the ring, with a sizeable entourage of large men trailing in his wake as well as his formidable coach, Johnathon Banks. Joshua himself wasn't without friends close by. His old amateur coach John Oliver was in the ring with him. His sparring partner and former team-mate Frazer Clarke, who worked on his off weekends for the security company that handled such events, was stationed at the corner post on my right-hand side.

The hostility between the principles charged the crowd. The grudge was real, their old score palpable. They touched gloves as referee Howard Foster gave them their final instructions, the last veneer of civility.

Joshua hit him like a hurricane. A snarl on his face, he flew out of his corner from the opening bell. Whyte detonated a right but Joshua came on. His cross blasted down. Whyte tried a jab, throwing the punch to keep Joshua off. It did not deter him. Anthony hooked in his left, getting needlessly close. But another right hand worked as a range finder. He lined up a quality one-two combination, powering into Whyte, driving him back across the canvas.

For a moment Whyte found a pocket of air, cleaving a left hook into Joshua's body. The Brixton man swept an ungainly right at him. Joshua knocked him back with a left hook. The shocking strength of the blow wobbled Whyte. It put him on the ropes, the place where Joshua had hammered so many of his previous victims to defeat. Then the Watford man opened up on him, ripping in punches with either hand. His left banged in and he looked for the right uppercut, the shot he had been trying to time against Jason Gavern a few fights earlier. Joshua wanted to finish Whyte there and then. His hands drifted down as he threw. Another big left shuddered into Whyte's guard. But beneath that awful pressure, in his home city, with his men and his supporters watching, his bitter rival looming over him, Whyte would not permit himself to fall. He simply would not allow it. He stood up to the hits, taking the kind of punches that would have levelled a horse.

'Why didn't I catch him? Why didn't I knock him out in the first round?' Joshua asked himself later. 'I had him hurt. It was just silly things, like rushing, swinging. But that's why I learn you've got fighters who can soak it up for the first one to four rounds. You can hurt someone but they've got enough energy, because it's early on in the fight they're not exhausted yet, to recover very quickly.'

And then all hell broke loose.

Joshua had been reckless in contests before. When he clicked into fight mode, he was going to keep slugging until his opponent broke or the referee got in the way. With blood still pounding in his ears, he ignored the bell chiming to end the first round. Joshua swung at him. Whyte, in the fog of that furious round, processed it for a moment. In that fraction of a second he decided he wouldn't take it. He reared up, attacking Joshua well after the round had ended. Howard Foster, the referee, knew at once that this fight was getting out of hand. He flung himself between the two heavyweights. At that moment Joshua nimbly ducked a wide arching blow. For Howard's trouble that punch scraped across his nose as he manfully tried to separate the two men, both of whom were far bigger, far stronger, and had no interest in stepping off. At that moment I thought Whyte was about to get himself disqualified.

As though enough pandemonium hadn't been unleashed, Whyte's entourage, seeing that the normal rules had fallen apart, elected to charge the ring, piling through the ropes, looking to brawl. Joshua's team, fearful for their man, followed that lead and rushed in from the opposite corner. This, on live television, could have turned nasty very quickly.

At this moment I deemed it appropriate to take a note, scrawling the single word 'pandamuninnm' (my attempt at pandemonium) across my pad in thick black pen. Security, with big Frazer among them, however, were quicker. Bursting in between the two rival groups, they kept the interlopers apart. Frazer, holding his arms out wide, ran towards the largest member of Whyte's crew, shouting the first and in fact the wisest thing that came to mind: 'He won't get paid. He won't get paid.'

It was enough to make them think twice. Whyte's men retreated. Joshua was hustled back to his corner. Banks stomped across the canvas to take hold of his man by the glove, for an instant looking like a parent grabbing a wilful child by the hand. As quickly as the chaos had exploded, Howard Foster was suddenly left alone in the ring, taking a deep breath and wiping blood from his reddening nose with a white towel.

Veteran sportswriter Colin Hart, sitting alongside me, leaned across to mutter, 'At least we know the referee can take a shot.'

'I wasn't thinking anything. Listen, Joshua hit me after the bell, two punches after the bell and it kicked off. This is boxing. If you want to hit somebody after the bell then there's a high chance it will kick off. And that's what happened,' Whyte said afterwards. Of course, from his perspective, with his back to his own corner, he would have seen Joshua's team piling in first. 'His people run in the ring because it's kicking off, then my people run in the ring, my people's coming in to protect me because his people's all come in. My guys have run in to protect me. It's boxing. These things happen,' Whyte continued. 'In the fight everybody's on edge so anything abnormal happens, then everybody piles in. That's just boxing. That's how it goes unfortunately.'

Joshua was equally sanguine about the affair in the aftermath of the fight, reflecting that in times like this the 'Dillian Whyte that wants a scrap comes out'.

'It's only Dillian. It's the same stuff I deal with all the time,' Joshua continued. 'That's fighting, isn't it? It's not like this is golf. This is fighting.

'It's what you've got to expect, you've got real bad blood on the line and stuff like that happens in the ring. Security done a great job of calming it down, get each of us back to our corners and continue the fight.

'I was thinking it could kick off. But that's the passion,' he went on. Becoming British champion was forgotten. 'It was more about bragging rights and who's the man.'

Personally, I was thinking surely, after a ring invasion, that the fight had to be called off. Eddie Hearn saw a disaster at first before he swiftly calculated just how lucrative a controversial rematch could be. 'I've never seen anything like it. I was sat there thinking, "What is this? WWE?"' he grinned. 'Can you imagine the rematch numbers if it was a no-contest after a brawl in the first round?'

But eventually the bell clanged once again. They went out for the second round. That's when everything changed. Joshua tried to continue this session in the same vein as he had conducted the first round, but Whyte struck his left hook into his opponent's attack. The shot hit Anthony's chin clean. It staggered him, loosening his arms. For a moment Joshua's defence fell away. Whyte was now in the ascendancy; he heaved his fists furiously at Joshua, trapping the big man in a neutral corner.

'Just cool, ride shots, slip shots, hit back, hold,' he thought. 'Some people get sparked out at that stage because they haven't been taught these fundamental things in the ring.

'Keep my composure, just get through this round and rest. So same mentality in the gym, same mentality I took into the ring and that's just down to good coaching.'

The danger for Joshua was real. The crowd sensed it, you could hear the edge in their cheers and chants now, a thrilled note of anxiety in that communal voice. This wasn't the first crisis Joshua had to manage. In the amateurs Medzhidov and Cammarelle had both hit him hard, then, caught between caution and the urge to counter-attack, Joshua had allowed further punishing shots through. Now he drew a breath and drew his gloves back up, getting that guard back together. He stepped in close for a moment, too close for Whyte to connect, and then a moment later pulled himself away.

It could have been a crisis, especially after the mêlée at the end of the first round, with Joshua now having been hit, having been hurt amidst all the chaos. If Joshua lost now, the golden future that beckoned him would be snatched away.

Tony Sims kept his cool. He at least wasn't feeling the pressure. 'I've been a trainer for twenty years now. I can't even think how many corners I've done. I've done all Froch's fights for him. I've been involved in so many big fights,' he said. 'It's just my job now. The crowd, I don't think of the crowd any more. In the early days you'd have got nervous and wound up getting to the ring, same as the fighter. But it don't happen any more. Whether it's York Hall or the eighty thousand-seat stadium, it's just all the same boxing ring.'

Joshua had felt the punch. He was disrupted, stunned, ears ringing, eyes wide. Tony needed to steady his charge. So he slapped him. 'It didn't do him no good,' Sims shrugged. 'He was still, his eyes were like a deer's in the headlights. He just had one thing in his head and that was to go out and destroy him.

'It was a little bit hard because it was more a personal battle between them. So it was a little bit hard keeping him calm.'

'He slapped me a few times,' Joshua recalled, almost taken aback. 'I'm, like, Tony, I'm still a bit dazed, stop slapping me. He's like, "Josh, you've got enough power to hurt him but you need to box. You need to do what you do best."' Anthony repeated the same mantra to himself: 'You can make this an easy fight. Keep your head up and do what you do, because you're making it a harder fight.'

But, he reflected, 'At the same time this is why these fights are so explosive, this is why these fights have so much more build-up. No matter how much you train to be a boxer, when you've got someone you don't like in the other corner, you go to war. I had to clear the red mist and get back to being simple and doing what I do.'

In the third round Joshua had to calm his mind and get the reverberations of that power punch out of his head. But Whyte was looking increasingly dangerous. He sank a cruel left hook into Joshua's body. Those punches were heavy. Anthony touched him with the jab, trying to rediscover his range. Both kept busy, punching at a high volume for such big men. Heavyweights aren't normally so active. A left-right from Joshua obliged Whyte to back off for a moment, but at once Whyte bounded forwards, in close, hacking punches at Joshua's trunk.

He barrelled in behind a big right. A backhand hook collided with Whyte. He in turn swept a right uppercut at Joshua, catching him with the shot. Joshua slugged back, but Whyte took it. Joshua aimed a one-two at him. A right did slam in flush. Joshua repeated the same shot but Whyte bounced off the back foot to go forward once again. He still didn't want to yield an inch of ground. Joshua had to work for every forward step he gained. He pushed himself out to the centre of the ring, looking to stake his claim to the territory. Hold the centre and he could dictate a fight like this. Anthony's left hook began to creep round Whyte's guard. Those shots, coming round the side, initially from outside Whyte's field of vision, would prove crucial.

In the fifth round Joshua maintained his efforts to repel Whyte, not simply looking to brawl, instead using long, straight shots to establish a gap between them. He jabbed Whyte's body, to strike his right to the head. Those jarring blows must have hurt Whyte, but the proud Londoner gave no such indication. He answered a cross with a cross of his own. Another shuddering Joshua left hook opened the path for his right. They glared at each other as the bell rang to call them off, but their ferocity was contained now within the rules and strictures of the sport.

Joshua came on still in the sixth round. Whyte targeted diligent hooks at his body. Joshua had to suck in air against them. Whyte looked to intercept him, leading off with his jab. Joshua powered in with his left hook. He shrugged off another right that Whyte slugged across. That left hook set up another of Anthony's increasingly effective crosses. All these hits chipped away at Whyte's uncanny reserves. Joshua grew confident, perhaps overconfident. As he warmed to his task a smile stretched across his face, and his hands began to drift ominously lower. But easily he popped in his right.

Joshua was taking his moment to talk to Whyte now. 'I just told him, when he was doing certain things, that's not good enough to beat me. It's funny. I just enjoy boxing, that's all. So I just talked to him in the ring.' For Whyte, if he did register this, it must have been maddening.

The bell ended the session, each wanted to walk through the other to get back to their own corners. Mr Foster had to move in deftly to guide them apart.

At the start of the seventh round they touched gloves, a momentary gesture of respect almost entirely at odds with the whole character of this confrontation. Joshua, though, resumed his work with gusto. For the most part he had been sending his backhand straight through the middle. He turned it in suddenly as a right hook. The shot hurt Whyte badly. He wobbled away, under enormous pressure at once. Another thunderous right hook blazed across. It left Whyte shaken but, clinging to the last remnants of that stubborn resilience, he would not fall. He had only his gutsy defiance keeping him upright, until an uppercut from hell plucked him off his feet. That shot, now honed, cut through, catching Whyte beneath the chin with such force that it lifted the 245-pound heavyweight clean off the canvas and flung him down heavily into the ropes. He was out cold, on the seat of his shorts, caught up in the rigging, his right arm twisted unnaturally over the lower rope, pinning him there. Whyte was groggy, trying to look around, trying to look out. But unmoving, his eyes dull and glassy, he was not getting up.

The score was settled. The fight was over.

Fallen Champions

Even as Whyte lay back, caught up in the ropes, Joshua roared in triumph. It's customary to wait for a fallen opponent to recover before celebrating, but now his mood switched from fury to sheer joy. It was a mental release as he bellowed, exulting, to his crowd. Attempting to rise, Whyte stumbled heavily down, hitting the deck a second time before he was helped on to a stool. Joshua had no thought of restraint, shrugging off even the general secretary of the British Boxing Board of Control. He leapt on to all four corner posts, answering the shouts of the crowd, springing his 245-pound bulk up on to the ropes. He angrily waved away Whyte's knot of supporters, savouring the raw adrenalin of the moment. He'd given the thousands in attendance the knockout they craved. He hadn't been as demonstrative when he'd won the Olympic gold medal. The crowd erupted all around him and he echoed their cheers.

Eventually Joshua returned to the centre of the ring. His team gathered round as he claimed the Lonsdale Belt, among them his father, beaming with unmistakable pride at seeing his son become the British heavyweight champion.

This was the first defeat Joshua had avenged. It was a weight off him and, pumped up, his celebrations in the ring had been clear for all to see. Sitting back in a side room an hour later for his media audience, those passions had cooled. 'I don't really do that stuff but I was happy. That's what I mean, it came out,' he said. Joshua was the new British heavyweight champion but he'd remember this night for what it meant to him personally. It had been his most emotional fight.

'I think more the fact that it was more about bragging rights, there was a lot of talking, all the way back since 2009. We were waiting patiently for this moment and I just enjoyed being victorious and showing that talk is cheap. You've got to back it up when you're in that ring.'

The brawling side of his character had been drawn out. 'I was working around with the left hook a lot of the time and trying to throw Mike Tyson hooks. But when I started boxing a bit more, and I started coming round the right side, that's when I caught him with a few more shots and that's why I worked more with the overhand right,' he said. 'Anyone at heavyweight can knock someone out. Dillian can take a shot. He was taking a lot of shots. But sooner or later you can keep on chipping away and then it's the first one to switch off. Every heavyweight from elite level down to novice is going to have knockouts on their records and I've always said it. It's not about "I can take a shot". It's just if I take stupid shots I'll get knocked out and that's why I had to regroup and get myself together. It's about skill.'

However, it wasn't as though this contest had soothed the animosity between them. Neither shook hands, let alone embraced afterwards. 'My life and my career doesn't revolve around him,' Whyte would gruffly maintain. Then he added, 'But I definitely want to fight him again. And bust his head.'

Joshua admitted, 'I'm a cool person but he can throw that off because I want to hurt him, get him out of there. He's the perfect fighter for me, someone who can give me what I need.'

Speaking to me later, Tony Sims saw a lesson for Joshua there. 'I don't think he'll become emotionally tagged into anything again. So that was a brilliant thing that happened to him early in his career because he's now going to fight people who are going to antagonise him. Say he fights Deontay Wilder, say he fights Fury; I don't think he'll ever be like that again. He won't emotionally attach himself to that again. That was a different thing for him there,' his cornerman said. 'With him it was more calming him down and getting on his boxing. After a couple of rounds, got caught in one of the rounds as well, he was piling in, pressuring all the time, got caught. I think it livened him up a bit. Once he started boxing he calmed himself down a bit. Once he got on his boxing it was like a no-contest, do you know what I mean? The first couple of rounds was mayhem but it was just about calming him down.'

Risks in boxing can be controlled. But not all of them, not all the time. There were always dangers lurking in the professional sport. Luke Campbell, Anthony's Olympic team-mate and fellow London 2012 gold medallist, had been on the same card at the O2, before Joshua's grudge match with Whyte. Campbell was a vastly more experienced amateur. He'd become the first Englishman to win the European Championships in forty-seven years all the way back in 2008, when Joshua himself was just getting into the sport. Like Joshua, Campbell had won World silver and Olympic gold medals, making him at that time the most decorated amateur in British boxing history. He looked more complete as a professional, turning over with those sharp, slick amateur skills but adding the power to take opponents out. The London 2012 side was Britain's most successful Olympic team of the modern era, and Campbell looked to be the best of the bunch.

I have almost complete faith in Luke Campbell. You would, too, if you'd seen some of the battles he'd won in the GB vest. But a slight doubt first crept into my mind at the weigh-in the day before this fight. Campbell looked fine on the scales, trim at the weight. He'd been matched against Yvan Mendy, a French fighter with a solid record, a failed European title challenger with few losses on his résumé. He was nevertheless the kind of opponent someone with Campbell's talent was expected to beat. Yet standing on the scales Mendy looked carved from solid muscle. It sowed a nagging thought in my mind, that Luke would have a real fight on his hands.

I still believed Campbell would be able to contain the Frenchman, but on the night he was not punching with his customary authority. He rushed himself, throwing clusters of quick, light punches. Mendy, the seasoned pro, could cover up, tough enough to let those shots bounce off him. It meant that he could himself counter the counter-puncher, ripping in left hooks, and Campbell, increasingly overanxious, worked forward, working himself on to those punches. The weight of Mendy's left even deposited Campbell on the canvas. In all the years of watching his amateur career that was something I had never seen before. But Campbell showed his true grit. He clambered up and threw himself back into the fray but he couldn't recover his position on the scorecards. He lost a split decision, his first professional defeat. In professional boxing so much is predictable, so often the opponents in the away corner are doomed to lose. But this sport could still be a theatre of the unexpected. The defeat would set Campbell back a year. He would go abroad to seek out a new coach, putting on hold his world title ambitions as he rebuilt and worked his way back up the rankings.

It was a shock for Joshua to see Luke Campbell beaten, so soon before he himself had to go out to face the crowd and his old rival. If Campbell could lose, anyone could. Joshua knew first-hand just how good Campbell was. 'Luke Campbell's the best British fighter that we've ever had,' Anthony said, recalling Campbell's exploits for the GB team. 'It shows that as a pro you can't just go from amateur level and turn pro and just shoot your way up to the top of the ladder. Luke will still go on to do great things but he just needs a bit more experience before he gets to certain levels. That's what I'm trying to say; it's good that I've got the potential but I really need to keep on grafting in order to get there the right way. I learned a lot from Luke's mistake tonight.

'It can happen to anyone. You've just got to keep on pushing. It's all good for me right now, everyone's applauding me, but I've got to keep my feet on the ground and understand any time it could change. I've just got to keep on working hard to try and keep it a smooth road to the top.'

Personally, that was a surprise to Joshua, but professionally he had to turn his attention to the global developments in his own weight class. A major shock had torn through the heavyweight division like a cyclone, spinning out world titles, altering reputations, all ushered in by boxing's king of chaos, Tyson Fury.

Wladimir Klitschko had ruled the heavyweight division since Joshua had first taken up the sport. His dominance had become indisputable. It had been years since he was in an exciting fight, such was the control he exerted. I first saw Klitschko ringside in 2010, the first heavyweight world title fight I attended. He was having a rematch with Samuel Peter. The heavy-handed Nigerian might not have been the reincarnation of George Foreman that some thought he could have turned out to be, but nevertheless five years earlier he had managed to drop Klitschko three times as the latter outpointed him to complete a rickety return to world level. In 2010 the Ukrainian was the holder of two world title belts and he gave Peter a punishing reminder that his command of the heavyweight division was not to be challenged. In Frankfurt to see Klitschko perform, for my first foreign assignment for *Boxing News*, he seemed to me to be at the peak of his powers. He had broken his boxing down into its essential elements. He made it look simple. Klitschko measured Peter out with his thudding jab. It stopped the Nigerian in his tracks. So much taller than most, Klitschko had mastered the art of just taking a step back, sliding out of distance from his opponent, but still able to hammer in that range-finding left. He used that lead to tame Samuel, beat the resistance out of him before bringing in a battering-ram right cross. Beginning to do damage, he slowly built up his work, adding in his hook now, bringing it round the side, striking in when he saw the openings, wasting nothing. He had Peter reeling, like a bull exhausted by the strikes from its picadors. Then and only then did Klitschko press his advantage. He strode forward, punches crashing in on the inside now to finish Peter with a right uppercut that levelled him with a crushing finality. The word that came to mind, that headlined my cover story in that week's issue of *Boxing News*, was 'invincible'. It was hard to see a flaw in the methodical, merciless approach exercised by the heavyweight king.

For so polite a man, Klitschko was intimidating. Outside the ring he was the model of what a champion could be. He'd conduct a press conference in three languages, German, English and Ukrainian. He cut an impressive figure. My first major interview with a star name for *Boxing News* was an hour-long audience with him in a hotel suite in Cologne. It was a marvellous experience as the champ discussed his inspirations, fighting, relived the Orange Revolution in Ukraine, a mesmerising tale. (It's just a shame that, since my Dictaphone failed to operate, it would be a story that only I would hear.) Indeed, so mesmerised was I that as I reached to shake his hand and thank him for all his time, I didn't realise he was holding out his first to be bumped (Wlad, it turns out, is a fist bumper rather than a hand shaker). In slow motion I watched, aghast, as I reached out my hand inch by inch as if all of its own accord it was going to shake his fist. I did manage to save it at the last moment and turn it into a fist bump. If I was unnerved just saying goodbye, imagine how disconcerting it would be having to face Klitschko in the ring. He was built like few heavyweights before, the breadth of his shoulders heightened by the cut of the scarlet robe he wore into the ring. A light show and an elaborate entrance always ushered him into an arena. He could fill a stadium with supporters almost regardless of the opponent. What he did between the ropes might have looked straightforward enough, but it was far more difficult to deal with in practice. His latest reign at the top of the heavyweight division would continue uninterrupted for eleven years, so far ahead of the chasing pack was he.

In 2015 the familiar Klitschko light show flickered across my jetlagged vision as his entrance music, the strains of the Red Hot Chili Peppers' 'Can't Stop' blared out at ear-splitting volume. The heavyweight champion had returned to America, boxing at New York's Madison Square Garden, a historic venue in the sport that had hosted the Fight of the Century between Muhammad Ali and Joe Frazier and many more legendary nights. A huge crowd had turned out to see the champion, who had now unified three of the major titles. The Ukrainian diaspora, with flags waving, were there in force, packing out the Garden. An immense roar greeted the arrival of Klitschko. Back in the United States for the first time in seven years he was taking on Bryant Jennings, a rugged American from Philadelphia who was by far the cruder fighter when you compared his abilities to the more refined skills of Wladimir Klitschko. At least they should have been. Klitschko, I thought, ought to have been able to walk through him. But Jennings didn't follow the script. He shouldn't have been able to get close to the great Ukrainian. Instead, he bounded underneath Klitschko's punches, eluding his long straight shots, stepping into clinches. The champion couldn't repel him on the inside, a sight that had once been so familiar. He didn't blast Jennings out as I'd expected, although the American could by no means wrestle a decision away from the Ukrainian. Klitschko won clearly enough on points but the cracks in his iron command were starting to appear. The heavyweight division, I thought, was about to get very interesting indeed.

Not that I was expecting Tyson Fury, of all people, to be the man to topple Klitschko. A lot had happened in the six years since Anthony Joshua and Fury had sparred. Fury, a brash Traveller, was unbeaten in twenty-four fights, even though admittedly some had hardly gone smoothly. Heavy overarm right crosses had dropped him in a couple of his previous contests, just the kind of shot Klitschko deployed so well. Fury, who proclaimed himself the 'Gypsy King', was tall, even taller than Klitschko, and he moved well for such a big man. He could at times look ungainly – a six foot nine man can do so when he's moving at a certain pace. His hands were good, he appeared increasingly to be punching his weight. He had skills reminiscent of the bareknuckle boxers of old.

Fury had worked his way up the rankings until he was Klitschko's mandatory challenger. The champion was no stranger to the odd soft touch but he was committed to the three world title belts he held and serious about defending them. It might sometimes have taken him plenty of time to get round to them, but in the end he always met his mandatory obligations. After a lengthy period of wrangling, the Fury fight was eventually made for Düsseldorf in Germany. In the build-up Fury unleashed the full force of his madcap persona. Their first announcement press conference, at a Hilton hotel in a quiet park near Twickenham, was not the sombre affair Klitschko perhaps expected. Fury kept the champion waiting. And then, with his own sound system, played himself in with the classic Batman theme tune, Fury, in full Batman costume, burst into the press conference hall. With his cape flapping behind him he charged round the hall full of journalists and television cameras, performing a quasi-victory lap before taking his seat at the tables on a raised platform. Alongside him Klitschko smiled tightly. He tried to resume the press conference with his customary dignity but Fury would not permit that. Another costumed figure appeared in the doorway. It was Fury's cousin, Hughie, a rising heavyweight prospect himself, dressed as The Joker. He approached the top table, muttering whatever line he had been instructed to reel off. Fury elected to fling himself over the table, not even noticing that in doing so he knocked Klitschko's three world title belts to the ground, and wrestled The Joker to the floor. They rolled over the title belts before barrelling into the bank of cameramen until the two of them fetched up at my feet. It was a stroke of good fortune that I'd elected to sit in the second row. 'At least I got to touch them,' Hughie laughed afterwards about landing on the world title belts.

The two made off and eventually Fury, now in a suit and sweating slightly, returned to the room. He apologised for being late and asked what had happened before denying all knowledge of any Batman sightings. That is the kind of mayhem Fury, if he had half a mind to do so, could unleash.

Klitschko insisted coldly that Fury was entertaining. But he cared little for the challenger's behaviour. The champion did want to teach the upstart a lesson. Klitschko, however, postponed their fight for a month after sustaining a slight calf injury. Fury's team crowed that they'd rattled him, that Klitschko was buying more time to prepare for this challenger. The champion did expect to be in control, even if Fury was not the type of man to be tamed.

But eventually, in November 2015, Tyson Fury and his team descended on Düsseldorf. It would be a surreal week. At a public workout a few days before the fight Fury took up a microphone and decided to serenade the champion. No one had approached Klitschko in such an insolent manner before. In the remaining few days the rival camps argued about the gloves that would be used in the contest. In boxing pretty much everything is up for debate. On the day of the fight itself Fury's trainer inspected the ring canvas and objected to it that afternoon, threatening that they'd all walk. They might not have operated at this level before but they were fighting their corner in spite of the mind games beyond the ropes. Eventually they forced the Klitschko group to remove a layer of padded foam that had been placed under the canvas. Fury for his part seemed to let all this drift over him, unaffected, at ease amid the disorder.

On the night Fury took his time in arriving. He walked slowly to the ring. In fact, he didn't seem at all fired up. But he began the first round boxing easily, not overawed at all. He was almost unconcerned. Fury was even winning the early rounds. With scarcely credible insouciance, he began to showboat as he got his punches off. Roy Jones-style, he held his hands behind his back. Daring to do that in the face of Klitschko was unbelievable. The champion himself couldn't grasp it. He couldn't seem to catch up to Fury. As Fury moved off, Klitschko could not land his jab. Without using that lead to measure out his opponent he barely threw his right hand. Klitschko was going forward but he was not connecting. The Traveller was weaving his magic over him. Few punches were thrown, but he was shading it as the rounds progressed. Fury did not apply huge pressure to Klitschko but occasionally he cantered forward, landing single shots that disrupted the champion. Klitschko did not react well to the hits.

Yet he was on his feet at the final bell. Bleeding from a wound beneath his right eye, Klitschko cut a tired figure. This was in Germany, a land not known for fair decisions, and the popular Ukrainian had been the one moving forward, arguably more aggressive in that sense. But Fury had been the more effective of the two and the decision, rightly, went his way. Klitschko was stunned. Most of the 50,000-strong audience were stunned. But Fury's supporters close to ringside erupted. His team leapt through the ropes to celebrate. Fury snatched the microphone from the ring announcer and, with no musical accompaniment and in the singular tones of someone out for karaoke on a Saturday night, turned to his wife and belted out Aerosmith's 'I Don't Want To Miss A Thing'. A final, surreal moment to end a week of surprises was entirely appropriate. Fury, unpredictable, maverick, infuriating, was the new heavyweight champion of the world.

That was the high point. The picture quickly became vastly more complicated. Ahead of the fight Fury had spoken of how the highs of previous fight nights often quickly gave way to bitter lows. The triumph, as soon as he had it, was slipping from his grasp. Even in the post-fight press conference he was already beginning to look agitated, frustrated.

On his return to England Fury perhaps expected to be celebrated. But his weird knack for issuing sometimes deeply offensive statements had been neither forgotten nor forgiven. In some corners of the press he was vilified. More troubling for his boxing career, he seemed increasingly uninterested in the sport. Klitschko for his part was left hurt but determined to rediscover his old self. 'It woke me up,' he said.

Fury's contract with Klitschko had a rematch clause, which

the Ukrainian decided to execute. That meant Fury had to box him a second time, a useful enough showdown for the new champion to prove the first victory had been no fluke. But it meant he could not meet the mandatory challenger, Vyacheslav Glazkov, for one of the three world title belts he had so recently won. Hastily the IBF stripped the Englishman of their title.

That was a disappointment for him, though Fury professed to being unbothered. But it took a long time to negotiate the rematch. Eventually it was set for July in Manchester, essentially Fury's home turf. It should have been the chance for the Englishman to celebrate a homecoming. They held a press conference at the Manchester Arena. The new champion didn't summon up quite the same madcap enthusiasm of his appearance as the caped crusader, even though he went through the motions of mockery. He danced next to Klitschko, the latter clearly ill at ease alongside his antagonist. But Fury's antipathy to the press, to the duties of the heavyweight champion of the world, was soon apparent. It tinged the event with a sombre sadness. Fury leaned on the desk in front of him, sullenly gazing out at the cameras and journalists arrayed on the seats in front of him. 'I'm like a performing monkey, aren't I?' he reflected morosely. 'Every single press conference, every single press event, every single time I'm on the camera, music plays, silent music and Tyson Fury performs. Like one of those snakes in India going round like that to the music or a dancing monkey.

'Because every single time I play at being the bad guy, the villain, the outlaw, the outcast, person who don't care, every single media event and all that. So it is what it is. People obviously like to see that. Some people don't like it but the majority of them do.'

He seemed utterly ambivalent about the sport and his career. 'I hate every second of it and I wish I wasn't a boxer but I'm in this position and I'm going to do it. I hate every second of training, I hate the boxing, I hate the lot. I hate speaking to all you idiots. I hate the lot. I don't want to be here. I'd rather be at home with the kids watching television. I'd rather be at home eating some chocolate and eating some sweets than be here talking about boxing. I hate boxing, put it that way, but I'm just too fucking good at it to stop and I'm making too much money.'

If boxing fans expected a champion to be packed with solid muscle like Anthony Joshua or to embrace his public profile, Fury greeted them with something very different. 'I don't live a strict lifestyle. I don't even live an athlete's lifestyle. It's an absolute disgrace to call me an athlete. You couldn't call me an athlete,' he declared.

After explaining how he'd eaten every pie in Lancashire and drunk every pint in Britain, his mood swung to the opposite extreme as he rounded on Klitschko to gleefully declare that a fat man had beaten him. Suddenly Fury leapt to his feet, tore off his shirt and let his voluminous belly protrude over his belt line. 'What's the point of practising your job for forty years if you can't beat a fat man?' he cackled.

Yet that fight did not come to pass. Fury postponed it after an ankle injury. Shortly after, he reappeared in France, buying Jägerbombs for English football fans at Euro 2016, which may have burnished his credentials as the ultimate lad but set a worrying tone for his championship reign. An allegation surfaced that Fury had failed a drug test for a performance enhancing substance. A UK Anti-Doping panel said he would have to go before a hearing but did not ban him from the sport. The rematch with Klitschko was still rescheduled. But with a date nailed down for it, Fury withdrew due to medical issues, with concern about his mental health now widespread. To add a further level of complexity to the murky situation, the Voluntary Anti-Doping Association, who had been employed to regulate the rescheduled rematch with Klitschko, accused Fury of testing positive for a recreational drug, cocaine.

In order to concentrate on his own health Fury relinquished his two remaining heavyweight titles, the WBO and WBA belts, without a fight. Beset by issues, it was a tortured end to his title reign. For some being the heavyweight champion of the world is a burden, rather than a blessing. It's not easy being king.

Let's Roll

The spectre of drugs haunted boxing. It is unacceptable in all sports to dope, to take illicit performance-enhancing substances. But in boxing it is a real crime. This is a dangerous sport. People can be hurt. The rules must be adhered to. There are weight classes for a reason, for safety. A drugged-up boxer going up against a clean fighter: it's as bad as if he 'loaded' his gloves. It was a grim element in the sometimes lawless world of professional boxing.

A worldwide, coordinated strategy was needed to tackle the problem. Cheats needed to be caught and subjected to sanctions that were actually punishing. Instead in this fragmented sport each outpost of order had to regulate itself. At least in England the British Boxing Board of Control could work closely with UK Anti-Doping. Anthony Joshua would enrol in a special testing programme which was all year round, just like the anti-doping scrutiny GB's Olympic boxers had. On this count it is important to have such a high-profile athlete setting a good example.

Joshua explained some of the detail. 'You have to let them

know in advance every three months where you're going to be sleeping and where you're going to be training or what you're going to be doing, and then you have to give them a one-hour slot each night or each morning where you're going to be so they can randomly turn up within the hour,' he said. 'You can change, you're allowed to change where you're going but they have to know exactly where you're going to be.

'If I forget, it's on me, I get a strike. I think it's two strikes then you get a ban. It's another job in itself keeping on top of that.'

But he was fine with it. He wanted to see real bans for drug cheats. 'It is a problem,' Joshua maintained. It wasn't right. It had to be a fair fight. Or it ought to be. 'You've got ten weeks to prepare yourself in the best way possible,' Anthony continued. 'When the ref gets together, says, "Touch gloves, I want a clean fight," you want the best man to win because he's trained hard not because he's given himself an unfair advantage.'

The hard work should be rewarded, not gaming the system. That was the morality of training. 'Some people do make general mistakes, but you can't put everyone in one box. I think it should have a board, a court system where they judge each person individually and make a decision. If there is anything that is giving you general advantages over your opponent, a hundred per cent you should be banned for life.'

Rightly so. This was too dangerous a game. In 2016 the sport saw too many accidents. In March Nick Blackwell was gravely injured in a high-profile bout against Chris Eubank Jr. Blackwell suffered a bleed on the skull and was placed in an induced coma. He survived but was never able to box again. Horribly, months later Nick began to spar in secret. It put him in hospital. He should have known the cost, he must have known, after coming so close to the brink. It was a frightening hold that boxing had over him, which Blackwell, inexplicably, hadn't been able to resist. It marked a dark period for the sport. In the same year a Scottish boxer, Mike Towell, tragically died. Such events in boxing are thankfully rare. But they cannot be ignored. There are rewards; indeed, for a boxer in Anthony Joshua's position those rewards can be great. The risks, however, are real.

Anthony had no interest in making a wrong move. 'You just have to be very appreciative of what's on offer and what you get from them and be very smart,' he said. 'It's not like other sports, like football. That's what I'm saying. It's not glitz. You've got to do what's right and make very, very savvy decisions because it doesn't last forever, and even as you plan, what, I've planned another ten years in the game, that's like at best, who knows how short it will be cut? These fighters get their careers cut short three years in, just at the start. It's tough, it's not all glitz and glamour. It doesn't put me off but I just make sure while I'm here to try and make good decisions.'

Those close to him had a vision of where they wanted him to be eventually, how he might be set up for his life after boxing. But he himself didn't want to dwell too much on what lay beyond his fighting days. 'It's easy to drift away and say I want to be some entrepreneur or someone's called me with this great idea,' he mused. 'I said, you know what, forget all that.'

He'd keep himself rooted in the fight. 'Everyone loses a bit of focus some time,' he said, but added, 'I said, you know what, just get my mind straight back in this boxing.

'That's it, just back to focus.'

Joshua had every reason to concentrate his thoughts. His burgeoning fame, his ability to sell a fight as a pay-per-view off his own name alone, made him a desirable target. With half a million tuning into Sky Sports Box Office, factoring in the gate and sponsorship an Anthony Joshua fight could generate something in the region of £15 million – before, that is, the money was parcelled out to the broadcaster, promoter as well as all the fighters on the card. But that kind of heft would draw champions and their titles to him.

The IBF had swiftly stripped their heavyweight world championship from Tyson Fury when, due to his commitment to rematching Klitschko, he could not meet their mandated challenger, a little known Ukrainian. By January 2016 Vyacheslav Glazkov was already boxing America's Charles Martin for the now vacant IBF world title belt. It was a curious event. Martin, a hefty southpaw who had been working his way dutifully through the professional ranks, seemed to be gaining some measure of control in the opening couple of rounds. He was the bigger man and his punches carried a greater weight. Whether Glazkov would eventually be able to work him out was soon rendered moot. A shot from Martin might have grazed Vyacheslav but, regardless of that, the Ukrainian's knee gave way beneath him. He collapsed. He could not continue on one leg and just like that, inside three rounds, Charles Martin was a world champion.

'It didn't even get time to unravel before it was already done for. I really don't want to touch upon that because I was disappointed in how it went down and how it went out. If anything, even if that had happened to me, I would have went out on my shield, I would have went out swinging,' Martin railed. 'If you're in there for an IBF, I would have went out swinging. That wasn't his heart, that wasn't his mentality so it ended the way it did unfortunately. But the belt is in the right hands and Charles Martin is the IBF heavyweight champion and we're going to keep it that way.'

His ascension to the title, though, was not conclusive. What kind of a champion Martin would be was not clear. We knew little about him. He had not fought anyone of note until Glazkov. He had halted a worn Tom Dallas, on the Klitschko–Jennings undercard at Madison Square Garden. But for a fight that Martin had ended in one round, it had been a strangely unexplosive performance. Instead of a clean demolition, the kind of finish in fact increasingly expected of Anthony Joshua, Martin, swinging languid punches, had eventually clobbered Dallas who wilted inexorably into the ropes. It could well have been a lot worse for Dallas if he'd been in against a more devastating contender. Martin did have an opponent in common with Joshua – Raphael Zumbano Love. Martin had knocked him out in ten rounds, Joshua in only two.

When Martin's fellow American Deontay Wilder had won his world title, the WBC version, he still took low-key fights in the USA as defences. Wilder's team wanted to continue to develop him. Would Martin take a similar route? Or did he want to go big and go quickly?

He made his choice apparent soon enough. Martin had no wish to wait around. They had seen the kind of numbers and the kind of cash Anthony was generating in Britain and they wanted in on that action. His emissaries enquired about making a world title fight with Joshua. Staying put and taking a few easy defences to mark time and eke out a few more paydays didn't appeal to Martin. 'That isn't what I wanted. I don't want to be in the sport forever fighting,' he told me. 'So I'm going to take all these guys out while I'm here. There's a hype job around Anthony Joshua.'

Injecting an edge of personal animus, the American continued, 'They treat him like he is more special than what he really is here, because that's like their golden child out here. They're going to put a lot of hype around him.

'I see different.'

For Joshua the opportunity was there to fight Charles Martin for the IBF heavyweight title. But stepping straight up to world level was not a simple call. Anthony had only had fifteen professional contests. He'd only entered thirty-two competitive rounds in his whole pro career to date. Tyson Fury, for example, had boxed 132 professional rounds before he went in with Wladimir Klitschko. Not that Martin was the most fearsome operator in the division, far from it. Indeed, it was hard to tell how good the American was at all. But if Joshua started competing for world titles, and especially if he won, there was no going back. It would catapult him into championship class, when he hadn't had the customary grounding in the professional game. His amateur career had been breathtakingly accelerated. If he went too far, too fast as a professional he could be left without the necessary experience, the necessary foundation for the higher level. It gave Joshua's whole team pause for thought.

Anthony wasn't expecting a world title fight to be an option so soon. 'You don't really think it's possible because of the stage you're at,' he thought. 'The great thing about it is it's an opportunity. Whether we want it or not.'

There were other options, defending his British title, for instance, going for the European belt or even chalking up a couple more wins against contender-level opposition. Ultimately, though, it was Joshua's call. His promoter Eddie Hearn didn't want to let this window of opportunity close. Eventually he sent a message to Joshua, asking for his decision. He replied. The text simply read 'Let's roll'. And, like that, the fight was on.

'That's how simple it is,' Anthony said. 'I've got an opportunity. I just need to turn it into reality now. You know how boxing is. You take fights you're capable of winning, you feel you're going to win. You have to be confident.

'Take the reward away, look at the opponent. I feel I'm capable of doing a job on Martin and with that comes the heavyweight championship of the world.'

That, though, would put him into a wholly new situation. That belt would lead inexorably to fights with the likes of Fury, Klitschko, Deontay Wilder. The world class. 'It was kind of going in that direction at some stage anyway. It just fast-tracks these type of fights,' he said. If he could get through Martin, that would truly put him into the big league. 'There's no hiding,' he confirmed. 'We know what we're getting ourselves into and we know what's going to come after. We're looking forward to another explosive year.'

The Unknown

Joshua would increasingly have to get used to backhanded insults. 'He's beatable to me, so that's why I chose him. Personally I think he's too smart for his own good,' Charles Martin confided to me.

It was a curious kind of jibe, but I could see what Martin was trying to say, in a way. In boxing, in the heat of action, you can't afford to overthink things. Sometimes you don't have the luxury of analysing your options for too long. Taking a second to decide what to do can be a second too long. Sometimes you simply have to react. Other times you can't think, you just do.

'You want to just react. Just all round, overall type of deal. Study long, you study wrong. He's just too smart, too smart for his own good,' Martin added, somewhat unconvincingly.

We spoke in the lobby of London's plush Landmark Hotel. He'd flown over to seal the fight, perform his media obligations and, for the first time, come face-to-face with Anthony Joshua. Maybe it was jetlag, or general disgruntlement, but his eyes narrowed as he talked. He tried to stare down Joshua when the two did their head-to-head. Looking up at Anthony's implacable gaze, Martin rocked curiously from side to side, muttering soft threats to himself, to Joshua, as the cameramen took their shots.

'He just called me a bitch, he was going to knock me out. All that,' Anthony chuckled. 'Just said that he's going to show me what levels is about. The kind of stuff I normally say to my opponents,' Joshua added with a laugh.

Joshua couldn't be sure what to expect from the American. But Martin at least carried himself like a champion. 'They're hungry, they don't waste time, they know what they want and they're going to get it by any means. That's what I see with Martin, the jewellery and everything like that. I think he may have come from a certain background. Now he's achieved heavyweight championship status that comes with certain rewards. He's enjoying that and I don't think he wants to let that go so soon. So he's game,' the Londoner observed. 'Becoming a champion does something to you. That's why I can't take him for the same man I saw months back. He's a champion now and that does something to your confidence and gives you a bit more fire in your heart. So I've got to be very careful, very wise and not make any mistakes because he's a counter-puncher. A counter-puncher is someone who capitalises on mistakes,' and Joshua concluded, 'he's a different level now.'

Not that any doubts had crept into Joshua's mind. 'Let's detach the championship belt away, that belongs to me, realistically, that's my destiny. He's just holding it. He's got it. But when we look at technical skills and that, I think I've got one up on him and that's why I think I can be victorious.'

For whatever Martin said about their relative levels of

intelligence, the ability to 'react' in boxing wasn't God-given. It was acquired. Through those hours of unremitting practice in the gym, Joshua was making the unnatural techniques of a boxer become second nature. That was skill.

However, he needed to make adjustments for the weeks of training ahead of him. 'This is serious,' Anthony reflected. 'It's only going to get bigger and better. It's serious business.' Martin, for instance, would be the first time Joshua as a professional had faced a southpaw. His promoter was hiring in southpaw sparring partners, given that Joshua's old GB colleagues, Joyce and Clarke, were orthodox boxers. Eddie Hearn promised, 'These guys are all world-ranked fighters, a couple of undefeated fighters. We're going to invest a lot of money in this camp because there's so much on the line.'

It would be a case of making and breaking habits. The last southpaw he'd boxed had been none other than Roberto Cammerelle in the Olympic final. And that had gone rather well. 'Being a southpaw never blessed you with an extra arm, an extra five inches on your reach. You've still got two hands, same heart, same feet and that's the same with me. I've just got to go in there with the same objective. Obviously there are still certain things you do to adjust but don't adjust what's been working. I've boxed southpaws before, I'm boxing Charles Martin, it's a boxing match. That's how I'm thinking,' he said.

The fight was made for April 2016, at the O2 once again. Joshua didn't intend to overhaul his approach to training, but if he was going to be competing at world level he would make this a world-class training camp. That meant taking everything up another notch of intensity, punishing himself just that little bit more cruelly. It was tough. It was repetitive. 'But I'd rather be a master of one than a master of none,' he shrugged. 'So where I've been doing repetitive stuff and it has been mind-boggling sometimes, I'm starting to perfect my style, my skill. I'm starting to understand myself more, rather than moving from gym to gym.'

In this way, four years on from the Olympic Games, Joshua had changed from the man he once had been. He had got through London 2012 without experience, making do on athleticism, raw, brute force sometimes. But he wanted to be more refined. That extended to his training practices. 'I was learning my trade and why I'm doing it. So this time around I understand why I'm here and what I've got to do. Before I didn't know what I had to do. I was just going through the motions, just learning my trade. Now I know my trade and I know what to do in order to improve it,' he explained. 'So it's the same situation, just with a better mindset.'

He could have been diverted. He could have made things easy for himself. Being a successful amateur boxer was no guarantee of professional success. Britain had had Olympic gold medallists before, but it took until 2015 for a GB Olympic champion to win a professional world title. That James DeGale was the only one who had managed it and that he, a superb talent, needed to go to America to achieve the feat, was an indication of the scale of the task. Joshua had had to tear up trees as an amateur, to go from a standing start, with absolutely no experience that is, to winning an Olympic gold medal in only four years. That was remarkable. Now, four years on, he was gunning for a professional championship. 'I've managed to phase out the bullshit and keep the good shit in order to produce what you see on fight night,' he said. 'So I've learned over time to just fizzle out the bullshit and focus on how I become the best athlete I can be. Whether that's British level, world title level or unification, I'm just trying to find my level, where I'm at and, who knows, I might just keep on going for a long time. We don't know where that stops, that's what's interesting about this journey at the minute. As you said, people are seeing the progression. From 2008 to now you can definitely see a progression. So it's interesting to see where we can go with it.'

Joshua had vaunting ambition, the kind of ambition he needed. He wasn't satisfied with his accolades or even the titles he'd won. He wanted appreciation for his qualities as a boxer, the skills that he had laboured so hard to acquire. That, at least, was where he wanted to be. He knew he was having to make up for lost time. But he thought of Vasyl Lomachenko, the lightweight gold medallist at London 2012 who was widely regarded as one of the best boxers in the world at any weight. He wanted to catch up with the likes of him. 'Lomachenko's phenomenal. I was thinking, why don't people say that about me. I'm serious. Because he's been in the game for a lot longer,' Joshua said. Unlike most elite fighters, he hadn't started boxing when he was a child. The span of his entire career, amateur and pro, was only a few years. 'From 2008 to '16, what's that? Eight years. Imagine I started at ten and went through everything and I'm eighteen now. By the time I'm twenty-six I would be talked of like Lomachenko. So by the time I'm thirty-two, thirty-four, and if I keep the same discipline, I'll go down as a Lomachenko. For me it hasn't been quick because I know the reality of my journey. I've still got eight years before I get to be one of the best fighters in the world. I'm not this style that everyone thinks I am or may think I am or they perceive me to be. I'm this hungry, grafting fighter that wants to prove himself still. I'm not at the top of the pecking order yet.

'So that's why I think they're ahead of their time. I'm not ahead of my time.'

Then he added, 'Sometimes it does get hard.'

Joshua had kept himself in a similar routine in camp since he'd been on the GB Olympic programme. His working day began at 7.15 a.m. sharp. He'd be out on the running track at 7.45 warming up. His cardio work was based around swimming, running or cycling. 'Back in the day it just used to be ten-mile runs. Times have changed,' he explained. 'It will be quite intense. Boxing's quite simple. Three minutes' work, one minute's rest. So if you can replicate that in your cardio sessions. So we work on that – those kind of rounds structure.'

That would be the first of three sessions in a day. At 11.30 a.m. he was in the weights room 'grinding, doing a lot of strength and conditioning, core work, sand drills to get your legs strong, anything to condition your body so, number one, you don't get injured, number two, you ain't going to get manhandled in the ring because in heavyweight boxing you need to have a bit of grit and a bit of strength about you'.

Late in the afternoon, at half past five, it was into the boxing hall. 'You warm up and then you've got to get ready for intense sparring. When you're with coaches who are taskmasters you have to make sure that your sparring is elite, is on point, so you just have to kind of make sure you're resting well, you're eating well so you've got the energy to perform when you're back in the gym. Because, even though you've done your running, your strength, your boxing, is the most important session of the day so you want to be fresh and you want to be able to perform. It's a really tough time because you've done two hard sessions but you still want to make sure you get your boxing right.'

He made additional tweaks. Normally he trained in large twenty-ounce boxing gloves. This time around he used the lighter ten-ounce gloves, just as he'd wear in the fight, for padwork and on the bags, to make sure on fight night there were no surprises, so that he was used to the tiny, comparatively hard gloves for battle.

The work fuelled his confidence. At each stage of this camp he was ahead of where he'd been last time around. He was building on his times, the weights he was lifting and rate of work put in. Physically he was on point and he'd been learning from his new sparring partners. 'Early on I was getting hit with the backhand a bit. I was thinking, this is going to be tricky. Now, two weeks later, defending it, slipping it, can counter, bang, bang, and that's what's helped me develop over the time. It's having key sparring partners over for the full duration of my camp,' he said. 'Just switching on to certain shots, that's all it is. They're no different but you're just unaware of certain shots and now I'm a bit more live to big hooks coming round that way, defend that and come back, defend the jab. At first it aches your arm a bit because they're always pawing so it aches my arm keeping it there solid. As camp's gone on it's got my muscle in there developed a lot more strong so I can keep it up, counter. It's really good. I'm happy with the progression over the last eight weeks.'

So active with his training, and so often in camp, he still lived with his mother when he was at home. 'Before I spend a ton of money on a big pad or something,' he joked. 'Property, it's a risky investment.' A sentiment all Londoners could empathise with no doubt. It was a mark, though, of a simple and singularly disciplined life and a family that had grown closer through boxing.

He descended on London for the pomp and circumstance of the events in the final days before the world title fight. He was full of vim and vigour. He was the star now. 'This is different, definitely. The Olympics was good but it feels like more because there were so many other sports. This is specifically boxing,' he said. 'That's what I think makes it a bit more interesting and the magnifying glass direct on me and Charles.

'This is just me and him.'

Joshua sat in a dingy side room up on the first floor of York Hall, the classic boxing venue in the East End of London. He had won his first ABA Championship here, he'd had his third professional fight here, but he was far too big a star now to compete here. Today, five days before his world title fight, he was merely performing a public workout, the kind of ceremony he'd carried out in shopping centres and even the plaza at Covent Garden to capture the attention of passing pedestrians and to entertain the hardcore supporters. But on this occasion it was different. A public workout, a session of skipping and cryptic padwork, was enough to fill out the hall. A queue of people wanting to see him stretched out down the pavement, extending out of sight down the street for this free appearance, which all served as clear evidence of Joshua's burgeoning popularity.

'Even walking out then, it gets you up a bit because you're

tucked away for so many weeks in training camp, so you don't really see much or do much. Your days off you're resting, then it comes out into all of the atmosphere, then it's "all right, cool, this is what it's all about". Everyone feels the pressure so he'll definitely feel a different pressure with that negative energy being chanted down on him.'

It's hard to read much into a public workout. The fighters aren't willing to give much away. Joshua, for instance, cracked some hefty punches into his padman's mitts, drawing a few cheery gasps from his audience as the impacts reverberated around the hall. But generally he was content to limber up and smile for the cameras without delving too deeply into his repertoire. And Martin, although he had been hired to be the villain for this occasion, didn't seem enamoured of a crowded room roundly booing him. He kept his workout brief, sidling round the ring shadowboxing, perhaps an indication that he planned to move, rather than trade with Joshua, in the fight. A sensible course of action, I would say.

But Martin was an unpredictable character. In some public appearances, he was almost quiet, keeping his own counsel. At their last press conference two days later, Martin elected not to stare Joshua out, looking instead into the big man's chest. Was that a hint of submission? Or was it pointless to try to interpret their mind games? Martin for his part claimed, 'I'm like an X-ray. I didn't see no heart in there. I know I'm going to catch him because I'm a southpaw, because I'm strong, because I'm tall, because I'm smart' – though not 'too smart' presumably – 'We got that jinx.' On television, in the full glare of the cameras, the American would abruptly declare that 'he walked this earth like a god' or bark 'I'm keeping that belt'. His temperament was unreadable. He insisted he was now calm and composed. He maintained, 'I used to be a hothead. I would get mad real easy. I'm going to say I was mad at the world, just a down individual, a loner type of thing, but it came sporadically.'

Now he warned, 'That anger that I have, I know how to direct it.'

He had good reason to be more content now, too, considering that for this payday his purse would be considerably larger than anything he had earned before. Strangely, when he had come to London a couple of weeks before the fight, he had to buy equipment, including new boots, for the big night, in the days before the title fight. Perhaps that was a sign of a relaxed mind. Or maybe it was a worrying indication of disorganisation for a heavyweight world champion.

Joshua couldn't be sure what Martin would say or do next, or how he'd approach the fight itself. And fighters do not like unpredictability. Take Klitschko versus Fury as a case in point.

'You've got to be careful with someone like that,' Joshua warned. 'I don't know what his game plan is . . . He's not really an explosive fighter but he might come quick. He don't want to be in there long with someone that can knock him out. It's a dangerous place to be for twelve rounds.'

'Very strange character,' he continued. 'Just out of the blue he says things randomly. I don't know whether it's nerves. It is a big occasion, you can't deny it. The UK scene is big now, you know what I mean. I think that may be the nerves where he says certain things. But that makes a dangerous person because they come out and do reckless things. Unpredictable things.'

Martin was adamant about one thing. 'This is self-pride. I ain't going to let that man embarrass me,' he swore.

They confronted each other again the afternoon before the fight. The weigh-in was set up on a stage in the concourse at the O2. A crowd flocked round the bank of cameras, their cheers lost beneath the high dome of the roof far overhead. Martin spoke of pride but he looked nervy at the weigh-in, shifting from side to side. Jumpy maybe, or perhaps primed and ready to fight there and then.

'I can only look how I look,' Joshua said. 'So I just stand up, brace myself and just say this is it now, soul to soul, eye to eye. It's the last time I see him before we step in the ring.'

Martin could not boast the same physical definition as Joshua. He was a single pound heavier than Anthony at 245 pounds but physically he was not as imposing. He had drafted in a new conditioning coach for this fight, but strength is not the kind of thing a boxer can cram in, trying to get up to speed at the last minute. He needs to put that work in over years. That's what Joshua had been doing.

Joshua hopped down from the stage. If I'd been fighting for a world title the next day, a contest that, if successful, would earn me millions and a championship, which would stand to make me a fortune, I wouldn't have hung around. But Joshua stayed put. Facing him was a vast line of supporters and fans, hoping for a picture, an autograph, maybe just a handshake or a fist bump. Joshua started at one end and worked all the way along. It took a couple of hours.

'Like a mayor, I'm campaigning,' he laughed. 'They waited three hours for me, I'm just giving something back.'

Through these last few weeks, though, there was an increasing air of serenity around the challenger. Joshua wasn't engaged emotionally with Martin. He went through his mental checklist.

'It's always a new experience really, seeing where your nerves are going. Do I feel any different from what I felt in the 12 December fight? So you know you're always trying to assess yourself but I feel calm, I feel relaxed. If I can go in there with the same attitude, controlling my nerves for the fight, I should be in a good place.'

He needed to get his head in the fight, though there were family, friends and well-wishers to see. 'It's a circus, you're an entertainer, I'm entertaining everyone's needs,' he smiled. 'So until you can get yourself away and just focus on yourself, that's when you lock yourself in for the fight.'

He had Saturday to gather his thoughts. A walk by his hotel along the Thames. Normally he slept during the afternoon before a fight, but on this occasion he could not, even though he was, to a surprising degree, untroubled. He lay down, shut his eyes but could not sleep. Rather than visualising the contest itself or how he thought the fight would go, he kept thinking about what he'd say afterwards, what he'd say if he won. In fact he sent a message to Chris Marshall, one of the psychologists from the GB set-up, asking simply if that was wrong. Chris said, 'No, don't worry too much about that. But try and focus on the moment.' Joshua locked in.

Anthony rose at six o'clock in the afternoon, spent an hour getting himself together before setting out to the venue. He still had hours until the fight. By the time he got to his changing room at the O2 he had an utter certainty about him. Tony Sims, one of his cornermen, led the whole team in a prayer before the fight, praying for a successful night and for everyone to come out healthy. 'That's all I worry about really and pray for is that the kids don't get hurt when they get in the ring and they come out all intact,' Tony said.

Joshua might not have been religious, but he had a sensitivity for faith. The prayer had become part of his pre-fight ritual. 'It's a form of meditation,' he said. 'It's whatever you put out to the universe is what you receive.'

Years before, after the Olympics, Joshua had told me how he thought as he waited backstage, about to go out beneath the lights, in front of the crowd for a major event. 'You're mainly always checking how your body's feeling. My hands are good. My elbows are good. Am I loose? Good. You do a whole body check.' That physical awareness feeds through to your mind. 'A whole mental check, a whole body check. You do a whole body check mentally. Is my mind good? Yes, great. Am I still here? Great,' he explained. 'Just always checking your body to see if things are all right.'

The fight came, as they inevitably do. Michael Buffer, who by this time had become the voice and mascot of big-time boxing, appeared illuminated at the centre of the ring. The moment would be incomplete without a montage. Joshua, the tannoy intoned, would tonight be the 'prophet of destruction', an almost biblical reference which at that moment in the heady atmosphere of the O2 seemed somehow appropriate. The roar of the crowd rolled round the arena, over and over, their anticipation palpable, their demand simple and clear. A knockout was required and a world title for their champion.

Amid the maelstrom Joshua waited backstage. He had warmed up on the pads; he knew he was sharp, he just knew. He attained that serenity and kept it, even as 20,000 people stood from their seats and roared. He was clear and for a second he took in that moment, the flashing lights and the crowd's peculiar fury. Four years ago, at the Olympic Games, he had stood and seen a similar scene. Four years ago it had shocked him. The weight of that expectation had been heavy. But now he was a different kind of fighter and this crowd, these people, were his.

'I was in my own world but I was aware of what I wanted to control, what I wanted to let in,' he said. 'I just felt very relaxed, very in control of the moment, nothing was going to get to me. That's how I've got to keep on going into every fight.'

Old faces were in the crowd, friends from GB, smiling at the sight, willing him on; even Dominic Winrow, the man Anthony had knocked out for his first amateur title was there. Fireworks crackled on either side, a final touch of stagecraft for his arrival, and Joshua had kept us all waiting long enough. He jogged in, high-cut boots on his feet, a long, white robe hanging down from shoulders and he smiled, easing away the tension of this final countdown.

He stepped lightly into the ring, shadowboxing. Up in the ring under the lights, he thought of his last fight once again with an unusual clarity. 'That fight with Dillian, why did we go to war in this ring? I could have just outclassed the guy. Why did I fight like that in this ring? Boxing is a sweet science, why did I go to war with Dillian in this ring when I could have outclassed him,' he wondered. 'This is the time to show how good I really am.' If the dark shorts he had worn before were intended to channel the furious spirit of Mike Tyson, these gleaming white shorts were a nod to the champions of a more distant, graceful past. Joshua didn't want to fight him tonight. He wanted to box him. Joshua, the challenger, walked slowly from side to side, pacing out the canvas, waiting for the champion.

'Even Tyson said he's scared walking into the ring,' Joshua had observed.

Charles Martin progressed down the gangway. For this occasion, his first defence of the IBF heavyweight title, he had elected to wear a crown of dubious craftsmanship and drape a purple robe over his shoulders. The whole effect did not manage to convey a regal air. Quite the reverse: it made him look like a pretender to the throne in a crown that did not fit.

Joshua stationed himself in his corner, jaw jutting out, broad across the chest, his entourage fanning out behind him. While he stood at the head of his team, Martin found himself positioned behind his cornermen. He eventually sidled out, to get his feet shuffling across the ring. All the while he kept the absurd crown on his head, a sign perhaps that he had balance or at least posture.

Joshua planted his hands crossed behind his back as the national anthem struck up. You wondered whether he was nervous or not. Stony-faced, breathing in deeply through his nose, he gazed down at Martin as the referee issued his final, scarcely heard instructions. One minute the ring was filled with their entourages and backers. Now all those bodies had drained away, leaving the two fighters alone together, but for the diminutive figure of the referee standing between them. Framed by the darkness, Joshua stood side on in his corner. His gloves hung low but he was primed and ready. With his right glove dropping behind him, he rapped it twice on the corner post and stepped out and forward to meet the world champion.

While against Whyte and Kevin Johnson Joshua had set a frenetic pace, now he did not rush. His serenity extended to the fight itself. Patiently he edged forward. His right shot out, a warning. He brought that glove back, to shield his chin while his lead left swung dangerously low at his waist. But he fired his right at Martin's body, tapped his left to the American's head before the two crunched together in a clinch. It was a reminder, when they crashed together, that these were big men with large bodies. When they hit, with their weight behind their punches, they did damage.

Another right to the body was heavy enough to force Martin back a step. Joshua's jab flashed out. He fired two right hands at the champion's head. He curled the right round as a hook. It prompted Martin to back off with indecorous haste, so much so that he tripped himself on the ropes, missing a step. The pressure made him ungainly. 'Prince' Charles slung out a cross of his own, Joshua stepped back with it, letting the shot fall through empty air. He had the first round won.

Martin came out for the second round, scuttling forward behind his jab. Joshua stuck in his left to the head and body. The champion wheeled away, clipping Anthony with a lead right hook as he tried to hook in his left. Anthony swung out wildly with both fists, just in that instant wanting to slug. Martin had been staying away, trying to keep mobile, perhaps thinking he would be able to drag Joshua into the unfamiliar late stages of a fight and finish him there. But if he did think such a thing, he soon lost faith in his own plan. He blundered in off the back foot. Joshua had his focus, had his eye in, and saw the opening. He released the shot. The right hand arched slightly and struck the target, clean on Martin's chin. It deposited the American on the seat of his shorts. The punch had shaken him to his boots. He stood, eventually, too slowly to inspire confidence. Charles, it seemed, had lost faith in himself, too. He abandoned hopes of staying mobile and keeping clear of Joshua. He gave up on a plan. He threw himself headlong at Joshua, headlong on to the same punch. Anthony nailed the shot instinctively, planting Martin back down on the canvas. The blow had knocked him silly. He sat up, a dull grin on his face. It had knocked the fight out of him. The referee shouted out the count but Joshua was walking away, already smiling. Martin stood too late. It was over. Joshua was the new world champion. It had taken him four minutes and thirty-two seconds of action, and a short lifetime, to complete the job. To be a champion.

Joshua was relaxed. He had thought the fight through and carried it out just as he'd seen it. He barely needed to celebrate. His emotions were, unlike after his last fight, in check. He afforded himself a broad grin and once again stood on the turnbuckles of a corner post, orchestrating a deep, guttural cheer from the crowd. Ticker tape burst open overhead, little squares of paper drifted down over the ring and over the crowd, emblazoned with the words: 'And the new'.

All was as it should be.

Inescapably Himself

'We can all do it.'

I don't know if Joshua delivered his victory speech exactly as he imagined it. Up in the centre of the ring, illuminated under the lights, he took the microphone from the television interviewer and spoke directly to the crowd. He was thinking of his friends on the GB squad, at that moment out in Turkey for a key qualification tournament for the Olympic Games, thinking of himself and those trying to make it in the sport.

'All the hype is good for everyone in boxing,' he beamed. 'Keep on embracing it. Everyone get behind every boxer, not just myself, keep on pushing this.'

It was an exhortation to those cheering, to those fighting, to himself, to keep this wave going. He had made his history. He had won a heavyweight world title in fewer rounds of a professional career than anyone had before.

For Charles Martin the sport would be unforgiving. While Joshua would be feted, Martin was humiliated. Until the first bell had rung the American had been a heavyweight world titlist with the apparent confidence to take on a dangerous overseas assignment. Before the fight he had promised that Joshua would not embarrass him. He had been unable to uphold that pledge. A champion one moment, Martin's swift downfall made him a sudden laughing stock, his plastic crown discarded somewhere in the chaos of his collapse.

Joshua for his part hardly got carried away. 'I knew I wasn't losing so I'm calm,' he said matter-of-factly. 'When you win I think you've got to keep it balanced and if you lose you've got to keep it balanced. You can't let it get to your head when you win and you can't let it get to your heart if you fail. So you just got to take it as it comes.'

Joshua did not celebrate that night; he hadn't even packed a shirt for the occasion. The following day he took his seat at the head of a boardroom table in the smart Four Seasons hotel in Canary Wharf, debriefing a collection of journalists the day after the night before. His ambition was clear, nodding to himself to wind up the conversation he intoned his mission statement, 'The kingpin of the division. The kingpin.'

Gathered round him were his promoter, manager, close friends, family, even Ben Ileyemi, the man who took him down to Finchley ABC in the very beginning. Big Ben declined to accept any credit for setting this express train on the rails.

'I think he created himself,' Ben told me. Ileyemi brought others to the gym. As it had got harder and harder they had dropped off. Joshua was the one left standing. Then they'd been boxing for the national amateur title. Ileyemi hadn't imagined he'd see Anthony crowned world champion so soon after getting involved in the sport.

'Yesterday was amazing, it's indescribable . . . I think all the work that he put in from the amateurs, the runs he didn't even want to do, the running in the rain, everything, it built up to yesterday. Now it just shows hard work does pay off.

'He's always got that winning mentality in him. I always knew he would do good things . . . Boxing he picked up quick. I think he's definitely got the heart for it, the mentality as well, that's when I knew he would definitely do something great.

'On the outside it does look easy but I know on the inside it can sometimes be hard. But he did make it look easy. But then again it goes down to the training.

'Preparation is the key.'

Joshua's life had prepared him for this moment and he welcomed it without surprise. I wondered if there was a moment when Anthony had *decided* to make himself extraordinary. When the sparring and the training got tough in Finchley and he decided to embrace it wholeheartedly maybe. Or perhaps after his suspension from GB, his defeat in the European Championships when he decided to come back stronger than anyone had suspected of him. Or maybe when he turned professional, he decided to take his boxing up yet another level. Joshua for his part didn't see himself as anything special. He had just held on to the vision. 'We're on a mission,' he smiled.

'I don't think it's about making myself extraordinary. I think we're unique in person anyway. I think I want to do extraordinary things. I don't like the normal. There's a time for everything. I could rush everything,' he said. 'We like doing everything to a certain level of extraordinary. So it's not me that I'm looking to be extraordinary, it's the thing I lay my hands on, I want that to be extraordinary. I want my boxing to be extraordinary, I want the people I'm around to be extraordinary.'

It wasn't a day or a particular moment of revelation. It was a process. 'It's not just about me, it's about everything. Everything needs to be extraordinary and that's what I like,' he continued. 'It's just whatever I involve myself in, I like to push that to the limit. That's a representation of me.'

I found myself walking alongside Anthony as he strode out of the meeting room and along the hotel corridor. I was babbling. I talked about first seeing him in the amateurs and how, on my return to the *Boxing News* office after the ABAs, the editor asked me if I'd been watching the future heavyweight champion of the world. Back then, only six years ago, I had laughed at the thought. In 2010 Joshua was strong but hardly slick. The thought of him, the thought of anyone in such a brief period of time winning a heavyweight world title, was far-fetched. Yet here he was, chatting with easy authority with the IBF title in his possession. It had never been inevitable. As I rattled on aimlessly, about the ABAs, about not thinking he was that good, Joshua looked quizzically at me, perhaps perplexed as to why now at this moment I appeared to be questioning his boxing abilities. But that wasn't what I meant. I had become a believer. Having watched him beat Cammarelle in Azerbaijan, now seeing him fling himself with clear eyes wholeheartedly into the job, I did not doubt him. The road would always get harder, the battles more vicious. But the point was he was here and he was going to fight. Then I had no way of knowing where he'd end up, if he'd be remembered for great victories or have to face terrible defeats. What would be would be. But however it all unfolded, I knew it would not come to pass through any lack of effort on Joshua's part. And that's what counted, to get in there and to try. Just fight.

I remembered something he'd said before, looking towards the long fight ahead. 'There's times when I get caught, I've got to bounce back and I'm going to go through many moments like that in my career,' he'd smiled. 'Just stick behind me and we'll get through.'

When he won the 2012 Olympics, to me he looked like he was the one, the man to take over from Klitschko, the iron ruler of the division. Joshua seized his world title in a situation no one had foreseen; he won it more quickly, too, than anyone had anticipated. I had thought that eventually he would win a world title, but I expected that to be the finale, the last act of his labours. But now he had it, I realised it wasn't the end of the story. It felt like he was, only now, just getting started. He had become Joshua.

Boss

I worried for Eric Molina. The Mexican-American seemed, overall, too nice to contend with Anthony Joshua at this point in his life. Anthony was in magnificent condition. Broad across the back, his body thick with muscle shone under the lights at the Manchester Arena. Joshua had already defended his IBF heavyweight title once, when he dispatched Dominic Breazeale in June 2016. He had looked near enough in complete control then but later admitted illness had plagued him during his training camp. 'I was wounded ahead of that,' Anthony laughed ruefully, confiding that he'd had glandular fever. He'd been advised not to take the fight but insisted on going through with it. He added, 'You forget about all the pain you went through and all the rounds, it's just getting that win.'

Now, in December 2016, he had suffered no such affliction in his preparations. And he had standing at his shoulder trainer Robert McCracken, a mentor for so many years. Now he was stepping into Joshua's corner to be alongside him for his fights. 'You know he's a massive asset to what we've been doing for so many years. He's guided me from the background. Having him at the forefront now should be a massive asset to my team,' Joshua said.

He may have been a world heavyweight champion taking Rob on to his staff but McCracken worked with him just the same way he always had. Joshua still followed those instructions as diligently as he had when he'd joined the GB squad as a fresh-faced amateur. 'I can't lose that respect for him. I've got ultimate respect for Rob.'

McCracken, who would work with Tony Sims in the corner, saw himself as part of a continuum of coaches who had helped Joshua. 'I was working with AJ, three really experienced coaches at GB, Paul Walmsley, Dave Alloway and Lee Pullen put a lot of work in with AJ as well on the Olympic journey where he went on and it culminated in him winning the gold medal. There's a lot of good work done by the coaches at GB. They deserve a lot of credit in his development to Olympic champion and obviously Sean Murphy and Jonny Oliver have done a fantastic job with him, making him national champion. He came to Sheffield a real good prospect and we were fortunate enough to work with him and try and take him to the next level. That culminated in Olympic gold and he's moved on from there and took the pro game by storm and he's developing well and nicely. But there's still a way to go and a lot of learning to do, and he's the first to admit that,' Rob said.

'Tony Sims – a hugely experienced trainer, but I know AJ very well. We're pretty close with the advice and mentoring and stuff I've always done for him over the last few years. Any advice he's needed, any tips, anything, he's come to me. We'll move on from this stage and hopefully my guidance and my help can culminate in him getting to the very top and being undisputed champion.'

He shared the dream of Anthony Joshua unifying the heavyweight championships. 'It would mean a lot to me to see AJ go to the very top, i.e. win an undisputed title, and to be part of that would be fantastic. My role is always to try and coach them the best that I can so they can win their contests, and guide them through them and try and avoid pitfalls along the way. And learn while I'm on the job and he's on the job. Ultimately the real pleasing thing for me is when you see the boxer succeed and fulfil his potential and that's what it's all about for me. Being part of that is really enjoyable but ultimately it's about the fighter.'

The exciting thing about Joshua was that we had yet to see just how far that undoubted potential could still take him. With characteristic restraint, McCracken added, 'But he's a pretty decent fighter already and he's got real power.' That was about as effusive as his praise got.

McCracken had been working with Joshua on precision and discipline. He had shown a tendency to drop his hands, loosening his guard, as he waded in to crush some of his professional opponents. You could see him now, on the pads with Rob, keeping his gloves up high, close to his eyes, throwing his punches sharply. 'It's sometimes easy to box like that,' Joshua said of his hands drifting low. 'You've got to keep it up, parry, that's important. It's simple. You either move out the way of a shot or you block it and come back, block it and come back, it's simple. That's what we're working on. Get out the way or defend it. Keep your feet balanced, defend it and come back. Simple as that.'

He had to be precise. Unknown to the public, a monumental prize waited for him on the other side of this bout with Eric

Molina. A contract had been drawn up to fight deposed champion Wladimir Klitschko for Joshua's IBF title and the now vacant WBA belt at Wembley Stadium the following year. It was right there. It would be the biggest fight in British boxing history. It would draw the largest gate since the Second World War and would generate more money than any prizefight in the UK had before. That concentrated the mind wonderfully. 'I need to win,' Anthony shrugged. 'It's a good thing because it obviously means I'm not overlooking him because, as you said, it's the final hurdle to the big fights and it's what people have been waiting to see. But you know every fight is a big fight because every fight could be the end. It makes sure I'm not complacent.'

This did not bode well for Eric Molina. It was hard to dislike the Mexican-American. He had been graced with a heavyweight frame and some boxing ability. It was enough to get Molina an unlikely world title shot. He grappled manfully with Deontay Wilder in 2015, lasting nine rounds with him in Alabama, far more than anyone expected. He managed to knock out former world title challenger Tomasz Adamek in Poland to keep himself in the division's top ten and bring him to this fight with Joshua. But deep down Molina understood his destiny was not to be a heavyweight champion of the world. Like Dominic Winrow, the opponent who had stood between Anthony and his first amateur title, Molina was a teacher and he knew life would lead him back to the classroom. In fact, to tug all the more at the heartstrings, he was a teacher of children with special needs. He was a good, kind man. But that wouldn't help him in the ring. Joshua was as intimidating as when I'd watched him in his first amateur championship seven years earlier, his blazing stare turned on Molina now.

Anthony was bigger, broader, more chiselled in muscle now. His power was greater, his technique vastly more refined and he had the strength of that howling 20,000-strong crowd behind him, all of it concentrated on Molina. Underneath that glare he folded.

Joshua boxed exactly as he said he would. His gloves stayed up. His arms tucked neatly into his body, protecting his trunk. He moved his upper body easily from side to side, ready to slip and slide past any shots that did come his way. He either stepped smartly back from Molina's punches, letting them fall harmlessly through the air or snuffed them out on his arms or gloves.

Molina quickly became a hopeless figure, his feet too ponderous to get after Joshua, his hands too slow to hurt him. Fleetingly at the start of the second round he summoned up some energy, bouncing his back off the ropes to muster a brace of counter-punches off his backhand. But they scattered wide, scarcely catching Joshua. All the while he had come on. His jab shuddered against Molina's defences. He looped his left through all too easily as a long, wide hook. The Mexican-American blinked beneath its weight, already feeling the hurt.

Joshua executed the finish mercilessly. In the third round Molina neared the ropes once again and Anthony stepped in. He loomed over Molina, completely in the ascendance, and in that snapshot, framed in an instant of time, he was by far the larger man. Towering over him, with Molina almost bowed over in his shadow, Joshua saw the opening and cleaved his right cross straight down. The blow to the head was tremendous. It flung Molina back into his own corner, stretching him out on the canvas, his head propped up against the corner post itself. Joshua just stood where he was, still poised, as if to emphasise his dominance, and only belatedly withdrew to a neutral corner.

Molina was barely conscious yet somehow managed to right himself inside the referee's count, a hint that he did have a bit of grit about him. But he was there for the taking and Joshua strode in, trebled his left hook to toss Molina aside and leave him hanging over the top rope, finished, as the referee called Joshua off.

'It's my job to make him look easy,' Anthony reflected afterwards. 'You've seen what he can do, and you can see what he can't do so you've just got to find your way. No fight's easy but we trained properly. I definitely trained properly for it.'

The formality of having his hand raised was scarcely completed when Klitschko himself took his cue to enter the ring. They faced one another, completing a solemn staredown. Joshua with sweat still glistening on his body, Klitschko casual, almost cheerful, in a dark shirt, returned his gaze. Looking at the old champion now, Joshua faced his introduction to the highest echelon of the sport. It was time to step forward.

'When opportunity presents itself you've got to grab it with two hands,' Anthony said. 'It's nearly there now.

'You best hope that you've taken all your time in the ring and learned something because you need it all in a fight like that.'

He did not see this next challenge as a final, climactic battle. It was the start of the path he'd now follow. 'It's more of a journey through boxing,' he said. 'It's about staying focused. Your class, your morals, what you're about, what more are you than just boxing. So that's why I'm on my grind.'

'Then,' he continued, 'I've got to prove it again and again

and again. That's why it don't mean nothing. You just got to keep on going and going and going. When I sit back and I'm done with it, then I'll be like, yes, I bossed this shit. But right now you just keep on going and going and going.'

This was not the end. There is always another fight.

Acknowledgements

There are almost too many people to thank that I don't know where to start. I have been lucky – lucky to be in the right place at the right time to see this great story unfold from so early on in the journey. I was lucky in the first place to get a job at *Boxing News*, the world's oldest, and, in my opinion, greatest boxing magazine, where I've always wanted to work. The whole team there has taught me a valuable lesson in dedication and passion for the job. A big thank you to the editor Matt Christie, Nick Bond and all my colleagues and friends at *BN*. And thank you, too, to former editor Tris Dixon, who gave me a job there in the first place.

Boxing News gave me a ringside seat for this particular adventure. Anthony Joshua's rise has been astonishing. He's crammed a lifetime of work into about eight years. It would be easy to think his rise was somehow inevitable, especially as he's crushed his early opponents so efficiently on his way to winning a professional world title. But nothing is inevitable, especially in heavyweight boxing. Joshua had the ambition in the first place but along the way he had to make the right decisions, keep faith in his vision and, when he reached turning points in his career, he kept on fighting. Joshua is the ideal subject for a sportswriter; as well as being articulate and thoughtful he can really fight. I am hugely grateful to him and for the time he's spared *Boxing News* and me. And I still have a feeling that Joshua's only just getting started.

It is a success story and, hopefully, this book gives an insight into how he's achieved it. Credit, too, has to go to the people he's gathered round him, men like Freddie Cunningham, Tony Sims, Ben Ileyemi and his whole team, not to mention promoter Eddie Hearn, who's always willing to oblige a journalist with a good line.

The GB boxing team has been a big part of the story and I've been fortunate to spend a lot of time at their gym in Sheffield and following the team through many international tournaments both in the UK and in some pretty far-flung places overseas. For an 'amateur' boxing team they are astonishingly professional. That professionalism is epitomised by Rob McCracken, who's always struck me as exactly the kind of man you'd want in your corner, and his team, including coaches Paul Walmsley, Dave Alloway and Lee Pullen. It's been great over the years to talk to GB's Matt Holt, Dr Mike Loosemore and Lee Murgatroyd, who have shared a great many insights into the boxing world.

Through my role at *Boxing News* it's been a privilege to meet so many boxers and hear their stories, so many of whom have been so generous with their time, especially the captain of GB Boxing, Thomas Stalker.

So many writers have been an inspiration to me, but I'd particularly like to thank Don McRae, whose help has been invaluable.

ACKNOWLEDGEMENTS

I've been working on this book for a long time and life helps you out. I owe another debt to my friends at my old boxing club at Oxford, who didn't just teach me how to fight but how to knuckle down, too.

A huge thank you to Tim Broughton at Yellow Jersey Press, the dream publisher, for all his help with this book, copy editor Richard Collins, proofreader Ilona Jasiewicz and my agent Richard Pike. It goes without saying the fault for any mistakes lies with me.

Friends and family have all been so supportive of my efforts to write, but, Katie, I can't thank you enough.

List of Illustrations

1. John Dennen and Anthony Joshua in conversation (Craig Brough/ Action Images); Dominic Winrow and Joshua at the ABA (Matthew Childs/Action Images); Joshua exercising after defeat at the European Championships (Craig Brough/Action Images)
2. Joshua at the ABA national championships, 2010 (Matthew Childs/ Action Images); At the Aliyev Stadium, Baku (David Mdzinarishvili/ Reuters)
3. Posing with the first GB boxers to qualify for London 2012 (Scott Heavey/Getty Images); Anthony Joshua vs. Zhang Zhilei, at London 2012 (Scott Heavey/Getty Images); Anthony Joshua vs. Erislandy Savón, London 2012 (Scott Heavey/Getty Images)
4. Becoming super heavy-weight champion at London 2012 (Scott Heavey/Getty Images); On the podium, London 2012 (Scott Heavey/ Getty Images)
5. Anthony Joshua and Nicola Adams, London 2012 parade (Richard Heathcote/Getty Images); Receiving his MBE, Buckingham Palace (Steve Parsons, WPA Pool/Getty Images)
6. With Eddie Hearn (Ben Hoskins/ Getty Images); Professional debut against Emanuele Leo at the O2, 2013 (Scott Heavey/Getty Images); Training with Tony Sims (Richard Heathcote/Getty Images)
7. Anthony Joshua vs. Dillian White at the O2, 2015 (Leigh Dawney/ Getty Images); Anthony Joshua vs. Charles Martin at the O2, 2016

(Justin Tallis/AFP/Getty Images); Celebrating after defeating Charles Martin (Richard Heathcote/Getty Images)

8. First world title defence. Anthony Joshua vs. Dominic Breazeale at the O2, 2016 (Richard Heathcote/Getty Images); Anthony Joshua floors Eric Molina, Manchester Arena 2016 (Richard Heathcote/Getty Images); Anthony Joshua and Wladimir Klitschko readying to showdown at the Manchester Arena, 2016 (Richard Heathcote/Getty Images)

Index